THE LIFE FOR ME

'Georgian, that was the point'

THE
LIFE FOR ME

by

RUPERT CROFT-COOKE

LONDON
MACMILLAN & CO. LTD
1952

PRINTED IN GREAT BRITAIN

TO
JOHN RISELEY PRICHARD

CONTENTS

ILLUSTRATIONS

Out of London

I

I COULD see over the slates and chimney-pots as far as Russell Square. A church spire or two, the pretentious dome of a petrol-filling station and some high blocks of new tenement flats were all distinguishable in the ochreous light of a misty morning in spring 1950. I had just pulled myself out of bed and with stale eyes was staring from the window of my bedroom in Doughty Street.

I was lucky, I told myself shakily but for the thousandth time, to *have* a bedroom in Doughty Street.

For four years, since I had come out of the army in 1946, I had been the tenant of two floors. Two floors, made separate from the rest of the house behind their own front door, are called by estate agents a 'maisonette', one of the most fatuous of the terms which have become current in the last few decades. I never used it, preferring the obvious misnomer 'flat'. But two floors I had, with three rooms to each, at a pre-war rent, and I was told by everyone who saw them that I was the luckiest man alive to have secured them.

'No one can get any sort of flat at less than seven or eight guineas a week,' my friends said. 'And that usually means sharing. Even if you can find such a place. You *are* lucky.'

Till now I had complacently accepted their assurance. But on this spring morning, as I peered at the smoky roof-tops, I was suddenly confronted by a new and startling doubt. I was lucky to have found this flat. I was lucky to have a home in London when so many people longed, prayed, searched and waited for one—and usually in vain. But did I want it?

Once I had faced that question I knew that for me a period of life had ended. I knew that I did not want it, had never wanted

it and should never be happy in it.   I had been fooling myself for
four years.

I remembered all the things that had seemed advantages.   By
living here I should be 'on the spot', whatever that might mean.
From the time I had joined the army in 1940 to my release in 1946
I had written nothing.   Whole reputations backed by vast sales
had risen in that time, and no one was much disposed to remember
a pre-war novelist whose books had never sold in vast numbers,
anyway.   I had been faced with the necessity of starting all over
again, and it had been reiterated to me that I must be in those
mysterious circumstances called 'on the spot'.

'Besides,' my friends said, 'you really should be in London.
Theatres, exhibitions, parties, meeting people—you need all that
after being away so long.'

It sounded very convincing, and I followed the well-meant
advice and believed that I enjoyed it.   But that morning, when
once the question was squarely asked and answered, the advantages of living in the constricted city of London looked suddenly
very silly.   I knew beyond question that I did not wish to
stay.

2

Doughty Street is that rarity, a Georgian street which is both
monotonous and gloomy.   The houses are built of bricks which
have become sooty-grey, the eight-paned Georgian windows
have been changed by the Victorians for their heavy single panes,
and there is nothing to break the street-long façades of house-
fronts facing each other across the tarmac.   Lawyers' offices
occupy many of these, their dirty ground-floor windows re-
vealing stacked files and skewered bundles of dusty documents.
The bombed shell of a black-walled chapel made a site for one
lonely preacher who on gusty Sunday nights would stand on its
steps crying our doom for an hour or more, though he never
achieved an audience, even of one.   Dust-carts and railway-
vans seemed to make up the principal traffic of the street, with
coal-carts and milk-floats.   The windows of my front rooms
looked down on this tired thoroughfare; from those at the back

I could see a row of smoky gardens, the one behind the house in which I lived being overgrown with dripping fig-trees.

Almost exactly facing my front windows was a house in which Dickens lived for a couple of years more than a century ago. Prints and contemporary furniture and bric-à-brac associated with the novelist had been installed and the place was open as the Dickens house—a euphemistic term when one considers how long he lived at Devonshire Terrace and Tavistock House. This meant that I could see a stream of hopeful visitors at a shilling an entry making towards the front door, while on summer nights the sight-seeing char-à-bancs chose it as a port of call. A sad business, that, for while a guide would shout that Charles Dickens lived here and wrote *Edwin Drood*, *Henry Esmond* and *Jude the Obscure* in his study on the first floor, the tourists would sit staring straight before them, too bored, or tired, or hungry to turn their heads. Shrines are splendid things, but I wonder what Boz himself would say if he knew that this sort of misplaced sentimentality was preventing the occupation of these premises, in which he no more than perched for a time, by two of the countless London families in need of a home.

The two floors below mine were occupied by the owners of the house, an organization called the Horace Plunkett Foundation. In the four years in which I lived in Doughty Street I never discovered what this title might portend; my only information, and that by hearsay, was that it 'had something to do with co-operative farming'. Had I heard this before I came to the house it might have led me to hope for jolly bucolic types in gaiters or to expect that riotous farmers' dinners might be held beneath me, the rattle of tankards and the noise of a shouted chorus rising pleasantly to disturb my evening peace. But no. Whatever connection the Horace Plunkett Foundation had with farming appeared to be an advisory one, for its staff was entirely and maturely feminine, and what little noise I overheard was of busy typewriters or, occasionally, a shrill but genteelly restrained argument. These lower floors, with their linoleum and green paint, their smell of the caretaker's cooking rising from the basement, their sounds of a flushing lavatory which seemed to be almost continuous during the day, their respectable dinginess, their effect on me of gloom, were places to pass through swiftly on the way to my flat. I am sure that the Horace Plunkett Foundation does yeoman service to co-operative farming, but its premises could scarcely be described as gay. That morning, in fact, I realized with a start that it would be a matter of some relief to me when I knew that never again would I have to climb through the musty cleanliness of that stairway, or pass the worried-looking ladies employed in those offices, or hear the wheeze of the constantly re-filling lavatory cistern, or see the sensible feminine coats and hats in the passage to the front door, or smell the caretaker's onions cooking persistently in the basement.

I was lucky, I tried to reflect again, to have this flat. The rooms on the lower of its two floors were reasonably well-pitched, and if I could touch the ceilings of those at the top with my hand so that my bedroom window seemed always too small to relieve the stuffiness under the slate roof, what was I to expect for three pounds a week? I was lucky and I ought still to know it. But that morning I did not. Indeed, I reflected as I yawned and looked towards Russell Square that I did not want this luck. I did not want to live in London. I did not want to be 'on the spot'. I did not want ever again to pass between the grim and looming house-fronts of Doughty Street.

3

My sudden nausea was not caused solely by the fact that I lived opposite 'the Dickens house' and over the Horace Plunkett Foundation in one of the gloomiest areas of London, but by London itself, the new harsh and bitter city which has so little in common with the pleasant London which was ours before the war. I realized that little of its degeneration was peculiar to it, that life itself and mankind had changed. Still, because I remembered another London, the sordid and unhappy way of life which was to be seen in its streets now seemed unbearable. In the 'twenties and 'thirties, I remembered, there was no need to plan one's evenings. With a few shillings in one's pocket one could slam the front door behind one and accept what London offered. Pleasure was cheap, people were kind. You could eat in a decent little French or Italian restaurant with a carafe of wine and your bill would be at the most five or six shillings. You could stand in one of a thousand pubs and drink bitter for fourpence-ha'penny a glass and find good company and civil, honest faces. You could go to the theatre for half-a-crown and expect not to be bored. You could drift about the lighted streets with your friends easily, happily, freely. You were not watched or 'canalized', questioned, restricted or robbed. Whereas in post-war London, though pleasure, or at least pleasure-seeking, persisted, it had been rationed and organized into the drilled misery of a holiday camp. Filthy food served without grace or consideration by insolent Cypriots seemed all that Soho offered, and the large and famous restaurants gave little more, though their waiters were patronizing, one might think pitying, towards their customers, instead of wilfully rude. To spend a pleasant evening at random had become an impossibility, and elaborate forethought, reservation, bribery and humiliation went to the planning of it. There were pubs, of course, but their bars seemed crowded with cadgers and crooks, or worse, with writers and pansies and girls with fringes and dirty hands. Theatres showed miscellaneous inanities at an hour when, in more civilized countries, the matinée would begin. All true gaiety had gone from the streets in which women's faces, trained to ferocity by years of competitive 'making ends meet', glared at you in troubled horror if you happened to be smiling. Up and down the West End at night marched groups of stony-faced people, among whom the most cheerful seemed to be the prostitutes, male and female, and the plain-clothes inspectors waiting to grab some unwary clergyman from the country and charge him with soliciting. There was, over the whole city, a pall of suspicion, of cupidity, of distress. No one knew how to enjoy himself; no one looked happy. Such laughter as there might be was too shrill or too forced or too drunken to come from any inner contentment.

Above all, one was confronted everywhere by the insolence of office, an insolence which most people seemed schooled to accept. Taking example from the more arrogant and ill-mannered Cabinet Ministers, every jack-in-office in every trade or calling had assumed what petty authority he could and from its shelter seemed eager to bully someone else. The commissionaire controlling cinema-goers, the bus-conductors, the countless officials in rationing offices, post-office clerks, shop assistants, ticket-collectors, behaved aggressively or patronizingly, and their victims accepted it. The old free-and-easy courtesy of the Cockney, full of good-humoured repartee, had given place to a surly defensiveness which made one's ordinary business and movement in London unnerving and distressful.

There was, too, a feeling that London was being run 'on the cheap'. When I remembered its dark magnificence in the time of my boyhood and the legends about it then, I felt something like shame at its mean and pinching economy. 'This building,' my father's old chief clerk had said when I was perched on an office stool in the City waiting to be called for by my father— 'this building stands on the most expensive few acres of land in the world—just round the Royal Exchange. Worth so much a square inch. The greatest city not only in geography, my boy, but in history, too. Don't just look at the buildings—think of the water, the electricity, the gas, the drainage for all that. Seven million people. What about the police, the post, the railways? Something to *be* a Londoner, you know.' And it was, I am sure. But would the Londoners of twenty and thirty years ago have suffered without some pretty forceful protest the power cuts and lighting regulations, the reduced and erratic postal delivery, the curtailed food supply, the housing shortage and the universal officiousness which are characteristics of our London? Would they have been ordered about, badgered and dragooned by posters, loud-speakers, inspectors of this or that? A petty meagreness has replaced the smiling munificence of Edwardian and Georgian London and made it a dour and difficult city to inhabit.

4

Once I had faced up to the certainty that my luck was two-edged, I began immediately to consider ways of escape. I was not quite simple enough to suppose that by merely ceasing to live in London I should elude the regimentation which I abhorred, but I did believe that there were places in which it would be less overbearing or less obvious. I wanted a civilized life. It even seemed to me of importance to us all that there should persist here and there dissatisfied and ambitious creatures like myself who were prepared to fight and make sacrifices to secure it, who would refuse second best, who would rebel against the pawky philosophy of an age which calls equity justice. 'So long as everyone else has to stand in a queue,' says my brow-beaten contemporary, 'I don't mind doing so. If we all suffer alike it is not so bad.' It is, in fact, far worse, and this pusillanimous acceptance of indignity poured over a man like slops thrown from a window is the most characteristic weakness of our time.

For thousands of years we have been crawling through barbarism towards some kind of civilization in which the individual can expand and create, can hold his own opinions and reach his own formulæ, and finally become an artist in living. If now we are to submit to the economic and moral slavery of Communism or, scarcely less insidious, to our own philosophy of acceptance of all substitutes, all mediocrities, all needless mortifications because our fellow men accept them, because we are no worse off than others, then we are veering back through one of the worst retrogressions in history.

From the little things to the great. We allow ourselves to be taxed or cajoled out of smoking and drinking, to endure an economy which makes enterprise, exploration, even freedom to travel the privilege of a few, and so go downward until we find ourselves dressing, eating, living by uniform and parsimonious standards in a grey and tawdry underworld in which creation is by rote and art by price and measurement.

A civilized life, I said that morning, and as soon as the words were formed I knew that their significance for me was momentous. For with them I recognized that my life then was unsatisfying and cowardly and that I would fight to make it more enterprising and emancipated. It meant, more practically, that I would at once give up my lease of the flat in Doughty Street and cease to be one of the regimented millions living in London.

What then? The most immediately tempting possibility was to go abroad. There are many countries in which flourishes the particular kind of freedom which seems most in jeopardy here : the freedom of a man to live as he likes within a minimum framework of law and order, to think, speak, love, write, paint, compose, eat, drink, laugh, travel, sleep where and how and when he likes, without being charged with being anti-social or eccentric if his taste is not the general one. Even the Fascist countries before the war, though they strenuously denied their citizens several of these liberties, never dared to impose restrictions on others, so that Nazi Germans, for instance, heard with disgust or incredulity of our licensing laws. Today I could think of a dozen countries where I might create the kind of life I wanted. France. Italy. Even Canada or Australia. Pakistan or—but for its Prohibition—India. Several countries of South or Central America. But they shared certain paramount disadvantages. To settle in one of them would mean the loss of most of my friends. And to leave England would be, in some sentimental sense which I did not wish precisely to analyse, to run away. I thought of the men of my own profession who, when the first bombs fell on London, skedaddled to America. It had been impossible not to feel a certain contempt for them, however much in the name of tolerance, common sense or charity one condoned their conduct; but would there not also be something cowardly in a similar desertion now? England was in worse case than during the Exodus of 1940 and 1941, possibly in greater danger and certainly nearer to bankruptcy. If every man who could earn his living wherever he happened to be took advantage of it to leave this most over-taxed, mismanaged and joyless country, its recovery would be even further postponed. I wanted no high-sounding name for what I intended to do and I knew I should enjoy it, but it was a kind of duty, too, and when sanity and gusto and guts would have returned, when England would again have become (as I firmly believed she would) a country in which people of independent spirit lived with dignity, happiness and pride, I should be glad to have stayed here during these cringing and melancholy years.

5

Thence it swiftly became clear. I would make my new life despite all the difficulties of the time, despite the discouragement, the grudging, the accusations of selfishness and the obstacles raised by those in power who conceived their duty to be the suppression of just such effort as mine; I would make it in that very area of England in which I was born and brought up : in Kent or Sussex. I would have a home of my own with a front door stout enough to exclude inspectors of all kinds—except those innocuous and civil souls who call to read the meter. Here I would accept no restriction which I could evade or challenge. Here I would eat and drink well, and instead of admitting this with a hushed voice and shame at 'selfishness' or lack of a social sense, I would proclaim it loudly and maintain that in achieving it, against all obstacles, I was being of higher service to the community than those who meekly took what butchers gave them and stewed it to an inedible salmagundi flavoured with patent gravy brownings, substitute pepper, *ersatz* thickening and tinned vegetables. I would make my home beautiful both because I liked beautiful things and because it was right to defy the Philistines. I would spend whatever money I could raise, because there was no better purpose to which money could possibly be put than to the making of such a home and such a life, surrounded with what elements of grace and good living could be salvaged from the past.

As I thought about it the idea grew more rebellious and more interesting. If I had been a rich man there would have been little to recommend it, ethically at any rate, for even in modern England there is not much that cannot be bought. It was the challenge in it that enticed me, a challenge to all the ingenuity and courage and taste that I could muster. I did not yet see how it could be done, for my resources in money were negligible, and although I had health and energy I was not sure that these would be strong enough to bear the strain of a protracted struggle.

B

I did not deceive myself. I wanted to do this. It would give me joy and entertainment. That came first, and I made no effort to deny it, even to myself. But I should, too, be serving a cause which I believed worth serving, defying what was most ugly and commonplace in modern life, and showing, I hoped, that there was no need to knuckle under to mediocrity while it was still possible for a poor man to defeat it.

Thus far I went in resolution before breakfast that morning.

Into Sussex

I REALIZED that in order to live in Kent or Sussex I should have to buy a house, for there was no hope nowadays of renting one. Moreover, a first glance at the advertisements of estate agents showed me that there was little likelihood of finding the sort of house I wanted at a price much lower than £4,000, and that for this sum I could not reasonably hope to have much choice of locality, situation, period or size. As I had only about £500 in all, the prospect would have seemed daunting to one who relied less confidently on his own good fortune.

It was not only a house that I wanted and meant to find, but all things in it and about it which were needed to serve my larger purpose. Useless to buy a house and then find that the purchase had so strained my resources that I could do nothing but live in it, parsimoniously and uncouthly. My move was not to be simply from London to the country, but from an unsatisfying life into one of more fulfilment. So I thought it time to make some calculations.

My list of debits and credits as it eventually took shape was not one that would have much impressed an accountant or bank manager. Certain of my assets would have seemed nebulous to business men, and these I put at the head of my list.

I had first of all a rather unusual amount of experience both of houses and of domestic economy. I had been brought up in the very thick of it. My father, who was a stockbroker, and therefore limited to areas from which he could make a daily journey to London, never lived in a house more than five years and never took one without meaning to remain in it for the rest of his life. I was born at Edenbridge in Kent, in a delightful Georgian place called Hatch House, from which, before I was a year old, we moved to a house on River Hill, Sevenoaks, called Parkside. A slump on the Stock Exchange took us back to Edenbridge to a thatched cottage named Little Mousehurst, after which we lived for a whole three years at Little Sunte, Lindfield. The next home, Wayside, Chipstead, broke all records, for it lasted for five years, till the outbreak of the First World War, on which we went to Cage House, Tonbridge. After that came a couple of years each in Eastbourne and St. Leonards-on-Sea, till my father was ordered by his doctor to cease spending four hours a day in travelling and we went successively to Forest Hill, Orpington, Longfield, Hildenborough. After retiring, my father speeded up the rate of moving until his death in 1935, so that my poor mother had scarcely finished unpacking when it was time to find a new home.

For each of his houses my father made a garden, for garden-planning was his abiding passion. It may be that this accounted for his restlessness, that his interest was in visualizing and constructing rather than growing, so that when his plan had been sufficiently realized he wanted to move on. At all events I had been brought up amid these changing environments, and when I reached manhood had watched more homes and gardens being made than most men see in a life-time. Since then I had remained interested in domestic architecture, in furnishing and what is odiously called 'décor'. I had not studied it as scientifically-minded or professional observers must, with note-book and reference book, but I had never ceased to look and remember and ask questions and learn methods. Moreover, a few years as an antiquarian bookseller had taught me to buy and sell, and a life-long habit of collecting had given me other valuable training. So I put down my first asset as experience, and added in brackets, and less modestly, a certain amount of taste.

Next came the five hundred pounds. It did not seem much when I thought of the price of houses and repairs, but it meant that at least I could pay a ten per cent deposit if I found what I wanted and needed time to raise more. It was, of course, a sum apart from the money I was earning. And now that I have mentioned it, I must add that it seems to me that the story I am telling here will lose all point if I do not indicate the approximate amount of this. If I am to describe frankly what I have tried to do, I must reveal such details of finance as are relevant to it. I had better say, then, that I was earning between £1,500 and £2,000 a year gross as a writer and had no other resources.

My third asset was my furniture. This I had accumulated very slowly and precariously in the ten years before the war, during which my average income was rather less than that of a farm labourer. Adding to it piece by piece—a table bought in auction, a chair brought from abroad—I had been able in 1939 to furnish a London flat. The periods were jumbled, the worm-holes, though they had been successfully treated, could still be seen. There was too much glass and not enough china. But, roughly speaking, I had accumulated a houseful of furniture when war threatened, and was sufficently attached to it to feel a certain special anxiety about it when it was generally supposed that London would be heavily bombed in the first days of declared hostilities.

At that time I was tenting with Rosaire's Circus, and lighting restrictions had closed their family show, so that animals and performers were idle and their waggons stood in a lonely Kentish field. On the first Monday of war, therefore, two of their pantechnicons and half-a-dozen acrobats and tent-hands went to London and in three or four hours removed everything from my flat. It was a strange occasion because the weather was warm and placid and in the streets there was little outward sign that the country was at war. To carry one's household goods to safety seemed a rather hysterical and stupid thing to do when so many people were going about the business of the day unmoved by the categorical change from peace to war which had fallen over us unseen. On the following morning we unloaded everything at a store in Tenterden, where it was to remain until hostilities were over. Although I felt a certain diffidence at the extreme cautiousness of this move at the time, I was glad later, for while one of the first bombs in the London blitz destroyed my flat, my furniture remained unharmed until I reclaimed it in 1946.

Experiment had taught me to limit the things I should collect, since too many could swamp any scheme of decoration, and with time limited by the necessity of working for the best part of every day, I could scarcely have learnt enough about more than one or two objects to form an intelligent selection of them. So I had contented myself with books, English water-colours and such European pottery as could roughly be termed old Majolica. Of these three I now had sizeable hoards, and considered them not least in importance as I counted my blessings.

I came again to less concrete resources. I could cook, for instance, not with the scatter-brained impulsiveness of the male given the freedom of the kitchen, but as a result of a good many years of study, practice and observation. I had a pretty good working knowledge of vintages, backed by experience of some highly curious drinks in odd places. I knew a certain amount— dangerously little in some cases—about gardening, domestic architecture, textiles, about silver, bottling, and preserving, restoring and polishing, bricklaying, plumbing, decorating. No profound or specialized knowledge, but enough to serve as a starting-point for enquiry. That I believed to be the essential kind of knowledge of all those things—enough to realize one's ignorance, enough to teach one what to ask, enough to enable one to use the information gained.

What more had I which would help in the pleasurable struggle ahead? Good health and gusto, I supposed, could be called resources. An interest in living and ways of living which showed no signs of slackening. And finally, most essentially, a German motor-car and an Indian secretary—remarkable products of remarkable countries.

That was really all.

2

On that same spring morning I drafted a letter to the appropriate house agents in Kent and Sussex and it was dispatched to thirty of them. This gave me a feeling of having started off, sailed, fired the opening shot or burnt my boats. Moving house was no longer a hazy ambition, but a course I was already following.

For that reason, perhaps, when the letters had been posted, I could not be content to wait for the replies, but had to start making enquiries from friends who might have suggestions. At some time towards the evening of that day I telephoned an innkeeper in an area of Sussex which I had known and liked for many years.

'Any houses for sale? Yes, there's one at Ticehurst,' he said. 'Too big for you, I should think. Right in a village. Shop windows. Cottage and a big warehouse go with it.'

I did not want a cottage or a warehouse. I did not want shop windows. I did not want to be right in a village. Still, 'How old?' I asked.

'Nearly two hundred years. Flat white front and slate roof.'

This was the first, the only thing in its favour. A Georgian house. 'I'll come down tomorrow,' I said.

3

Georgian, that was the point. The English countryside would certainly be poorer if it were not for our inheritance of countless Tudor cottages, thatched or tiled, brick or stone, their eaves wavering with time, their odd little windows peering out quaintly, their diamond panes and tall, sometimes seemingly twisted, chimney-pots. Their interiors, too, have delightfully unexpected angles, their vast beams hanging wearily and their fireplaces seeming to be separate apartments. I have stood on the brick floor of a sixteenth-century house and felt the past about me like an odour and thought that to such a hearth Bully Bottom would return after rehearsals, on that beam hams must have hung every winter for three or four centuries. The very shape of the roof is an invitation to painters, and there might be a historical novel in each room. But I have never wanted to live in the most attractive of these pre-eighteenth-century dwellings.

There are good reasons for admiring Tudor cottages only from a distance or during a visit. They are excessively uncomfortable. The wonderful old chimney recess with little settle seats inside it has to be treated in some clumsy way—an interior cowl or a bricked-in fireplace—before a fire there can be prevented from smoking. The solid oak doors and the little diamond-paned windows are draughty. The beams are too low and crack heads. The oak staircase, too beautiful to cover with a carpet, is a death-trap when it is polished. Moreover, if into this museum of old oak and historical associations the most commonplace of modern appliances is introduced, it looks shamefully out of place. A hand-basin in a low oak bedroom, central heating, however cunningly concealed, even electric light —these are anomalous and sometimes offensive against a Tudor background. As for furniture—every piece not strictly contemporary looks ridiculous, and even the earliest or the simplest mahogany cries out against the rough oak round it, while curtains, carpets, pictures are all restless and unhappy with walls that were never intended to harbour them. No, I had long since decided, let Tudor be for those who love it well enough to be half suffocated at night and smoked out by day, and who like the heavy oak furniture of the period. For me the matchless proportions, the airy grace, the bland and beautiful simplicity of outline which were achieved by domestic architects only once in all the centuries during which we have been building houses. For me a Georgian house. The eighteenth century was the period in which I felt blissfully at home—its art, music, furniture, its way of life, its sceptical courageousness, its elegance and good manners, its violence in personal issues, its reverence for all classical and exquisite things. So great was my faith in it that long before I had seen the house described as 'nearly two hundred years old; flat white front and slate roof', I was prepared to trust the age which had made it. I knew it would be all right. Ugly buildings might have grown up round it, senseless alterations might have been made to the house itself, but the framework would be faultless.

So on the day following my first resolve to leave London I set out for that area of Sussex which lies between Tunbridge Wells and Hastings—a wide, rich garden of hill-top trees and gentle green slopes, of scattered villages and little rivers with the hop-gardens and oast-houses of Kent running towards the bare downs of Sussex. The area in which I wanted to live.

The House Found

I

THE hedges were in full leaf; there was an almost blatant fecundity about the countryside as I drove by a narrow, wooded lane towards the village of Ticehurst. Beside me was the owner of the house I was to see.

I stopped on the crest of a little hill and looked across the valley.

'That's Ticehurst, on the hill,' said my companion. 'Usual sort of village. Couple of thousand people. Three pubs in the village and two more on the outskirts. No railway station for three miles. Eight or nine shops.'

I was trying to distinguish one building from another.

'That patch of white below the church is the end of the house we're going to see,' went on its owner. 'It's at the bottom of the village. Ticehurst is on a by-road running across between the Tunbridge Wells-to-Eastbourne road and the London-to-Hastings road. West to east, near enough, from Frant to Hawkhurst. Only has Wadhurst and Ticehurst on it.'

'All 'hursts,' I said.

'Yes. Hereabouts. Lamberhurst, Goudhurst, Staplehurst, Sandhurst, Salehurst. Soon as you cross the border into Kent you come to the 'dens. Smarden, Marden, Biddenden, Benenden, Bethersden. West of here it's 'fields. Mayfield, Rotherfield, Heathfield, Uckfield, Maresfield, Hartfield, Lindfield. But Ticehurst is right in the centre of the 'hurst country. There's nothing special about it. Just a pretty village off the main road and the main line.'

There was a steep downward slope, then we climbed the hill beyond it into the village. I saw that this was grouped, as most French villages are, about an open square, with the two largest inns, the Duke of York and the Bell, glaring at one another

17

across a central area of tarmac which had also a roofed seat, a war memorial and a few trees. Then we turned eastward as though to leave the village behind us and stopped outside a white building.

2

The house was built, as I had heard, about two centuries ago, or perhaps a little less, and for at least half its life had been occupied by one family. They were builders, and had carried on their trade here until about two months earlier. There were still many evidences of this, and the very lay-out of the place showed that it had been no mere residence, but a shop, an office, a warehouse, a workshop and a builder's yard.

The house stood in a triangle between a road and a lane, and stretched from one to the other, with its garden running down to the acute angle. Behind it was its own cobbled yard, wide enough for a lorry, and behind this stood the warehouse. Also in that triangle was a six-roomed white weather-boarded cottage, a row of garages and a long timber shed.

It needed all my faith in the house's period to see past the defects which were the result of alterations and additions made in the last century. There must, I argued, be a good façade, but how could I know this except by faith, when it was hidden behind curved hedges of *Cupressus macrocarpa* fifteen foot high, which not only made it impossible to see the house but effectively prevented more than the dimmest light from creeping into its rooms? The façade was intended to be a model of bare simplicity, I was sure, but now it had been broken by a hideous Victorian bay window jutting forward like a snout. There would be good lines from end to end, I supposed, but a dingy collection of decaying sheds and a misplaced greenhouse concealed what little was left exposed by the hedges.

The north side of the house, which faced the road, had, it is true, a pair of finely proportioned and unspoilt Georgian bays for its upper floor, but beneath these had been erected a piece of sloping roof running the width of the house, and under that were two shop-windows with a shop-door between them. The space which divided that from the road was paved with concrete.

The garden had suffered no less. It was about a hundred yards long, and with care and a simple design could be made to appear larger. But only a space a few feet wide was uninvaded by vegetables, and in this the hedges left little room even for the rockeries and asphalt paths which it contained.

The interior was complicated by the work of planners who had not been satisfied with the original, quite matchless, design. The front door opened on a minute hall and staircase, and although there were six bedrooms in the house, three sitting-rooms and a long succession of large back premises, a larder as big as the sitting-room, a roomy kitchen, a scullery of the same area and another larder, there was no one room of any size. Walls and divisions had been put up piecemeal, and there were dark passages. The most sizeable room, which had been used by the last occupants as a dining-room, had French windows, but as these opened straight on one of the taller hedges, the room was permanently twilit, while in case anyone should be able to see across it, its wall-paper was deep brown in colour. But the beautiful shell of the house was still recognizable. In five minutes I had begun to plan its restoration, and from that moment there could be no turning back.

3

It came, as most things must, to the hard and basic matter of money. I could buy the house with the garages and garden for £3,650. Or I could buy the whole property, including the cottage and the warehouse, for £4,500. It was explained to me that the cottage, although it had six good rooms, although it was built at the same period as the house, although its decorative simplicity was unmarred by alterations, although it had a good situation and a sizeable triangle of garden, could not be considered worth more than a few hundred pounds, since its tenant was 'protected' under the Rents Restriction Act. The warehouse was roomy and well-built, but as an adjunct to a private house, not highly valued. So that the two of them represented only £850 of the purchase price.

It was clear that if I was to buy the place at all I must buy it in its entirety. The question to be settled was not between the two offers, but as to whether the purchase could be made possible to me. Four thousand five hundred pounds, I repeated rather dizzily, and that before spending any money on the restoration and equipment of the house. Desperately I sought all the arguments to justify it. The price was, or course, phenomenally cheap, for once again my luck in such things had supported me. There were endless 'possibilities' to give me confidence—I could let the warehouse and garages, for instance, or sell some part of the place to pay for the rest. The price was little more than the current one for a semi-detached suburban villa. I should live much more cheaply here than in London. I could make it worth double its present price by the outlay of a little money. And so on. But against all these formidable polemics was the clear and undeniable fact that the price was £4,500 and I possessed £500. I wondered whether it would not mean a long, perhaps interminable struggle for solvency. Whether I should not be concentrating everything, every nerve and energy, on the long and uphill task of buying this house, making it habitable and living in it.

Then I saw how the front door could be taken from its present position and put at the back of the house in a little cobbled courtyard. I saw that this would make the garden free of all invasion from anywhere but the house itself. That the front door, instead of opening on the stairs, could face a wide prospect of hall running the width of the house. I began again to plan, in fact, and in doing so forgot the difficulties of finance.

I sometimes doubt whether money exists except in the form of the little metal tokens we exchange for food or clothing. The pieces of paper, cheques and treasury notes seem as fictitious as the visionary gold of Spain. What reality can they have when a man who asks leave to overdraw his account by ten pounds pending his receipt of fifty is practically thrown into the street by the bank's doorman, while a 'business man' who demands a loan of a hundred thousand to finance an expedition prospecting for uranium, has it thrust upon him? In a varied life of factual poverty and practical comfort and freedom I have made some curious discoveries about money as it is considered by those strange and able beings who accumulate or handle it in large quantities. It has little or no relationship with life, I think. When a stranger to wealth such as I am, says, 'I wish I was rich, so that I could buy this and do that', he is repeating the time-honoured gibberish of the poor. If he *were* rich he would not buy this or do that, and if he bought this or did that he would not be rich. I once knew a Stock Exchange millionaire who only had one holiday in his short and feverish life, and that, he said, cost him thirty thousand pounds because he was absent when he should have been selling or buying something.

One thing about the situation which seemed certain to me was that if I, a money-earner with negligible capital, begged from society or the bank, from the Government or from the professional usurers, from mankind or from the building societies the means of paying a cottage rent of fifteen shillings a week, they would scarcely even be amused by my temerity, but if I roundly demanded four or five thousand pounds to purchase a house, I should be almost embarrassed by their eagerness to accommodate me.

I began, therefore, with the present owner of the house.

'If I can get a mortgage of four thousand, will you take a second mortgage of five hundred?'

I had, you will observe, learnt the jargon. The clear-cut question seemed to baffle him for a moment. Then he said yes, that could be arranged.

4

The rest of that visit to Sussex was not quite real. The weather was radiant, I remember, for I had chosen one of the few fine week-ends of 1950. I came alone to the house with the keys, and in the hollow-sounding rooms and the shadowy garden began to work out the details of restoration.

I had been warned that I could not spend more than £200 on this without a licence, though this area had unemployment in the building trade and a housing shortage. By one of the major imbecilities of our stifling bureaucratic system, it was made difficult to render habitable any premises other than those required to house the vast armies of Government employees, or to provide offices for Boards and Advisory Councils, Research and Higher Education, Ministries and Local Authorities, or such bodies as would, in due course, no doubt, refuse an application from me for permission to spend a reasonable sum on turning a ramshackle builder's yard and offices into a home. I might spend £100 in what remained of 1950—that is to say, before June 30th—and £100 in 1951. The rest was problematic. Better, I thought at once, to make plans on the assumption that any application would be refused.

The garden at least I could cultivate, for by another legislative anomaly I was allowed to employ a dozen men and spend unlimited sums on that, while the more urgent matter of living accommodation awaited permits or licences. I realized that work here would be largely a matter of clearance, for the network of cupressus hedges and the half-dozen rat-ridden and rotting sheds would have to be removed before the ground could even be ploughed.

Indoors, I began to see, the work would be much the same—clearing away unnecessary passage walls and wooden partitions and letting in a little light. During the remaining hours of that week-end I worked out the first plan, I saw how the jumble of rooms and passages could be made a home. The office, with its magnificent pine cupboards from floor to ceiling, should remain an office, though the two outside doors opening, one to the street, the other to the cobbled yard, should be closed. The present sitting-room, with its shop-window, over which great mahogany curtain-rods with carved ends to them still remained to show where lace curtains had doubtless hung, should form an L end to the hall, which would comprise what was now the larder, the dark passage and the mean square of entrance hall. It would be a wide, light area running the width of the house. The room which was now a dining-room would be my study when hedges and trees had been removed and a new window made. The kitchen, with its vast dresser and ancient range and smell of blackbeetles, would be the dining-room. Thus the four rooms on the ground floor would be logically grouped about the entrance hall. I turned then to the regions beyond the present kitchen, and decided that the scullery, which was a large tiled room with a sink and boiler, should be the kitchen, while beyond that there was room for a fair-sized larder. Beyond that again I found what had once been a separate cottage—bedroom, sitting-room and kitchen. This, I decided, could be made into a comfortable and independent home for my housekeeper.

The first floor of the house would need few changes. There were six bedrooms which could be re-decorated later, a bath-room from which a rusty old bath would be moved, and a lavatory with a magnificent mahogany carved throne which must have been nearly a century old, a piece of furniture to match early pioneer sanitary plumbing. Reluctantly I decided that this rococo relic must make way for the more characterless fitting of today.

There remained the warehouse. Here the possibilities seemed endless. It was, I found, nearly forty foot long and, built at the same time as the house, it had its fine oblong, eight-paned windows unchanged, though on the top floor they had been supplemented with other glass.

I climbed the steep stairway to this upper floor and stood there examining the mighty beams and the high roof. The windows on the east side looked over the house to a pleasant but rather too cosy vista of oast-houses and fields; from those opposite I could see the red tiles of the village, while the single window facing north gave on to a cottage back garden far below. It was like being in a windmill or on a covered church tower, so high and windy, so light and spacious did the great room seem. The old gantry stood at one end, and behind it was a sliding door through which grain or timber had once been hauled. Since I had seen what lay in all the other directions, I decided to pull this back and look southward. This was not difficult, for in spite of its size the door ran on rails and slid quietly out of the way to leave me staring into the distance.

This was certainly a 'view'. When I was marched over the Surrey downs as a six-year-old boy by my sentimental Wesleyan nurse, we used to stop while she stood looking across country. I would ask what there was to see, and be told it was 'the view'. 'What *is* a view?' I demanded. This perplexed my nurse, who paused to think before answering, 'That's one. All over there.' So now, as I gazed from the sliding doors of the high warehouse at the bounteous slopes of Sussex billowing towards the sea, I knew that although I had seen more imposing views, there had never been one so richly characteristic of the countryside which I loved and had always known. I thought of famous views descried in the past—Rio de Janeiro and Fatehpur Sikri, Table Mountain and Prague from the Hof, the eternal snows from Mussoorie and Barcelona from Tibidabo. I could have continued to recall imposing and remarkable vistas, any one of which had probably more symmetry and grace, and certainly more grandeur, than this. But not more solace, friendliness, or kind, familiar beauty.

The foreground was intimate, formed by the outskirts of the village; chicken-houses, garden trees and one lush meadow at my feet, with large heads of clover visible in the grass to remind me of how once I had sucked the tiny tubes of their petals for a taste of sweetness, and marguerites and dandelions and vetch— a field smelling of summer. Away to the left were some pines and cedars shielding a house from view, and to my right was the grey squat tower of the church. The land fell away in the middle distance to a dip crowded with trees, and behind this there were folds of green fields patterned in odd divisions and fading at last into the blue-green distance, like shadowy, deep water. On the farthest ridge were groups of trees which might have been set there by Capability Brown, such stark tufts they made against the hazy skyline.

A chance, the merest fluke of circumstances, had added one more charm to this vista—it was wholly unexpected. I should have remembered that Ticehurst stands on a hill or noticed that nothing faced the warehouse on this side. I had forgotten both circumstances when I rolled back the door and found that green-and-gold map of summer.

A little impatiently I looked back at the long room. What

1. 'A pair of
wrought-iron
gates'

2. 'This was
certainly
a "view"'

should I make of it? A studio? A party- or a play-room? A club? I saw several ways of decorating it. But that could be settled later, I thought, and returned to the open doorway. Gazing across the fields and woods, I decided at last. Whatever the cost in anxiety and energy, I would buy the house and with it the warehouse and with that the 'view'.

Reconstruction

1

On Monday morning, back in London, I began to receive notices of houses for sale. They poured in from the agents to whom I had written, but my interest in them was now an academic one. None of them seemed to offer anything like the value I had already obtained; indeed, no premises of the same size as mine without the cottage or warehouse, were priced at less than £6,000. So it is the simple truth that I did not consider or even examine another house.

Negotiations to finance my purchase by a mortgage proved as easy as I had anticipated, though I was warned that, apart from solicitors' costs and surveyors' fees, there would be some infliction called Stamp Duty, which in this case would cost me the best part of £100. This, I gathered, had been made onerous by law to render the sale and purchase of houses more difficult and expensive. It was, it seemed, lacking in a 'social sense' to wish to possess one's own home. However, I was prepared to find obstacles of this kind, and they were offset to some degree by the ease with which the mortgage itself was negotiated. So I signed where I was told to sign and the house became mine.

2

At this point there arose a problem of nomenclature. In the village of Ticehurst the house was known as 'Startin's', because Startin was the good Sussex name of the family of builders who had lived and worked here for the last century and more. I should have liked to make this its postal address, but since members of the family still lived nearby it would have caused confusion and perhaps resentment. During the nineteenth century, the age of the first pretentious house-names, it had been called alliteratively

Laurel Lodge, but as it was not a lodge and there were no laurels, this was equally unthinkable.

Houses names are more important than might appear, and in England go down to the last depths of asininity. Worst, of course, are the 'funny' ones—Kuminside, Minsabitta and Sanfairyan. Not much better are the French—Sans Souçi, Mon Repos and Chez Nous. I dislike arboreal names, especially when they are irrelevant—The Larches, Chestnut Cottage or The Laburnums. Then there are those tiresomely coy and arty names which sound like quotations—Top o' the Hill, Wings of the Morning, Windy Brow, Dream Days, Nonegobye. Seventy or eighty years ago there was a fashion for grandeur in housenames: The Towers, The Manor, The Dower House.

It is a singular fact that many luckless people condemned to live with such nonsense on their gate or over their front door suppose that there is a prohibition against changing it. Accustomed to accepting vetos, sometimes real, sometimes imaginary, without examining them, they will tell you that the postal authorities do not allow them to change the name of their house. They should remember the words of Mr. Wackford Squeers:—'A man may call his house an island if he likes; there's no act of Parliament against that, I believe?' The postal authorities, I imagine, would say that in some cases there might be delay or difficulty over the delivery of letters to an unfamiliar address, but a man, even in a bureaucratic country, need not suffer his house to be called a castle.

So a name had to be found for the house I had bought, a simple and useful one, if possible composed of monosyllables. The shape of the place and the name of a previous home of mine, during an exile in Gloucestershire, gave it to me—The Long House. That was plain enough, accurately descriptive and free of preciousness. So I explained to the village postmaster at Ticehurst, and thereafter in documents the name was used.

3

The builders who set to work to exhaust the £200 which I was allowed by law to spend were astonished and rather amused by the alterations which seemed to me most urgent.

'Now, why remove the bay window?' one of them asked, referring to the misshapen piece of grey masonry which pushed its nose into the garden.

I had discovered by observation certain things about bay windows. The Victorians spread them on every house-front, apparently believing that if they extended the area of glass they increased the light in a room. In fact, the amount of light and air is governed by the size of the aperture in the wall, and all that the bay window does is to put an opaque roof over that, thus decreasing the amount of both. If it is argued that the bay increases the size of the room, this must be admitted—by its own floor space. But if anyone wishes to increase his room, let him do so by a natural addition to it, not by this roofed and lugubrious anomaly.

These lumpish bay windows demonstrate the nineteenth-century tendency to exaggerate to a point of ugliness the pleasant characteristics of their predecessors. The charming bow windows with which earlier architects had broken the flat surface of a house-front became in their hands gross pieces of masonry and blank glass, hooded monsters for which there is nothing to be said either æsthetically or practically. The one which defaced my house was therefore to be cut off as a first step towards symmetry.

Nor did it seem to the builders intelligent of me to insist on having eight-paned windows in place of the several single panes which had been put in at various times, and which showed an ugly contrast with the original ones remaining.

'Surely there's no hurry about those?' they said. 'Before you've got the inside of the house straight? What does the number of panes matter?'

It matters most seriously. Had I not suffered from this very anachronism whenever I had looked out of my flat in Doughty Street? I remembered that one house there had been restored or had never been changed in this essential, and it had looked elegant and correct among a crowd of ill-dressed, hustling relatives. In the last half-century domestic architects have made the inhabitants of countless new houses peer through diamond panes in mass-produced frames, because their imitation Tudor cottages demanded them; but they have not shown the same sensitiveness to period in the far more important matter of the long windows of a later date. I was convinced that I could never achieve the restoration of the plain and graceful façade which had once been here unless this change was made, and gave it as my second demand.

4

Inside the house the builders were less contentious, and showed me how we could clear away the labyrinth of dark passages and disused larders to make the central hall which was to span the house. They would have to introduce a couple of oak beams, they said, to carry the weight of the upper story and roof, and on one of my impatient week-end visits they showed me these stalwart lengths of oak. They suggested that these should be painted to match the woodwork in the hall, and when I begged them to leave them bare, with only some warm linseed oil rubbed into them, they demurred.

'Look much better painted,' one of the builders said shortly, looking at me in a kindly, apprehensive way, as though I must be discouraged from some special lunacy.

The phrase he used has ruined many decent pieces of furniture, many floors and beams, shelves and mantelpieces. What, I should like to ask the stainers and painters, the grainers and varnishers who are resolved to cover wood up—what is more chaste and handsome than an untouched surface of pine, or elm, or oak, its grain giving it an exquisitely natural pattern, its colour fresh and decorative? And how many fine floors in old rooms have been rendered patchy and unpolishable by some beastly sticky stain?

I never shared the general mania for 'stripping' and 'pickling' wood which was rampant in the 'thirties, and even, grotesquely, took the waxen glow, like dark sherry, from old mahogany. But when a surface, particularly of a beam or floor, can be left as God and the carpenters of a better age than ours intended it to be, why mess it up with paint? So my beams were oiled,

and took their places in the hall ceiling, and one day, not so
many decades after my death, will be smoked and darkened to
the colour of old oak as you may see it in houses in which it has
been exposed perhaps for centuries.

5

Then we came to the question of heating, an important one
to me, who have spent a good many years in tropical or hot
climates. Kindly advisers advocated this or that system of
central heating; strange devices by which electricity warms the
oil in a radiator, I gathered, had replaced the steam heat generated
by a boiler which was once more popular. To these suggestions
I was unresponsive and not, I hope, in a merely reactionary spirit.

Central heating is not a clever invention of modern times;
it is an insalubrious development of a Roman scheme. In high,
cool places like Scandinavia and Switzerland it is valuable; for
ordinary domestic use in England it is unnecessary, unsightly,
harmful to human beings and to furniture, books and pictures.
Unnecessary because all but the largest rooms can be heated to
the degree of greatest comfort by the means allowed to them by
their architect. Unsightly because not only are metal radiators
and pipes an eyesore, however they may be concealed or flattened,
but because they too often cause the abolition of that beautiful
thing—an open fire in a sitting-room. As for the damage done
by central heating here and in America—it should be a cause of
shame to all of us in this century that we have allowed so much
of the graceful furniture of Chippendale and Hepplewhite and
Sheraton and their versatile imitators and pupils to become
buckled and dried and rotted by the artificial heat of radiators,
which they are even, sometimes, used to conceal. Old bindings
have been twisted to the shape of potato chips and old textiles
filled with moth. Moreover, though perhaps in the long run
less importantly, human beings have been chilled or made feverish, prepared for influenza and colds by the contrast between
steam-heated rooms and the air outside their windows. Or,
keeping these tight shut, they have slept at night in the fuggy
atmosphere of a Turkish bath.

Yet worse than being stifled by central heating would be to live in a chilly house of draughts and cold passages, of icy bedrooms in which the sheets feel damp from the very churchyard chill of the place, and meals are eaten in shivering haste because the dining-room is cold. I have been a guest in too many such houses to wish that anyone I might ask to my home should suffer as I have done, and I was determined to have sufficient heating to make each room, as it was used, thermally comfortable and the hall and passages of the house permanently warm.

There was no room downstairs without a fireplace, while for the bedrooms the need was for power-plugs and electric heaters, preferably fitted to the wall. Then in the hall there should be, I decided, that useful and not unsightly thing, an anthracite stove, which I hoped one day to replace with one of those Dutch or German stoves with old tiles covering them which keep an area such as this warmed evenly and sufficiently and look cosy and snug. This would mean having two open fires burning for most of the day in winter. I decided to try this, and, as I have since found, it has been sufficient. It has not meant disproportionately heavy work, and at no time during my first particularly cheerless winter did anyone in the house feel cold, while the electricity bill, though heavy, has been less than if I had installed, at vast initial expense, some system of central heating by oil and electricity.

How infectious is a bad idea, how easily we accept one as an established fact. Because central heating may be almost a necessity in hotels, blocks of offices, schools and so on, it is assumed that it is an advantage in the home. Sales talk has made people believe that heat coming from a bunch of ugly pipes is more widely diffused than heat coming from the pleasantly visible red glow of an electric fire or from the bright beauty of a hearth. Nonsense. I still remember our fights at school to be one of two or three able to warm their backsides on a steam-heated radiator, and the fact that there is no glow or flame from them makes no difference to heat diffusion. All that central heating has given me when I have lived with it in England is a stuffy head, a sense of being forced up in a hot-house and a crippling bill for fuel. My home, I resolved, should be free of it.

6

Then the fireplaces. I looked at the bright mauve tiles round little ornamental grates with dismay. In this matter again, as in the larger one of domestic architecture, there seem to me to have been three periods: the Tudor, which is picturesque and inconvenient; the Queen Anne and Georgian, which is well-proportioned and practical; the Victorian, which is ugly and unscientific. One might add the neo-Tudor for the frightful modern replicas, like brickwork tabernacles, of so-called Devon or Sussex fireplaces, but these, it must be hoped, are too ephemeral to win the name of a period.

Those of my house were Victorian, and there were brass knobs, I seem to remember, and brass or copper hoods stamped in relief with floral designs. Yet in every case there was a marble mantel-piece supported by marble side-facings, and these were reasonably plain and shapely, while in one of them, in the room which was to be a general sitting-room—or, in the jargon of the estate agent, the 'lounge'—the marble was of a rich, decisive grey and beautifully grained.

There was clearly only one way to treat these fireplaces. To remove them all and replace them with the carved and stripped pine ones of the eighteenth century, or with the replicas of these which are being made by skilled craftsmen now, would be a far too costly affair. Besides, since most of these were intended by their designers and makers to be painted, I find that their bare wood has a nude and shivering look. To retain the Victorian grates was impossible, however far they might 'throw the heat', because mauve or blue or pink tiles round an iron grate look quite deadly. I told the builders, therefore, to leave the marble surrounds and cut out the interior of the chimney, after which I looked for basket or ducks'-nest grates, and was lucky enough to buy sufficient of them.

The result has justified this step. None of them smokes. They all burn coal or logs in moderation and warm their

1. 'The hall is as bare as possible'

2. 'Between the hall and its L-shaped end'

respective rooms. Moreover, though they are not truly in period, their shape and proportions are right, and they give a certain dignity to their rooms. To adapt them from their previous ugliness, and to purchase the necessary old baskets together with one fireback, has cost no more than £9 apiece—a modest average.

7

Beyond the removal of a copper, the closing of some of the eight outside doors which were around the house, the construction of a wall across the cobbled passage behind it, the moving of the old bath from my bathroom to the housekeeper's cottage—these completed the builders' work, and in a series of week-end visits I saw the changes slowly come about. The work in progress seemed to throw into confusion my sense of time. There were weeks when I felt that the house would never be habitable, that the builders had done nothing, that winter would come before a start could be made with the decoration. But at other times it felt as though the year was running by too fast, as though this mid-step existence of mine had lost me the months of summer. Yet with each week a little more of the original design appeared, and before July I had seen enough to know that I had made no mistake. The cheese-knife removal of the Victorian bay window and the uprooting by winch of all the trees darkening the windows, except one tall Irish yew and a couple of smaller clipped ones, gave back to sight the true front of the house. Its demand for interior decoration grew insistent.

Decoration

I

WE have always been a race of gardeners, and now there are signs that our interest, which has never ceased to be lively, in interior decoration may produce some interesting results. At least we have progressed from the marqueterie, the chinoiserie and the grotesquerie of the past to a neutral state in which there is less positive ugliness and here and there some real beauty.

It should not be difficult for us to have the best-decorated homes in Europe, for the French and Italians and Spaniards, who have made in the past the most admirable furniture and textiles, have become such café-dwellers, such diners-out, that their homes are often perfunctorily decorated. The Scandinavians, who, like us, are forced by their climate to spend more time in the house, have some original and traditional schemes for its embellishment, but they lack the influence of that great era of civilized living which preceded the French Revolution. We, as islanders and colonists, have not only had beautiful things from all over the world, have not only pilfered the ideas of neighbouring countries, but have created and adapted our own. We have everything in our favour, and should scorn to live in the squalid, gimcrack surroundings which would be ours if we accepted the easiest and most politically popular way, if we bought veneered three-ply furniture by hire purchase, slapped distemper amateurishly on imperfect wall surfaces, dropped scrappy little mats on the floor and reduced lighting to a minimum, all in order to aid an illusory export programme, the savings movement, the national economy, or merely to promote the popularity of some propagandist whose success depends on our mute acceptance of what we are given.

The happiest English interiors have often grown to a natural

and harmonious grace by a process more accumulative than
consciously discriminating. I am thinking of those much-
lived-in rooms in country houses, rooms which overlook a
pleasant garden whose scents invade it. Once, perhaps, care
and discussion went to the choice of paint or wall-paper, once
someone visited a number of shops to choose the curtains. But
these and the carpet and chair-covers have grown to maturity
together, and no one notices any more what colour or pattern
they may have. They are there as the mixed hedge is at the
bottom of the garden; they are taken for granted and un-
obtrusive. Besides, with time, so many things have been brought
in to cover the walls that there is not much of them visible. There
is the one ancestor painted by William Etty, perhaps, which was
left to you by Aunt May because, as she said in her Will, she
knew you would appreciate it; and there's that flower-painting
picked up at an auction which you believe rather good and intend
to have valued one day when you have time; your grandfather's
sword hangs there because he had it in the Crimean War and it's
a beauty, anyway; then that really lovely carved mirror (you
must get that piece of carving put back—you've kept it in the
bureau drawer long enough); the three Dresden plates which
are so colourful and fresh that you've sometimes thought of
trying to carry out in real flowers the design in their centre; the
water-colour—who did the Vicar say it was by? David Cox,
of course—the sampler which your mother is certain her mother
did as a child, though the initials are all wrong and you're sure
it's older; the pair of sporting prints which those rich people
who took the Manor furnished one year gave you as a Christmas
present and which are sure to be *good*, though you have never
been quite certain that you like them there over the bookshelf;
the perfectly exquisite old fan which you found in Cadiz that time
and nearly left behind in another shop; and the family silhouettes
and minatures—rather an undistinguished collection, you always
feel, though they do look nice over the mantelpiece. How
crowded the room itself seems to have become! There was
enough furniture to 'do' it with when you came to live here just
after the First World War, but more has crept in since then.

Some good pieces—well, that awful Mr. Thing who knew all about furniture said the walnut bureau was worth over a hundred pounds, and you know the little mahogany sofa-table is a fine piece. Then that silver rose-bowl—the Madame Edouard Herriots *do* look nice in it—George's cigar-box, the pewter on that shelf, a grand old oak Bible-box, the snuff-boxes which Charlie started collecting at one time, and—— But you can't catalogue it all. You feel happy and at peace in the room, and never forget to bring flowers into it.

There is no room more charming than one which has grown like that in the home of people with a certain amount of taste but not much specialized knowledge of decoration. But you cannot make it by deliberately bringing together good miscellaneous things. If you try to do so the result will be a stage-set or an antique shop kept by energetic ladies. It has to grow of its own accord, and will do so if you have enough natural discrimination and live another twenty-five years.

2

At the other extreme are those rooms which attempt fidelity to a certain period, so that everything irrelevant to it is severely excluded. The age which is most generally in favour at the moment is the Regency, for which the most I myself can say is that its productions are less ugly than those of the Victorians but too *outré* and Gothic in conception to be more than a decorator's fad. I know one house, built during the Regency, which, in the manner of its time, has pointed windows and, I seem to remember, a bit of faked battlement here and there. This is Norman Hartnell's home near Windsor, and he has most cleverly decorated all its rooms in the same manner. It has great charm, a voluptuous diversity of colour, and is almost flawless in its faithfulness to its school, but for me too rich and self-conscious as a background to the everyday business of life. Other rooms which I remember seeing successfully ape the interior of Brighton Pavilion, and some of them are attractively outlandish. But I have no ambition to create one, still less to apply this fashion to an entire house.

More gloomy and more difficult are truly Tudor rooms with their solid oak and heavy wrought-iron. Or Jacobean houses in which the oak furniture swells to housemaid's knees and stump pictures adorn the walls. Empire or Louis-Quinze rooms are no less difficult to achieve or to live in, and the few attempts I have seen to make Chinese rooms have ended in unmentionable disasters in which pots of lacquer and rice-paper prints have had their part.

Period, in decoration, should surely be a guide and an ideal rather than a rule or a criterion. After all, we shall not dress in period, or introduce the lighting, heating or upholstery which our Jacobean or Elizabethan ancestors used, so there seems little point in an absolute conformity. On the other hand, there are anachronisms which are as offensive as clashing colours or discords.

3

The worst period to revere is the present. There is always a thing called the very latest, and it is healthy to remember that Hepplewhite was a modern just as the makers of Victorian whatnots were. The only way to view the products of our own age is with detachment. Are they practical, æsthetically admirable or are they vulgar and misshapen? Speaking more generally than is perhaps advisable in such a matter, I would say that though our interior decorating is interesting and progressive, it is so only in so far as it avoids the silly and unsightly things which are sold as 'the latest' or the 'furniture of tomorrow'. Certainly the idea of having one room decorated and filled with the best of our own time is an attractive one. Its danger lies in the fearfully swift rotations of contemporary fashion. I know one man who decided when he bought his house in the early 'thirties to have one modern room and ordered chairs of nickel tubing, a mantelpiece of irregular design, cupboards flush to the wall, plastic curtains and a carpet which looked like a diagram to prove a Euclidean proposition. It was all right while it lasted; its inherent ungainliness could be forgiven while it was 'the latest thing'. But although it was arranged only twenty years ago, it is already out-dated by surrealism, and its chromium looks harsh, its woodwork misshapen, while the cramps and stitches caused by its furniture remind one that a chair, after all, is made to give ease and comfort, and not to be an item in an elaborate scheme of décor.

4

Compromise is the thing. If a basic style of decoration is adopted, be it William Morris or William and Mary, Queen Anne, Regency, Lyons Corner House or Elizabethan, Balkan or Dutch, Empire, Byzantine, Chinese, Edwardian, Surrealistic, Monastic, Rococo or Georgian, there is no need to try to make every article conform. An effect will evolve in which occasional breaches give a certain charm. What is needed is an over-all, fairly elastic scheme with variations which do not offend the spirit of it.

That, at least, was what I needed for my house. My furniture consists for the most part of country-made eighteenth-century pieces, mahogany or fruit-wood, though I have a few rather earlier bits of oak. With these I have to make blend several thousand books, a collection of English water-colours, a quantity of Majolica and other continental pottery and a number of pieces of carved wood, some painted and gilt, some polished. The decoration, therefore, might be said to be baroque; for the dull gold of an Italian carved mirror and the pink cheeks of painted *amorini*, and the gilt quiver and arrows of a pair of Adam wall-lights, and the pottery itself give a general effect of crude and faded grandeur such as one might find in a Spanish village church.

But not too much of it. I have seen this kind of decoration carried to a hideous absurdity. Once anyone starts *collecting* baroque items and looking round his room for a place in which to put a new one, he is lost. It can only succeed in an English room if it is used (as it was never intended to be used) sparingly. It was this that I meant to have it in my house, and so sought the right background for it, the right colour and finish for the walls, the floor, the ceiling.

5

There is a firm of wall-paper manufacturers in London which specializes in designs actually in use two hundred years ago, and in one case holds as a relic the original block from which paper was printed in Queen Anne's reign. I had seen their products in the houses of my friends and been delighted with the rightness and restfulness of them. I remembered particularly a room in John Rothenstein's home which had a scarlet-and-gold paper of a design used in Brighton Pavilion, and in other places there were stripes and stars and spots like the neat markings of hand-embroidered waistcoats in Beau Nash's time.

Wall-paper, until this firm and others revived the small regular patterns of the earliest makers, had become a grisly phantasmagoria stretched across the wall like a disease, and could be dangerous, if not fatal, when it surrounded a sick man of the slightest sensitiveness. I can look back to childhood and remember bunches of sickly yellow lilac round which, at regular intervals, wound blue and pink ribbon looking as though it had been pulled out of the lacework of women's stale underclothes. I still recoil from repetitive clumps of six pale blue cherries on a lace-work stripe matched with seven pink primroses on dusty yellow watered silk. In too many rooms have I woken to be greeted by alternate grey carnations and deep crimson lilies-of-the-valley to accept even the idea of wall-paper lightly. I can remember the jaundiced roses round me at my preparatory school, the nightmare of sweet peas in baskets or similar equidistant collections of formalized flowers and fruit which greeted my returning consciousness in each of the four preparatory schools at which I taught before I was twenty, the mauve network in which wild roses rambled, strictly according to pattern, in endless apartments and hotels here and abroad.

'But,' said the decoratiors, 'you've got to have something on these walls. Short of re-plastering them, which would cost a great deal of money.'

'What's wrong with them?'

'Nothing. Only age. They'll be all right for your lifetime, and more. But you'll have to paper them or reface them.'

So I thought of the firm that made the old wall-papers, and in their showrooms chose two papers: a cool lime-green with a small neat design of silver rosettes, each rosette being about half-an-inch in diameter with a clear inch between it and the next. It was a pattern such as Alexander Pope might have ordered for his house at Twickenham. For my study and the dining-room I varied this by having the same design in gold on an off-white surface. The price was moderate, but here again I had to pay my dole to the insatiable State in the form of purchase tax, for wall-paper with which to cover the scars of wartime and age in house walls is obviously a luxury which only the most grossly sensual sybarite could want, and so merits the heaviest taxation.

There is one other penalty for those who use a fine wall-paper —they must find one of the few remaining craftsmen paper-hangers to hang it. The paper-hanger of your building firm is a good chap, and has plenty of experience in hanging ordinary papers, but he will probably come to grief on a 'distemper finish' paper. However, this is not like so many crafts nowadays, and it is still possible, though difficult, to find a master of it.

6

With this green I decided to keep the woodwork ivory white, or—perhaps more accurately—a pale Sung cream. This meant another tussle with the decorators, who felt that a green wall-paper should have a green paint, but ceded the point eventually. So one week-end I saw at last the hall and the sitting-room in the L of it looking fresh and light, the cream and green demanding loudly the dark and seasoned wood of old furniture to be set against them.

But there was one thing to be added which, like all boldly attractive pieces of decoration, was not without an element of risk. It would either make a brilliant success of the whole scheme or it would look out of place, even a little macabre. I decided to take the risk.

A year previously I had purchased from an Oxfordshire

1. 'In the jargon of the estate-agent—"the lounge"'

2. 'A meagre collection of walking-sticks'

antique dealer a vast Florentine bed of the seventeenth century. It had been in pieces in his store-room, a discouraging collection of billowy gilt carving.

'If you will pack the thing and take it away,' he said, 'you can have it for a tenner. It's been here for years, and I suppose I should reconstruct it and show it, but it would cost the earth to put it together, and I've nowhere to let it be seen.'

I saw that it would be useless as a bed, for few modern rooms could hold it, and it would be necessary to have a spring mattress and bedding specially made for it. But there were other possibilities. Its four posts were finely carved; Ceres and Bacchus were at the head, Ceres rather brazenly using her cornstalk as a fig-leaf and Bacchus with the usual mass of grapes in his arms and on his head. At the foot were Jupiter and Juno. The gilt panels were enormous—there were giants in the earth in those days. The whole thing had an air of belonging so much to another age that it brought history down to us, the authentic aura of a good antique.

When I saw it there in the musty showroom I had no notion of how it could be used, but I recognized that it accorded with my general scheme of decoration, and bought it, and stored it. Now I saw its possibilities.

The dining-room, I have explained, was being adapted from the old kitchen, and the removal of the range had left a high mantelpiece and a cavernous grate beneath. This could be entirely reconstructed with two bed-posts and a panel to become an ornate whole. Yes, said the carpenter, he could do it. He was a Sussex man, born five miles away, who had no conception of what a Florentine bed of three centuries ago might be like, but yes, he could make a fireplace out of those figures and that panel. He did.

In the hall was a tumbledown fireplace of chipped and dirty marble in which my anthracite stove was to stand. I knew that when marble has lost its freshness and become grubbily rubbed and chipped there is no cure for it, and I had it painted, while Jupiter and Juno were cut to support the mantelpiece, and another panel ran between them.

D

That was not all. Long pieces of the carved panelling remained, the gold paint of a more rococo age still gleaming on
them and small fat angels with dogs distinguishable in the relief.
These were cut to fit the recesses on each side of the fireplace in
the lounge (as I must, I suppose, call the sitting-room L end of the
hall) and let in under the ceiling. Since the recesses were to be
shelved, these panels would be at about thirty inches over the
top shelf, and behind them would be electric lights shining down
on whatever I put on the shelf. So the whole bed was to be
absorbed into the general scheme.

I waited with anxiety for the week-end when I should first see
this done. Would it look pretentious? Over-ornate? Would
my Sussex carpenter have been too precise or unimaginative?

I need not have worried. When I saw it all, the fireplaces
and the light panels, I knew that they 'fitted', that this anomalous
gilt bed might, by some freak of taste or circumstances, have
been built into the house by its first occupant.

The whole place seemed ready, seemed impatient even, for
occupation.

Fittings

I

THE two monstrous and inescapable expenses of a new home are curtains and carpets. In these there are few bargains or means of economizing. Even curtains bought secondhand, though they may be of a quality rare today, are not often adaptable to other windows, and though Persian rugs may still occasionally be found at prices less than those obtaining in London, they must be set on a floor-ground, and this may mean cost untold.

Not, of course, if the purchaser or tenant of an oldish house is lucky enough to have, or knowledgeable enough to recognize, flooring of one of the woods which can be cleaned, oiled and waxed. These are far less rare than might be supposed. I remember finding in a Cotswold cottage a floor of golden pinewood. It had the usual border stained with some odious preparation claiming to produce an effect of oak, and the rest of it was so ingrained with dust that even after a first scrubbing it was hard to recognize its potentialities. But when the stain had been removed by a solution of caustic soda and the whole surface thoroughly oiled and polished there was a floor of soft texture and a rare sunlit colour which made the room beautiful.

At Ticehurst the floors were severely of deal, and had to be covered before I could put down the few Persian rugs which in a lifetime of search are all that I have been able to collect A one-coloured Wilton cut to measure would have been my solution before the war, but to do the hall and lounge, the staircase and landing in this with an underfelt would have cost nearly £300 at current prices. So I decided on a material called, in the detestable vocabulary of the department store, an 'art felt'.

I had used this 'art felt' in my flat in London, and found that its good qualities were many. It was less exorbitantly expensive

43

than most floor-coverings—a lapse on the part of the price-setters which has since been made good. It wears exceedingly well; better, I think, than many modern 'all-over' carpets. It is obtainable immediately in many colours. It is smooth, soft, pleasant to walk on. It shows off one's rugs far more effectively than does a carpet. It has, on the other hand, one paramount disadvantage—attempts to clean its stains result only in larger areas of discoloration.

I ordered it, however, for the hall in a deep Pompeian brown, which, so far from being gloomy, is a discreetly gay colour on the floor if it is to be relieved by the radiant geometrical patterns in Bokhara red and blue of a few rugs. The stairs and landing had to be carpeted, but I obtained a Wilton in the same colour. The felt which I already had would do the other rooms downstairs, and the bedrooms would have to be left bare until opportunity provided for them. Even so, the cost was over £120, and I still see no way in which it could have been avoided or reduced.

2

No less difficult was the business of obtaining curtains. When windows were draped with black sateen during the war, and women described to their friends the gay hues which would one day replace those black-out curtains and dreamed of long graceful folds of soft colour which would frame their daytime outlook and bountifully fall by night, they had not reckoned with the Cromwellian State which was to replace the England they once knew. They had naïvely supposed that they would be allowed a certain width of selection in the way they would live, that such things as purchase tax would disappear and that—for instance—they would at least be able to sling a few yards of cretonne across the sitting-room windows without being accused of an act of sabotage against the nation's recovery programme. How little they foresaw! For the first three years there were no curtain materials to buy, and when a few dribbled on to the market there was no money left in private hands with which to buy them.

I remembered, though, that it was precisely such drab inhibitions which I intended to defeat. If it meant appropriating all I should earn for a year, if it meant branding myself as a drone, a parasite, and an enemy of the workers, I was determined that my house should have pleasing and appropriate curtains, non-utility, egregious, unstinted in size or quality, of the right colour and texture, well-made, promptly supplied, imported if necessary, expensive if occasion demanded. No dyed sacking craftily sold as hessian; no ill-printed cretonne; no 'we think it's awfully pretty stuff—I wonder if you can guess how much it cost a yard'; no wonderful second-hand bargains made for larger windows ('We had to have those strips put down the side, but we really *like* them now'); no 'we got them in an auction—it's only in that *one* place that they're a little faded'; no second best, no making-do, no imitation this or that. Curtains, indeed, of which I could be proud, not only because they were right in my eyes, but because they were wrong, morally, in the eyes of people who accepted popular social doctrines.

Colour was the most important consideration, and at least in this I was fortunate in knowing, before I had examined a single textile, just what I wanted. Indeed, it seemed to me that there could be no more than one colour which would contrast happily with the green and cream of the walls and the deep brown of the felt, which would give the light entering an extra tinge of warmth, which would accord with the sparsely baroque decorations of the room. Gold. A rich, uncoppery, yellow gold, such as the Conquistadores coveted. A most non-utility colour, a colour to dazzle the eyes of neo-puritans. Saint-seducing gold, Romeo called it. Moreover, a colour which, rightly chosen, would be neither ostentatious nor unnoticeable, neither commonplace nor *outré*.

As to material—no cloth with a neat or fiddling pattern would hang in a room which had carved wood figures and country-made furniture in it. It must be bold, suggestive of old, coarsely embroidered designs; it must look weighty, and yet not flat or tugged, a material full of sunlight. It must gleam, but not glitter. It must be warm and light, but not fiery.

All this I meant to find in a curtain material 'released for home purchase' and at a price which would not be an impossibility for me. I was told immediately that if any such materials were in the course of manufacture in England now they were only to be shipped abroad, to bolster up the State's balance sheet. And women of experience in such matters were not encouraging.

'If you're prepared to pay about five pounds a yard,' they said, 'you might find something which you wouldn't hate in a fortnight. But don't expect to have any *choice* at that price.'

I remained undismayed. Having gone so far with a lucky wind behind me, I was not prepared to meet failure. But I expected a long and difficult chase.

As a preliminary to this I decided to look at the stock of a Tunbridge Wells shop. I peered a little bleakly at striped cotton and printed chintz. Then on a shelf above the salesman's head I saw a roll of something which looked woolly and mustard-coloured.

'What's that?' I asked.

In a moment it was unrolled before me. The woolliness had been on the wrong side of the material. Opened it was a gold brocatelle, its design raised in heavy silky thread. It was so exactly what I wanted that I could scarcely steady my voice to ask the price.

'Eighteen-and-six a yard', said the salesman calmly. 'It only came in today. It's a Dutch material—forty-eight inches wide.'

I demanded firmly that the whole roll should be put aside for me till measurements had been taken. A few weeks later the curtains were made up, lined with sateen, crowned with pelmets shaped to my own design, pelmets ornamented with a shining white tasselled fringe three inches deep. I wonder now whether Dutch housewives see this material in their shops marked 'for export only'. Perhaps they do, and hurry on to purchase what they want, fresh from an English loom.

3

There remained one essential fixture to be added before I could move in. Bookshelves.

The late A. J. A. Symons, an arrogant and hard-working

eccentric, once told me that he had not let a day pass without buying a book since he was seventeen years old. It did not occur to me at the time to ask how he stored the accumulating volumes. It is a problem for every book-collector, from the man who buys Everyman classics to the Directors of the British Museum. Some try to solve it with glass-covered oblongs which can be obtained in uniform sizes and added to at will. But that is impossible to one who thinks, as Sydney Smith did, that no furniture is as charming as books. Others go to the other extreme, and improvise endlessly with wood of varying thickness, length, colour and width, so that their books are in strange huddles and hoards. Yet others build their shelves to the ceiling so that a man feels threatened and overcome by the towering volumes around him, rising unrelieved by wall or picture, and demanding that perilous little step-ladders should be kept at hand. An error made by one is to have the divisions of his shelves too far apart, so that the unsupported line of books sags and wavers. Another is to put the shelves themselves too close together, so that arrangement by authorship or category becomes impossible. Or too far apart, which makes the books look lonely and scant, like a thin red line of infantry. Shelves too thick are cumbersome and buckle irreparably. A carpenter who has never collected books himself will make the divisions between shelves of curving design—useless to set a book against. An undomesticated man will design shelves to come down too near to the floor for a broom or vacuum cleaner to encompass. And so on.

As a bookseller and collector for some twenty-five years, I had made most of these mistakes at one time or another, and was determined now, as I was with so many things in the house, that my experience should be useful. I decided to abandon (selling them if possible) all the shelves that remained to me of a daringly designed set which had once covered a long wall in my little Gloucestershire house. They had been made of Japanese oak an inch thick and now were twisted, unwieldy and ill-spaced. To replace them I designed shelves to fit all the walls of my study at Ticehurst, rising to a height of four feet, except those against the longest wall, which were broken by a drop in the middle. This gave me four shelves for a total length of thirty-two feet and would hold about fifteen hundred books. A similar set along one wall of the hall would take another five hundred, and the shelves in the recesses on each side of the fireplace in the lounge would absorb a thousand. This would do for the moment, and leave the office free for files and stationery and that annoying extravagance, copies of my own books for reference, reprinting or, in cases of the greatest rarity, presentation.

I designed these shelves with care and, rather smugly, I believe them to be impeccable. The length of the shelves between divisions, which varies slightly, since the whole set is constructed to fit the room, is about forty inches. All the uprights are one inch thick, and the shelves themselves five-eighths. The top two shelves are nine and a half inches apart, the lower two ten and a half. The bottom shelf is four inches from the floor, but the base is completely cased in. The top shelf overlaps at the ends by less than half an inch. The depth of the shelves throughout is eleven inches.

The effect of such shelving in a fairly high room is of coloured panelling round its lower half. Their open tops give great scope to collectors of any kind of small ornaments, and there is ample space for pictures above them.

I had little choice of timber, and after some enquiry had the shelves made of a wood described as Tasmanian oak, which is good enough to remain bare. A year or two will tell me if it should be left as it is, or oiled, or painted. The total cost of the whole thing was £65.

4

So decoration was finished, carpets down, curtains up, shelves in place. It was time for me to move.

This, too, meant some thought. Moving can be done rashly and hurriedly with disastrous ill-effect, and I had heard plenty of stories of things 'lost in the move' or 'broken in the move', or of wild confusion at 'the other end' which could not be straightened out for days.

The scheme I followed is very simple, and not in the least

1. 'A miscellany of odds and ends, offensive and defensive'

2. 'There is a Flemish Nativity in oak on the bookshelves'

original. There are two moves, a small one with a lorry and,
a week or so later, a large one with a pantechnicon. The first
transports all carpets, curtains, bookshelves and fixtures of every
kind, so that these are respectively laid, hung, fixed before the
main bulk of one's possessions is carried to the house. The
advantages are obvious, but only fully so to one who is experienced in moving house. That the moving-men can put everything in place at once, that there is no question of—'leave that
here for now; we'll see to it later', that the work for them and
for oneself is halved, that one can settle down in far less time and
that there is not so much opportunity for breakages.

The Mortuary

I

BEYOND the kitchen were four rooms which had once been a separate cottage. The smallest of these and the nearest to my house had become my larder, but a door opened from it to a few feet of passage-way from which the remaining two downstairs rooms could be entered and from which a little staircase went up to a large, low bedroom.

When I had first seen these rooms I decided that they would make admirable quarters for my housekeeper. She would have her own front door and a minute square of garden between her sitting-room window and Church Lane, the quiet little road which ran behind my house. Moreover, the bedroom had windows looking in three directions, one of which commanded the view southwards. A bath was put into the back room downstairs. She would have, in fact, an independent cottage with a way through to my rooms. This convenient arrangement had seemed to be one of the main advantages of the house.

For I had at that time a housekeeper whom any man would envy, a Treasure, a Paragon, an Angel. Mrs. Deacon, as we will call her, was the third of three splendid and beloved women who had kept house for me in London. Asked by covetous friends how I managed to find these succeeding angels, I said, quite truthfully, that I put an advertisement into the showcase of a local tobacconist's, though I did not add that the key-words of the advertisement, the bait, the certain draw, were 'For bachelor establishment'. Women, it may be generalized boldly, will work for a man when they will not work for another woman. They explain this quite logically, 'You don't get a lot of fuss where there's only a man. I like my kitchen to myself. I can't stand interference. A woman is On At you all the time.' So when my little advertisement was shown three times in a shop in Theobalds Road, during my four years in London, each showing produced a number of applicants, from among whom I chose, successively, the three.

The first angel may be called Mrs. Curtis, a plump, talkative, cheerful soul who had once been in private service and secretly kept the prejudices and sentiments of a happier age, though contemporary influences, or her grown-up son and husband, had made a vociferous Socialist of her. How fiercely she would dismiss news of the Royal Family, which in her warm heart she longed to hear, by saying that she had no use for that sort of thing. What deep-hidden regret she felt that she could not join a cheering crowd milling round Winston Churchill, but angrily gave thanks that he was out of office. She longed to praise Lord Woolton at the expense of the Food Minister of the time, but she had adopted her party and remained loyal to it.

For a year she arrived daily in a bustle of cheerful talk and activity. The weather, the news, her husband's health, her son's career—and all the time her duster or broom at work as hard as her tongue. She had a happy laugh and a business-like way with a vacuum cleaner. She was entertaining and a scrupulous polisher. She might have continued to keep my flat clean until I left London if at the end of a year her husband had not died suddenly.

She was succeeded by Mrs. Siddons, an angel of another kind. Where Mrs. Curtis had been jolly and brisk, Mrs. Siddons was quiet and industrious, a gentle but no less happy soul who never left a rug unturned or a corner dusty. She would answer in a soft, rather musical voice when spoken to, but I could scarcely tell when she was in the flat, so discreet was she and so silently busy. She was as greatly appreciated as Mrs. Curtis had been, and would not have left, I am sure, if after a year she had not returned to her home one day to find her husband dead there.

Undaunted by this repetition of circumstances, I again showed a card in the shop-window, and this time secured the most remarkable of the three, the very archangel of that heavenly choir. Mrs. Deacon had the briskness of Mrs. Curtis with the discretion of Mrs. Siddons. She had been a sergeant in the A.T.S., and worked as though she wanted to do the jobs of her entire section. She was a good cook, and did not mind how long she stayed at the flat, so that for the first time I could have a friend or two to dinner. And if she had a husband she never mentioned him, and passed the danger period at the end of a year without comment. When I decided to leave London she had been with me for two years, and said without hesitation that she would like to keep house for me in the country. It was therefore for her, for this domestic functionary whom even Mrs. Beeton could scarcely have criticized, that the little cottage beyond the kitchen had been furnished, decorated and arranged.

'In fact,' said Mrs. Deacon, 'I've always wanted to get back to the country. I shall never really be used to London. I'm glad you've decided to move.'

Merrily she did the work of three moving-men as we prepared to leave London, then drove down with me and my secretary to Ticehurst. We arrived on a warm August evening, and for the first time Mrs. Deacon saw the house and her own adjoining cottage. Her enthusiasm was loud and sincere. She saw at once where she would put her saucepans, her brooms, her cleaning materials. She seemed almost instantly to have settled in. She particularly approved of her cottage.

On one of the occasions on which the previous owner had joined me in examining the house and planning its adaptation we had looked into this housekeeper's cottage.

'This,' he said with suspicious casualness, 'was the mortuary.'

'The *what*?'

'The mortuary. Most village builders are undertakers as well. It's not often they have a corpse on their hands, but they have to have somewhere to put it when it does happen. They used this little sitting-room downstairs.'

We went out to the yard, and I never gave the matter another thought. After all, death must have occurred in most of the rooms of a house of any age, and past history of such premises is of little account. 'Mortuary' was a cold and ugly word, but the sunny little sitting-room with its window facing South had

nothing in the least gruesome about it; indeed, like the rest of
the house, it had a friendly and contented atmosphere. Mrs.
Deacon, for instance, said she felt at home in it at once. Its past
was forgotten as much as that of the rest of the house. But not, it
appeared, in the village of Ticehurst, where people still shuddered
at the thought of it.

'I shouldn't care to go into it at night,' one might say.

'Not very *nice*, is it?' another would suggest, while the name
'mortuary' is retained with a certain unction. Perhaps in all the
century and more during which my house was inhabited by
builders this cottage may have kept a dead guest for the night on
half a dozen occasions, but there was the name, the forbidding
and awesome name. I was up against one of the greatest powers
on earth, that of words.

Had I guessed that anyone would give more attention to the
matter than I did, had I realized that the people of the village still
shivered and nudged at the mention of it, I should have warned
Mrs. Deacon. But I did not. What was more, there were local
men still working in the house when we moved in, local people
coming to the back door curious to see what strangely courageous
stranger had made a sitting-room of the unmentionable apartment,
and local shopkeepers serving Mrs. Deacon and eager to discuss
the grim matter with her. And on the fifth morning after our
arrival at Ticehurst I came down to find no breakfast laid, a still-
ness in the kitchen and in the rooms beyond, and a note on the
mantelpiece addressed to my secretary and stating simply that
Mrs. Deacon's luggage would be called for. A word, as potent as
a witch's spell, had been breathed into her ear, and my third angel
had vanished.

3

This early-morning departure, with all the circumstances of
mystery, left two distinct problems, one an urgent one, the other
more remote—how to replace Mrs. Deacon and what to do with
the housekeeper's cottage.

I do not regret the disappearance of domestic service as it was
in my childhood. Whether it is to be regretted as it was in the

Victorian age and before is a larger question, and depends on whether or not you consider, as the Greeks and Romans did once and as the Russians do now, that civilization must rest on a basis of slavery. I suppose arguments could be improvised in defence of the great household with the servants' hall having its own dynastic community, but surely there is no argument in favour of the precarious remains of domestic service which persisted among the middle classes until the last war. 'Don't do that—it will upset the servants!' was a parrot-cry of my parents. For the first forty years of this century life in middle-class English homes was dominated by the terror of losing some slipshod, ham-fisted slattern who had been induced to come and work against the advice of all her friends. The endless treks by harassed ladies of twenty years ago round the registry offices, the fruitless interviews at back doors, must still return to them in nightmares. Then the expected arrival which frequently did not after all happen, the first anxious days. 'Is she any good?' 'Will she stay?' 'Does she mind the kitchen being so small? Or so large?' The servile consideration which the household had to give to the lightest whim of their new acquisition. And with it all the struggle to persuade her to play her part in keeping up appearances—an apron in the afternoon, the handing of dishes when there were guests to dinner, the whole sickening make-believe and toadyism of the time.

I regret none of it, and I cannot see how any woman who has her faculties and reasonable health can regret doing the work herself rather than cajole and bribe some insolent slut to dress up as a housemaid. Honest labour is another matter, and that can still be obtained and paid for. It was not the hard work that made domestic service unpopular, it was the mockery of it in a society in which it had become a mere pantomime of what it once had been. There are plenty of women now who will work in a house, and work loyally and well, because they are not 'maids' or 'cooks'; they do not have 'nights out' and 'followers'; they do not have to conform to the trumpery standards of middle-class pretentiousness. They come in from their own homes and earn their two shillings an hour and 'don't mind what they do'.

There is a certain dignity about such labour, for neither employer nor employee is humiliated by it. It leads to greater knowledge and efficiency on the part of the housewife herself, through which it may eventually come about that the English will learn to cook. It is a decent, a democratic and at the same time comfortable arrangement which has relieved the mother of a family of her most acute worries.

How, I wondered after the departure of Mrs. Deacon before six o'clock that morning—how was I to reconcile my convictions about this with the making and keeping up of a home such as I meant mine to be? It was a question which brought no panic, for either I or my Indian secretary could, at a pinch, do everything in a house which she had done. But it was urgent because until it was solved my own work was at a standstill.

I thought first of a married couple who would occupy the cottage while the wife did my housework. But clearly only the housing shortage would drive any married couple to such an arrangement, and I did not want to take advantage of it. Or a married couple, both in my employ? The cost of this with food, light, heat and wages would, I calculated, exceed £10 a week. Another resident housekeeper, then? It was not an altogether attractive idea, for Mrs. Deacon would be hard to replace and I preferred to have the house to myself. That left only one course —to employ what are conveniently known as 'dailies'. I embarked on this somewhat dubiously, for I had not yet seen the whole question of service as clearly as I do now.

At first it seemed that supplies of angels were exhausted. Or, if they were still on the market, they were too easily enticed to highly-paid seasonal work in the fields. But after early experiments, tranquillity and content were brought back to my life with the ministrations of Mrs. Rummery and her daughter Mrs. Piper. 'Angels are bright still,' I said. 'Angels in broad-brimmed hats and russet cloaks.' For Mrs. Rummery and Mrs. Piper not only have the thoroughness, the humour, cheerfulness and punctuality of Mrs. Curtis, Mrs. Siddons and Mrs. Deacon, they have not only volunteered to come on Sundays—a rare concession in the country—they not only clean and polish and

scrub with care and competence, but also they make the phrase
'good plain cooking' less of a paradox than it appears.

4

There remained the housekeeper's cottage, which I will cheerfully call the mortuary, in case it may seem that I am afraid of the
word.   During the period of uncertainty and experiment before
God sent me Mrs. Rummery and Mrs. Piper, it stayed empty,
for it seemed that it might after all be necessary to use it as a kind
of bait to some hesitant house-worker.   Even then, unvisited for
weeks at a time, it never seemed derelict or forbidding : it remained an inviting little cottage.   The Virginia creeper on its
wall grew crimson, then naked, the box hedge, as high as it was
long, which divided its tiny garden from Church Lane, sprouted
untidily.   But still its bedroom window was the only one looking
south, and still a fire in its sitting-room brought the whole place
back to cosy life.

At last, when there was no more fear that I should have to use
it to attract some homeless family which might provide a housekeeper for me, I decided to let it.   But first, I knew, it must be
furnished.   I already had one six-roomed cottage let at a negligible
rent to a 'protected' tenant, and I had no intention of allowing a
part of my house to fall under the lunatic injustice of an Act
which frequently forces the owner of a house to suffer an annual
loss on his property.

So six months or more after I had moved in, I partly furnished
the housekeeper's cottage, and advertised it in a London daily to
be let at £2 a week.   The result was, of course, a registered
parcel from the newspaper containing over three hundred letters.
A most baffling situation, for I could not, after all, ask intending
tenants to give details about themselves as if they were applying
for a job, and I could not, on the other hand, ask them to spend
time and money in coming to see the cottage if it was unsuitable
for them, or they were unsuitable for it.   For a day or two I
stared uneasily at the stack of letters and telegrams, then began to
read them.

The next hour is one which I should like to forget.   To what

degradation are we brought by the failures of bureaucracy!
Six years after the end of the war, in a country ironically called
victorious, members of a race once renowned for ingenuity,
industry and independence are so pitifully in need of homes that
a Box Number advertisement such as mine, which specified as
many as possible of the disadvantages of the premises offered,
produced letters pleading, fawning, promising, letters which
told pitiful life-stories or boasted of exceptional personal qualities,
which shamefacedly confessed to their writers' possession of
children or pets, which complained that their writers' lives were
being wrecked for lack of accommodation or their marriages
threatened or their health imperilled. Apologetic letters: 'I am
sorry to say that we have a child,' one ran. Persuasive letters:
'Do please give us a chance; we have waited so long.' Pompous
or bragging letters: 'I can assure you we should be excellent
tenants and no trouble to you in any way.' Flattering letters:
'Your cottage sounds ideal and I'm sure you must be kind to let
it so cheaply.' I found it hard to believe, as I examined them,
that they came from my compatriots.

However, I was saved from embarrassment by the recognition
of a name. 'Richard Hope Hawkins' was the signature at the
bottom of a curt and business-like letter asking for further details.
My mind went back to the 'twenties, when, with memories of
Ruritania and my own Christian name, I had called the hut in
which I lived 'Hentzau', and someone had sent on a piece of my
notepaper to Sir Anthony Hope Hawkins, who as Anthony Hope
had not only brought that Balkan kingdom into being, but,
much more significantly, had written *The Dolly Dialogues*. He
wrote me a courteous little letter of congratulation on my feeble
joke, and now, twenty years and more later, finding his surname
at the foot of one of these letters, my choice was made for me. I
answered only one of the three hundred applications, and have as
tenants the six-foot-five son of the novelist and his wife and
young son, while in a spare room of this house, a gift in apprecia-
tion of my choice, hangs the original wash drawing of the Spy
caricature of Anthony Hope.

So the mortuary has become 'Church Lane Cottage'. My

E

tenants call their sitting-room the Laying-Out room, but add
that their bedroom is the Laying-In room. The shock of Mrs.
Deacon's mysterious departure is forgotten as I eat Mrs.
Rummery's *tête de mouton vinaigrette* and see Anthony Hope's
grandson rush by on his bicycle.

Furnishing

I

THE story of the mortuary has taken me ahead of events. My house was still in the chaos which must be left after the departure of even the best moving-men. The framework was complete and my possessions, scraped together during twenty years of unsubsidized collecting, were sufficient to fill it. There remained the long, delightful task of arrangement.

This, as I have suggested, followed certain broad lines in every room. Bookcases or other furniture against the walls left an area above them for my ever-increasing collection of English water-colours, and provided a top shelf at rather under eye-level for the old carved and painted wooden figures of saints which I loved and which I had brought home at different times from Spain and Italy. Between them, and in an open corner cupboard and elsewhere, could be placed the pieces of Majolica and other continental pottery, their rough designs in green, blue and yellow according well with the carving. There were drug-pots and plates and jugs, not only from the Mediterranean countries but from Germany and Holland, all of one character however, all crude, uneven in shape and pattern, all very notably the work of potters and not of artists in porcelain. Then the furniture itself, none of it delicate or too detailed, but country-made pieces of the eighteenth century which had neither the finished fussiness of Empire or Regency furniture nor the heavy oak puritanism of an earlier age. That was the general scheme, and I soon found that the house absorbed it comfortably.

Between the hall and its L-shaped end, which was to be the only general sitting-room, I had had constructed a pair of double doors which could be lifted clean off their hinges and removed for the summer months, or folded right back against the wall to

59

leave an open space, or closed to make the little room snug in cold weather. It was this little room, variably a part of the hall or an independent apartment, which I arranged first.

The fireplace here, it may be remembered, was of a fine grey marble, and into the space which had once been filled by mauve tiles and an ugly grate, I had put a basket-grate with a small fireback. Above the mantelpiece I now hung a gilt Italian mirror, a rather late piece of carving, but one of fair proportions and finish for the room. The little Georgian bow window, which had replaced the shop window on the street side, had to have glass curtains, and in this, I found, modern materials are a vast improvement on older ones. Those gloomy white hangings in patterned network which were almost invariably used till about 1910, and may still be seen occasionally, were for the most part replaced by the honest square netting of the 'twenties and 'thirties, heavy stuff and hard to hang, but less offensive than its predecessors. Now there are materials filmy and transparent as a bridal veil which hang gracefully, and allow the maximum of vision outwards and prevent passers-by from staring in. I found one called, rather theatrically, Ninon, and it hung over the windows behind the heavy gold curtains which cut out the shape of the bow at night and had pelmets broad and stiffened over them.

On each side of the fireplace was a recess, and these I had shelved to within two feet of the ceiling. I had chosen calfbound and morocco bindings for them, and above the shelves lighting was concealed behind two fairly narrow panels of carved gilt. On the top shelf, in the full glare of the hidden light, I set the warmest of my pieces of Majolica, and I am reminded when I see them of a remark made by a Rye antique dealer from whom I bought one of them. 'You know,' he said sincerely, 'you can tell that this stuff was made by people who loved sunlight, can't you?' The rich yellow and blazing blue of them realizes his fancy.

There is not much furniture in the room—a settee and two armchairs with white loose-covers, and against the wall a little Queen Anne fruit-wood table with a drawer and two false ones in its shaped front. There are some Persian mats, two standard lamps made of tall altar candlesticks, and a rather shamefaced radiogram in the recess of the bow window.

But as usual it is the one or two things which have come by chance or through an opportunity seized, things with something like a story to them, which mean most to me, and to the general effect. For instance, I have only to look at one object to remember a man and a landscape which I have not seen since the middle 'thirties. I lived then in a village of less than one hundred people in one of the loneliest rifts of country in the Cotswolds. It had no pub, but was one of five innless villages grouped round the Puesdown Inn, which itself had only one small cottage within a radius of two miles from it. There was a post office in my village but no shop, though the local road-mender sold a few articles from his cottage when he reached home in the evening. This road-mender was a picturesque anachronism who wore whiskers and a bowler hat and sat bolt upright on an ancient bicycle as he went to work every day. He was a widower who lived alone and did his own housework, a hirsute, solemn man with the intriguing habit of speaking in the first person plural.

'We haven't any cigarettes,' he would announce, standing in his empty house. 'We're hoping to get some in tomorrow.' Was it editorial, royal or conjugal, that 'we'? Certainly it was invariable. 'We had a puncture today, so we're rather late home.' His name I have forgotten now, but I can still see his bowler hat, and hear his loud and pompous plurals following me down his garden.

It was in the shed at the side of his house, where he had taken me to purchase some firewood, that I saw a round table painted white. I did not know enough to give it its name, a cricket-table, but I knew that it was old, and I liked the shape of it.

'Do you want to sell that?' I asked.

'We never use it,' admitted the roadmender. 'We would accept half-a-crown for it.'

At home I set to work, on that same evening, to remove the white paint. It came away fairly easily, and revealed a smooth top of some satiny fruit-wood—pear, I have been told. The three legs were oak, but there was a small triangular stretcher under them

of the same wood as the round top. The legs were so rotten at
the foot that six inches or more had to be cut from each of them,
and that made the table of fireside armchair height. With years
of polishing, its round top, which is now soft golden in colour,
has taken on a sunlit radiance. It has stood before the fire in my
home ever since that evening, and I know of no piece of furniture
I would prefer.

The corner cupboard, which is now painted with the rest of
my woodwork, was also bought somewhere in Gloucestershire.
It is of pine, and was painted brown when I saw it in an auction
room, having only its shape, the neat little side-panels and the
strongly curved fronts of its shelves to recommend it. Those
were the days of stripped wood, and for a long time I kept it
unpainted and with its four-panelled door, but it must be remembered that most pine panelling and fittings were made for
paint and in most rooms are improved by it. The removal of the
door gives point to its presence, for closed it is a somewhat
commonplace piece of furniture, but filled with pottery and lit it
can justify the space given to it.

There is a lampshade in this room which is amusing and gay in
itself and suggests interesting possibilities. Among the parlour
tricks of the last century was one of taking a coloured print and
pricking with a pin the windows and lamps, the outline of the
cornice and dome of some building which might be illuminated,
so that, held up to the light, it showed its subject sparkling with
lights, as if for an exhibition. The print used was most often an
aquatint which had been hand-painted in heavy colours for the
purpose, and the pin-holes were made in two sizes for the sake of
realism. Somewhere, in a portfolio of a crowded Edinburgh
shop, I had found such a print, professionally pin-holed for sale on
some special occasion. It was of Saint Peter's, with the Vatican
a darker outline in the background. The Cathedral and square
blazed with thousands of lights when the print was held up, or
faded into dark blue body-colour when unilluminated. This,
embodied into a lampshade, with an old gilt candlestick as its
standard, adds a touch of magic-lantern fantasy to the room's
decoration.

One other object in this room has its associations for me—
a pierced brass fender. This came from the scrap-and-metal
yard of my old friend Ned Skelton, whose Romani blood is
strong enough to give him a little of the gypsy in his face, and,
when he can be persuaded to reveal it, in his language, but will
die with him, for his children and grandchildren are gorgios.
Our English Romanies, who were metal-workers and wood-
carvers when they came from the East, have never lost their
aptitudes, and even today, when so many of them are settled in
houses and have forgotten most other gypsy attributes, they still
deal in metal and wood, so that the scrap-heaps and log trade of
rural England are still in their hands.

I have known Ned since I first came to this part of Sussex in a
gypsy waggon with a young gypsy as my companion before the
war—in which, incidentally, Ned's two sons served, as he had
done in 1914–18. I have bought a good many articles from his
yard and found him, as his neighbours say of him, straight as a
gun-barrel. Old wrought-iron firedogs from him are in each
of the rooms downstairs; a fine stone urn at the foot of my
garden was once lying near his pig-styes. There is some Regency
garden furniture, a 'conversation chair' for two and a plant-stand;
there are fire-irons and a basket-grate. Above all, through the
winter there are logs burning in every room, logs delivered by
Ned and one of his sons, for when Ned promises a ton of logs he
brings it, and not a mean cart-load with the logs underneath
twisted to make the quantity look greater. Any countryman
will know the value of a wood dealer who neither over-charges
nor bilks, who gives fair value for a fair price and does not depend
on door-to-door extortion. So there in my room is a pierced
brass fender on its claw feet which once lay, a dull piece of jetsam,
on a stack of rusted iron.

2

So in my study—once the dining-room, and so dark that
another person was visible only as an outline, now with an extra
window and a white-and-gold wall-paper—it is the oddments
and decorative pieces which have most character. Over the

fireplace, for instance, is a bracket of carved wood once painted with gold relief and now dully biscuit-coloured. It is shaped like the top of an ornamental column. On it stands a Bambino which I once bought in Lisbon, a little boy Jesus with the Sacred Heart in his hand and an expression of piscine complacency on his pink-and-white face. I found this in an antique shop when I was ashore for a day during a voyage to South America in the 'thirties. The child was dressed in shabby velvet and silver finery, but the craftsmen of the age of baroque were not the fellows to skimp their work, and under those dusty embroideries the whole childish figure was beautifully carved, so that he stands now naked, raising his right hand to throw a benediction on the room.

Down the wall on both sides of him are long three-branched Adam wall-lights, with the familiar design of arrows in a quiver round which ribbons wind from a knotted loop at the head. These I bought only a year or two ago in Grimsby. They were so coated with oily dirt that I did not know what colour I should find beneath it until careful cleaning revealed a dull old gold and green. There is another cricket-table here, and on the book-shelves are three long Sheraton boxes which puzzle even experts, particularly when I tell them that they once made one long box. What, in eighteenth-century England, could have demanded a box five or six feet long and only three inches deep and four wide, with the familiar white inlay edging of Sheraton boxes and an ivory keyhole escutcheon? It was a bow-case, for the toxo-philite, like everyone else in that age, demanded a certain refine-ment in the appurtenances of his sport.

In this room, too, away from the more brilliant colours of the Majolica, are three pieces of pottery which are of singular design and shape. About ten inches tall, they are of the crudest earthen-ware roughly glazed, terracotta and cream in colour, with black markings in the cross-lines and diamonds, the spots and rough geometrical figures which are found in the ornamental designs of the most primitive peoples. I judged them to be at least five hundred years old when I first saw them, which meant they were not African. They had none of the characteristics of Arab or

1. 'My study— once the dining- room'

2. 'The fireplace with its opulent embellishments'

Oriental design; they certainly were not Chinese or European. Their price was nominal, and the Hastings shopkeeper explained that she did not know *what* they were. They were not quite as I guessed, for I had supposed they were Aztec, whereas they have been identified as pre-Columbus Inca pottery. In spite of their remote origin, they do not clash with their more civilized fellows across the room.

3

The dining-room, formerly the kitchen, is still in embryo. It has been made tolerably cheerful and orderly, but that Florentine bed which has become a fireplace five foot high needs more living-up-to than at present it has. Its opulent embellishments must one day be matched by Spanish leather or some bold rococo furniture, and the windows of the room, which now look on to the cobbled courtyard behind the house, must be lowered so that this courtyard becomes almost part of the room, confronting those sitting at table with a nonsense of some sort, a trickle of water or faked iron-barred windows. Just now the fireplace is complete in itself with two plaster baskets of fruit on the mantelshelf—the same two which once I remember in the Randolph Hotel at Oxford. Above it hangs an oval carving, a woman's head in relief. The hair is dressed in the style of Napoleon's day, and the ribbon among the curls, the low neck and even the profile suggest that it might be a contemporary portrait of Lady Emma Hamilton. But no, it is French, say experts, chilling these romantic suppositions, but raising others as enticing. Whoever it may represent, it worthily crowns the tall fireplace.

Until the rest of the room can be made appropriate to that fireplace the furniture consists of a spinet, used as a sideboard, a little painted dresser which I bought in the Forest of Dean, and on which is arranged a Mason's Ironstone dinner service in red, gold and black. The six chairs are in three pairs—all country-made Chippendale—and the table is the same, a weighty piece of very dark mahogany. It is a warm room in winter, appropriate in size and atmosphere to a small dinner-party, as though some of its previous life as a kitchen persisted to give it the benison of an age when food was not shaken from a tin and a man might drink a bottle of wine with his dinner without being considered a glutton, a sybarite or a drunkard.

4

The hall is as bare as possible from the front door on one side of the house to the window overlooking the garden on the other. It is the largest room I have, even without the sitting-room, and this gives the house a spaciousness beyond its true measurements. There are bookshelves again, inevitably, along the first half of the wall to the left on entering, the second half being cut by the double doors.　In a corner at the garden end the staircase comes down in a wide, gentle curve.　This room, twenty-eight feet by fifteen, of almost empty space, is what is usually called by visitors 'the making of the house'.

This again follows the general design, bookshelves surmounted by pottery over which are hung water-colours, and here again it is the smaller details which save it from the commonplace. Just inside the front door, for instance, is an old well bucket which still has its iron loop.　In it is my collection of walking-sticks— a meagre one compared with that of G. B. Stern, but cosmopolitan for all that, and including African dancing-sticks and bead-sticks and a miscellany from Madagascar and India.

There is a Flemish Nativity in oak on the bookshelves, which seems to me the most truly creative piece of carving I have—its faces, someone has said, tell the story of the Crucifixion as well as the Birth of Christ.　But beyond a coffer or two against the walls, a Jacobean oak corner cupboard, an early Italian chair, and an old oak school desk with sloping lid and the illustrious initials W.S. on it, there is no furniture.

Thus the rooms downstairs were arranged, excepting those highly functional rooms, my secretary's office and the kitchen. Thus I set my house in order and began to live in it.

The Indian Influence

I

When I arrived in Bombay on a troopship in 1943 I perceived within a few days of landing that India was not the best country for soldiering in the ranks, and although I had spent three intensely happy years as a Sergeant and had intended never to be anything else, I put in for a commission, and was sent to an Officers' Training School at a small town called Belgaum. I wasted six months doing an Infantry Course, but found it tolerably agreeable in spite of the rains.

There was little to do in the town at night except go to the two cinemas which showed English films, the one owned by some young Mohammedans and the other by an imposing Parsee woman. At the latter was a bar serving soft drinks, and in charge of it was a sixteen-year-old Indian boy who formed a habit of confiding in me while I was drinking gassy orangeade.

For instance : 'I'm a Catholic. Yes, I'm studying and, like most students in India, do a job at the same time. In my case two —I teach Tamil at an Infants' School in the morning and run this bar at night.'

Again : 'But of course I'm not going to be satisfied with *this* for a life. I want to see some of the world.'

Or : 'My name? Well, my Christian name is Joseph, and my Indian name is Sussainathan. You don't really use the two together, like your Christian name and surname.'

Or : 'Tamil? It's supposed to be one of the oldest languages in the world, quite different from Hindi or Urdu. It's spoken in South India with other languages from the same root, Telegu and Malayalam. There are several hundred letters in our alphabet. Yes, I suppose it's my language, but I probably speak more English in a day than that.'

And finally : 'When you get your commission and leave here I'm coming with you. You'll travel about, won't you? I'm not going to stay in Belgaum all my life.'

This, I thought, was Joseph Sussainathan's idea of a joke. He was earning two salaries and he had a good home and fond parents. I accepted it as a flattering piece of flippancy, and standing at his bar with other cadets would say facetiously that when I left Belgaum, Joseph was coming with me. But I knew less of Indian character then. The seemingly too pliable and imitative nature of Indian youth had a steel-wire quality which I never suspected, a tenacity and resolution quite foreign to its volatile surface. When Joseph made up his mind that he would hitch his waggon to my star, because he wanted to see beyond the little provincial town of his birth, there was nothing much for me to do about it. When the long Course was at last over and, wearing my single pip, I went down to Belgaum railway station to leave for Bombay, I found him there with his boxes beside him. He has been with me ever since.

That Indian tenacity, infinitely flexible but not to be broken, was demonstrated several times during my remaining two years in India. Installed as a civilian clerk attached to my Field Security Section in Delhi, Joseph disappeared into the city in the evening, and when I asked him where he went, he replied unexpectedly that it was to a school of shorthand and typing. I pointed out with some amusement that it was not necessary to take his job as clerk quite as seriously as that, but was told firmly that it was not his present job that Joseph was considering.

'You're a writer, aren't you? When the war is over you'll need a secretary, and I shall be coming with you to England.'

This prognostication was more startling than the previous one, for although returning Englishmen have occasionally, and almost always without success, made the experiment of bringing home Indian servants, I had never heard of one with a secretary from any country east of Suez. But the way in which the plan was announced seemed to leave little room for argument, and when Joseph explained that he would like to see London and the English countryside and perhaps some other European countries, experience taught me that by one means or another he would do so. When my time was up his passage was booked and he came to England rather more comfortably than I did.

He adapted himself easily to life in London, but the move to Ticehurst meant a greater uprooting for him than his journey to Europe had been, and at first it seemed that it strained even his versatility too far. I saw English rural life afresh through his eyes, and realized that although for me there was occupation, interest, entertainment in it, it had less to offer to a town-bred Indian. The people of Ticehurst, after a first incredulous shock at his exotic appearance, accepted him warmly, but it took some months for him to find pleasure in country pubs and games of darts and shopping in the nearby town and occasional small parties at neighbouring houses. However, the larger aspect of the thing appealed to his imagination and, coming of a race which learnt to be civilized while we were still living in caves, he saw the significance of my experiment and threw his own talents into it.

Curiously mixed talents, too; some racial, some individual. I might have expected him, for instance, to be a master of the spiced cookery of India, but how could I guess that in making European dishes he would develop that daring and flair which are rightly called genius? I might guess that, like many of his race, he would be able to grow flowers, but I did not suppose that he would have green fingers. Most Indians can dance a bit and most can mimic movements, but one could not foresee that Joseph would do both at the expense of Ram Gopal so successfully that that famous dancer would invite him to join his company, and that he would spend his holiday on the stage of the Adelphi Theatre. Moreover, his handling of my affairs, his orderly collocation of my published work so that second rights and third rights, foreign rights and reprints are sold where before all lay dormant, shows talent of another, but no less oriental sort. In a word, the boy who decided to join me when I left Belgaum, now a maturely intelligent man of twenty-four, quickly became an essential factor in my new scheme of things.

2

Which brings me to the remaining room on the ground floor of the house—the secretary's office. If you find that a somewhat pretentious term for a room in a writer's house, if you think that my profession could be carried on with little more than a writing-pad on the knee, let me justify both the name and the appropriation of the room to which it is applied.

In order to make the sort of income I need if I am to keep up payments on the mortgage, it is essential for me to maintain a business as comprehensive as one which, in the easier field of commerce, would cause its proprietor to lease a London office and engage a staff of clerks. The writing of new books has, in a way, little to do with that business, and for me the two are divorced as widely as possible. And that in spite of the fact that I have a good agent who justifies his drawing of ten per cent of my income.

What business? I have a filing system with over thirty headings, all of which are active and some of which have been filled six and seven times in the last five years. Articles for newspapers, short stories, foreign rights, broadcasting, serializations, correspondence on topics in which I am particularly interested, like the circus and gypsies, film work, one-act plays, cheap rights in books, correspondence connected with my book page in *The Sketch*, correspondence with American agents and publishers—endless hu-ha for very little calculable result, but letters one cannot ignore or lose. I challenge any writer to simplify all this more than I do, to write less personal letters than I do or to give less time to it than I do, and yet for anything up to two or three hours in a day I am dictating letters and memos necessitated solely by the merely commercial aspects of my work.

Short stories, for instance, demand a filing system of their own, for if one were to be satisfied with a single sale of each, the craft, considered commercially, would be unproductive. A story may be sold a dozen times so long as the editor buying rights in it is not misled into supposing that he has been given first use of it.

It may be published and re-published, translated, broadcast, televised, dramatized, filmed; it may appear in America, Australia, South Africa or India; it may be entered for a competition, it may—as happened to a story of mine—be published twice by the same periodical in error. To keep track of this with the hundred or two of short stories which a fairly prolific writer may have achieved in his time, a cross-filing system is necessary, under title and under the name of the periodical publishing, while I personally keep a loose folder for each story.

There are box-files for unfinished work or for material on some subject to be tackled one day—in my case these run to a score or so—and piles of old typescripts and manuscripts which cannot quite be thrown away. All this is apart from the business connected with my home, rates, electricity, gas, fuel, food, insurance and heaven knows what applications for permits or registrations or ration books. Income tax alone would provide a full-time job to most clerks in business offices, while answering letters from strangers would occupy another one.

I do not grumble at the constructive part of all this business; to be truthful, I enjoy handling it with as much efficiency as if I were an executive official in a department store rather than a writer. I resent it when I hear it said—as I frequently do—that no man occupied with such commercial flummery can possibly be an artist. History has shown, I think, that some creative writers were good business men, like Shakespeare, Trollope, Dickens, Arnold Bennett; some were not, like Chatterton, Shelley or Goldsmith. Whatever a writer may be, he cannot be disqualified from merit because, having done the best that he is able in writing, he wants to turn it to the maximum commercial advantage, any more than he can be criticized as an artist because he has no business sense.

To deal effectively with all the commercial etceteras of writing, then, a great deal of space, paper and equipment are necessary, in addition to an orderly mind, time and patience. My secretary had the latter qualities, and the room which had once been the builder's office was adapted to provide the former. With what delight did I first see its deep cupboards stretching from floor to ceiling and lining every wall of the room. Like all things which any member of the building family had added to the house, these cupboards were solid and well-constructed, if not handsome. There were in all eighteen separate cupboards, two foot deep, heavily shelved, lightly doored, practical and inviting.

Joseph, with his oriental sense of order, took possession of them with gusto, laying out our files and stationery according to a plan of his own. To be able to line them up and see their labels, to have everything docketed and in place, has meant a shortening of the time given to them and all that they represent.

For the rest, the room is free of encumbering furniture, has a desk and typewriter and chair and little more. But its proximity to the front door solves another problem. On the only short piece of wall from which I have cleared the cupboards is a row of hooks, and here are hung our own and visitors' coats and hats. This enables the hall to keep its character as a part of the house in which to dawdle and talk unlittered by odd clothing, an improvement on either the pegs near the WELCOME mat or the dark cupboard smelling of raincoats and mothballs in which it is impossible to find what one wants.

3

For two hundred years and more the English have been bringing home souvenirs from India, and these have so far degenerated in quality that during the last war they scarcely rose above models of the Taj Mahal or purple cushion-covers on which its outline had been crudely embroidered in silver thread. The houses and antique shops of Cheltenham and Tunbridge Wells are crowded with the bric-à-brac which soldiers retiring from the Indian Army have brought with them in the past: oddities in brass, over-carved wood, Benares ware, ivory inlay, Kashmir rugs, Mirzapur carpets, silver boxes with elephant designs beaten into them—a vast collection of over-ornamental junk which gives the stay-at-home English the idea that nothing beautiful is produced in the country. That, I remember, was the argument put to me by a knowledgeable antiquarian. 'When you think what China has given us,' he said, 'Indian art seems

'His handling of my affairs'

fussy and trivial. What has it brought to Europe? Some Mogul water-colours, some carving in stone, some early brass and bronze. India's goldsmiths and silversmiths have failed in the same way as her musicians, by complicating and over-complicating, elaborating and embellishing till the design is lost in detail and twiddling complexity.'

True, of course, that much Indian art lacks simplicity of form, but it must be remembered that the whole culture of the Hindus was nationalistic to a degree that forbade Indians to leave their country, and so produced art which was immovable. The great temples with their fantastic richness of stonework, the gods carved in stone, twice, five times as large as man, the friezes and monstrous carved pillars—these were for their own place and no other, so that a man cannot speak of Indian art who has not been to one of its ancient centres such as Khajrao, where, many miles from a railway, rarely visited by tourists, three hundred temples are grouped on a lonely slope of wild country, and each of them has as much statuary and carving in relief as the British Museum, and as one walks among them one is almost frightened by the nearness of the ancient world.

Moreover, putting the matter at its lowest, debasing it to a mere collection of *objets d'art*, India has been misrepresented in Europe by the fact that such a collection will have been made by soldiers and business men whose standards are of exoticism and novelty rather than of beauty. Seeing a brass bell whose handle was formed by a small figure of Hanuman, the monkey god, a young Englishman, already bedazzled by the strangeness of everything about him, might buy it as a 'curio', and during his years in the country add to it a gong, a piece of blatant embroidery, a pair of coloured shoes, and some objects in roughly carved ivory and sandal-wood. All these, with time, would be dispersed in England and be despondently neglected in the less expensive antique shops, the proprietors of which know only that 'Indian stuff isn't much good'.

Yet it is still possible to collect in India, to avoid things made for souvenir-hunters and to find beauty and character in brass, stone, silk, silver, wood. During my three enchanted years in the sub-

F

continent, buying only from army pay and without unlimited
time to give to the search, I managed to get together enough to
send home in three large metal boxes, enough to make Indian one
room of my house at Ticehurst.

For these Indian relics will not 'mix'. They can be kept in
great profusion, god nudging god, silver and ivory surface to
surface, and will thus achieve a kind of ornate unity. But put
them among European things and they will at once appear
outlandish, even grotesque. I deplore, somewhat, the necessity
of having an 'Indian room', for if the principle were extended it
would lead to that most affected kind of millionaire's decoration,
a division of one's home into centres of ancient culture—a
Byzantine room, a Chinese room, and so on, as though they were
museum galleries. But if one has this 'thing' about India, if it
is a vital part of one's life, there is no way of avoiding the isolation of its relics.

I found that two of the smaller bedrooms led one from the
other, and at once decided that they should be mine. The
first of these, which has fitted cupboards extending the length of
one wall, would make something I had coveted all my life, a
detached dressing-room, and this should be Indian in its
decoration.

So here is the little brass head from Nepal, eight hundred years
old, smooth and sleepy and beautiful. Here are the five Mogul
water-colours and the four little miniatures, Mogul kings painted
on ivory. Here are those shapely jugs in brass or zinc and copper
and silver which I bought in the bazar at Bijapur one evening, the
Hindu metal-dealer selling them to me by weight, unaware that
they had been in this town since the Muslims ruled it and built the
Gol Gumbaz, the third largest dome in the world. Here is the
beaten silver hookah which a havildar in my section used to fill
and light for me in Delhi, here is the lute-playing winged angel,
so like an Italian one, which I bought from an old antique dealer
in Bombay who used to give me a pale green drink made from
almonds. Here is an ancient papier-mâché box on which
crowned noblemen mounted on caparisoned horses play polo,
while around the lid in old Urdu script are the words: 'The

glory of KAIQBAD and LAURASP is known to all. Emperor! Your honour and splendour are from the heavens. Your magnificence is of this world and the next. On the last day the sleeping people of the world shall be lit by your effulgence. As long as the moon remains, the earth and the bright stars shall your honour increase. May your kingdom be secure and your pen continue.' Here is that dancing Shiva, the little graceful figure with the minute waist and powerful shoulders whose leg is high in a dance which symbolizes the rhythm in the universe. 'In joy and sorrow he dances. He dances over the body of the Asura he kills, the symbolic dance of the ultimate triumph of good over evil.' Round him, in my bronze, is a ring of flames.

I should like fondly to catalogue all the small pieces in my Indian collection—another Shiva is mounted on Vahan Nandi, his bull, and this little brass from which all the lines are worn by time must be as old, almost, as the Aryan race. But there are too many of these pieces, as there are too many gods perhaps in the Hindu pantheon. It is with one article which comes from another culture, which may be found only in remote parts of the Punjab, that I must end this gloating over Indian possessions. (I am using the word India, of course, to apply to the whole sub-continent whose boundaries I knew.) This is a *khés*, a vast spread of hand-woven cotton made up of two pieces, each seven foot by five, which are stitched end to end, and so make a double blanket. The design is two-sided, so that the Punjabi who owns a *khés* has four surfaces to show in turn, as though possessed of four garments. The weaving is in squares and oblongs, in a minute white and red and yellow pattern which makes the whole effect one of brilliance and order.

It is hard to obtain one of these lustrous sheets of woven colour because they are made on the hand-loom for a specific person and never for sale to shops. The long work of them would be impossible as a commercial proposition, and only by chance or favour can they come to be in the hands of a European. I am both proud and appreciative of mine, which brings India into my house more radiantly than the sombre eccentricity of some of the Hindu gods.

4

So the Indian influence in my home is not something which impregnates the whole place, but instead fills certain compartments of life. There is nothing Indian in any room except the one in which it is collected—not even a carpet or a piece of copper. And meals are either wholly Indian—a curry to satisfy the most pepper-loving and spice-bewitched—or they are European. No mixtures, which ruin both. But that isolation of all the things which I have brought from the East does not mean their oblivion or neglect—on the contrary, they are real and alive to me. An Englishman's home, I like to think, should not be so much a castle as a storehouse for which he has foraged the world, bringing home the best examples he can find of the cultures which have impressed him most, so that its very decorations are in a sense his past. Thus I can still see Indian temples and smell the rich night, hear the lazy sea indolently plashing home, taste the hot and heady spices, listen to the harsh cries of nightbirds, feel the cool and pliant dark flesh under my hand and respond to the whole sad glory of Hind, when I find myself, on an English morning, staring into the mysterious brazen face of one of my little gods.

Drink

I

THERE is another collection of objects which have to be isolated, which bring with them to England the colour and strangeness of a distant country and people, but which, unlike most of my Indian possessions, are more curious than beautiful: the beadwork and skins, the carved masks and dancing-sticks, the brilliant and primitive things which I amassed in Africa. Between them and the polished extravagance of Indian art there are the widest differences in spirit and conception, of course; but there is another, a more personal distinction; for while my Indian possessions were honestly earned, by long, dusty journeys, by years of effort to understand them and the country which produced them, by hard work and arduous bargaining, these things from Africa are mine only through wildly improbable good fortune. I was lucky first to all to be in the Force which went to Madagascar. I was lucky when it was decided that this Force should go to the Union to recuperate from the fevers and infections of that malarial island. I was again lucky when, through a slight recurrence of malaria which took me to hospital in Pietermaritzburg, I was left behind for two months by my unit, which had gone on to India. I was perhaps most lucky in that deep-voiced, gawky Brigade-Major, the only person I could find who seemed suitable as an officer to whom to report when I came out of hospital, and who said, 'You'd better run away on leave and come back when you want some money.' So I found myself with the freedom of Natal and undisturbed weeks ahead of me.

That anomalous holiday, a peaceful summer in the middle of the war, I shamelessly enjoyed, and although from other countries I have perhaps learnt more and with other peoples achieved greater understanding, from nowhere else have I brought with me such brilliantly coloured, such acutely cut impressions. India is a golden dust turning to a violet-and-green haze, Argentina is an ocean of grass, Hungary a weird plain and Spain a terra-cotta afternoon; but Zululand is a series of sharp photographs, each recollection vivid still as a landscape seen through the window in a Dutch painting.

I can see Durban itself with the bougainvillea threatening, it seems, to throttle the other vegetation, in such lavish masses does it spread in suburb gardens. The little town of M'tuba Tuba, from which a friendly police officer took me out to the Hlue Hlue game reserve, where hippopotami nosed out from the roadside. The Kraal of old M'tuba Tuba himself, where I drank Zulu beer and was ceremoniously presented with a goat by the chief, some of whose sixty wives stood calmly blinking at us from their doorways. The little Catholic mission in the hills beyond Mapamulo, which could only be reached on horseback. I spent Christmas there at the invitation of the tall, white-bearded priest who had built the church, the school, the house, with his own hands and with blocks of stone carried on Zulu heads, one by one, from a quarry ten miles away. He had started with a dozen converts and had now a congregation of two thousand, most of whom crowded his church and the approaches to it for midnight Mass. The little courtroom where a Boer magistrate dispensed decent rough justice to a long string of garrulous litigants; the ebony shepherd-boys with their home-made flutes; the mad, beautiful dances in the huts; the Indian stores where the Zulus would pass a whole day in contemplation of the commodities offered. Then, too, the gentle-eyed old witch-doctor with whom I spent a day on foot, tramping ten miles to the kraal of his brother, who put on his warrior's dress for my admiration. The old man opened his fortune-teller's bag of miscellaneous objects and told me the significance of each of them, warning me that he was giving me knowledge of the future which no white man should possess. The veldt, so oddly like and unlike our Sussex downs, the long, graceful bodies of the men, the plump-breasted, all-but-naked women, the wire-haired children. And over it all something wistfully macabre, something occult, as though reproachful eyes were on you as you walked among the trees or forded the wide, shallow rivers.

So now I had in my very four-square Sussex house the impedimenta, the souvenirs of that visit, the bead-work, the carvings, the clubs and shields. Such quantities of things made from beads did I accumulate that I have been reduced to mounting them on round plaques which become polychromatic, geometrically designed shields to hang on the wall. Then there is the tall wood carving of a heavy-lidded mother with a baby on her back, the fearsome spotted masks, the elegantly plaited grass skimming-spoon, the bead-covered gourd snuff-box, the walking-sticks which are one brilliant surface of beads, the little cow-horn *gri-gris* from Madagascar, the whole gamut of primitive and exciting design and startling colour in all these things. How could they be kept here, in this quiet eighteenth-century house in the Home Counties of England? I wanted them; they were more than curiosities to me. I wanted the sunlight which they would bring here when rain was shouting outside, I wanted the sad aboriginal music from a lonely flute which they would awaken in a silent English evening. But where? Away from the rest, certainly, yet somewhere frequently visited and brightly lit.

I had it at last. Perhaps it was the association in my mind between South Africa and its good wines which suggested it. The bar! The bar should be garish and prismatic with the bright beads. My wooden mother and child should stand among the stone jars, and the bottles would reflect the blue and red oblongs in the necklaces.

2

Now, the bar was the cupboard under the stairs. I had learnt this trick in London, when space was scarce and every kind of ingenuity was needed to avoid wasting a cubic foot of it. What else is to be done with that cupboard, which has a man-high door at one end with a ceiling which starts above it and slopes down to floor level? Brushes and brooms? But in the darkness there will accumulate with them dust and a musty smell, or objects will be put behind them 'just for the moment' to rot and mildew in obscurity and oblivion perhaps for years.

Five things I learnt to do with the cupboard under the stairs, none of them expensive, none unpractical. First, to light it with a bulb over the door which shines on the interior as one opens. Secondly, to paper it in some gay design, a contrast to that of the room which surrounds it. Thirdly, to shelve the wall opposite the doorway and the wall beside it, making the distance between shelves sufficient to enable a tall bottle to stand there. Fourthly, to shelve the rest of the cupboard, as far down as possible, with pigeon-hole squares, to make bins for wine-bottles. And fifthly, to put outside the door and beside it a shelf on a swing bracket, large enough when it is up to form a counter on which to mix drinks, or decant, or pour out for a number of people. By these simple expedients the whole problem of where to keep liquor handy for hospitality but under lock-and-key, in an orderly and attractive yet unostentatious way, is solved, while the best and greatest use is made of what otherwise becomes a dingy cubby-hole in which one gropes amid dust and cobwebs for a missing broom.

The glasses, with a few pieces of coloured glass among them, bottles, decanters and fittings are decoration enough, for the strong light on them produces a flash and sparkle and makes even labels look brilliant. I had already set among them some odd-ments of advertisement and decoration cajoled from publicans— a porcelain Tuborg crest which a Copenhagen barman gave me; a small sherry barrel on a wooden stand which I bought for a few pesetas in Cadiz; a plaster negro rolling a barrel and advertising a brand of rum, and so on. But until I reached Ticehurst and found that the cupboard under the stairs was a particularly large one, it never occurred to me that any pronounced scheme of decoration would add much to this. Not until the beads and masks twinkled and grinned among the bottles was I sure that the bar was the place for relics of Africa.

3

A bar sounds, perhaps, an extravagant or grandiose addition to a modest private house, for alcohol has been the butt of all the

tax-gatherers, and a man's right to drink it the most brutally
infringed of all human rights, not only during the orgies of
restriction and legislation which have followed the last war, but
ever since successive governments failed to repeal the Defence of
the Realm Act of 1914-18. Politicians have rivalled pro-
hibitionists in giving to something as healthy and natural as
drinking a sort of stigma of corruption and guilt, as though a glass
of wine were a drug or a cocktail-party a black Mass. They have
taxed liquor beyond all sanity; they have initiated fatuous but
enforced time-tables for its consumption; they have given to
whisky the name of an evil spirit, to wine an aura of immorality,
and they have only been less vindictive towards beer-drinkers
because their number in England is such that no political party
could be elected which had penalized them. 'Spirit-drinkers',
as they have called those of us who prefer that most splendid
production of the stills of Scotland to the chemicalized and
watery swill which passes too often now for beer, 'spirit-drinkers'
are greedy, unethical, unhygienic and selfish, and no amount of
taxation is too heavy for them to bear. 'That will teach them!'
have said successive Budget-makers of all parties, 'that will
bring them into line!' until now the retail price of a bottle of gin,
containing spirits to the actual value of a florin or so, is thirty-
four shillings and whisky is obtainable almost exclusively on the
Black Market, costing there from fifty shillings to three pounds a
bottle.

This makes drinking a duty, in more senses than one.

4

No, I find nothing pretentious or guilty in my bar, and shall
continue to stock it in preference to meeting the demands of the
Income Tax Collector while I have a home of my own. That
so ordinary a matter, a few shelves of liquor for my friends, should
lead me or anyone else into these defiant polemics is in itself a
black reflection on the times. And while I never buy a bottle of
spirits without resentment towards the extortioners who pocket
a high percentage of the price, and a warm sympathy towards the
smugglers who operated in this village less than two centuries ago,

I still manage to have a drink at hand for myself and my visitors and accept the reproachful name of spirit-drinker without shame.

A habit formed in India, however, serves me well in this. I never drink spirits till the evening, when, splashing the soda-water on my first whisky of the day, I remember the nectar of a sundowner under the early stars in the Deccan or among the pine-trees of the Himalayan foothills. But yes, soda. The Scot, I am told, who is born to whisky, drinks it neat or with water and regards effervescence as the ruin of good liquor. He may have been right when there were varying qualities of whisky, when fine old blends were boasted of by their careful owners, but now that all whisky of what are curiously called 'proprietary brands' is of much the same quality, and that sound rather than exquisite, it seems to me that whisky need no longer be treated as a fine liqueur.

There was a time when I should have doubted, in fact, whether I or any man of my generation would recognize the glorious whisky of the past if we came on it, so standardized has it become in our time. But I know better since 1942, when I spent my embarkation leave at the home of Compton Mackenzie on the Isle of Barra and was offered, without comment, some of that ambrosial spirit which he made famous in one of his gayest and most farcical novels and over which cinema-goers licked their chops in the film *Whisky Galore*. No hint was given me that I was drinking anything unusual, but with that liquor, at least, there could be no doubt.

'What is it?' I asked, breathless with interest and not from swallowing the creamy draught.

'God in His infinite mercy looked down,' Monty Mackenzie explained with a satyr's chuckle, 'and saw this little group of islands which have never changed their Faith.'

I knew that Protestantism had failed to reach the Outer Hebrides and that Mass has been said in the villages without interruption from the time of their first conversion to Christendom.

'So?' I prompted.

'So He arranged that when a ship which was carrying to America all the finest and oldest whisky in the British Isles was

destined to be lost, it should be on our coast. Our faith is
rewarded.'

Sipping the amber ecstasy I believed his parable. And it
taught me that although in my lifetime that noblest product
of Scottish industry has become almost as indistinguishably
standardized in quality and taste as everything else, I could still
recognize its aristocracy.

Probably I shall never again drink whisky like that, and for the
rest of my life shall continue to consider myself fortunate to
purchase a bottle of the uniform stuff at the standard price, that
is to say without paying impost to the Black Market. But it
remains my drink. Give me, as evening falls, an unmeasured
quantity of whisky, a rough two fingers of it, in the bottom of a
tumbler, and let me pour soda-water on it till the glass is two-
thirds full, and I am a happy man. It is a long drink, a clean one,
a healthy one, and as it goes down the irks and fatigues disperse,
and a warm light rims the world.

If our supplies of whisky and gin are both of standard quality,
there is far greater variety among the various brands of rum.
'I can't drink civvy rum,' I heard a naval rating say in a bar
the other day. 'It *stinks*!' And certainly some rum has a
retching smell, instead of the invigorating and pleasant tang of
molasses. When I discovered that it was inadvisable to buy
rum without discrimination, I set out to discover something
about this essential liquor and the distilling of it, and found that
two distinct kinds are on sale here—rum which has been matured
and bottled in Jamaica, and rum which has been brought from
various parts of the world and is blended, matured and bottled
in this country. There is as much difference between them as
between a cigar rolled in Cuba and one manufactured in England.
Of the various rums bottled in Jamaica, my own preference is
for one called Captain Morgan, partly because I like to see the
name of that old buccaneer on a bottle, and partly because it
seems to me the lightest in aroma and the least sickly to drink.
But all these island-bottled rums are good, and drunk out-of-
doors on a summer evening or with hot water by a fire in winter
are kind and friendly spirits which would be greatly missed.

5

I am not going to write here of wine, which is of another tradition and must be considered separately, or of liqueurs, but of all the good drinks which can come from such a modest and unextravagant bar as mine. The hospitality it can provide, the friendliness it can inspire, the pleasure it can give, the splendid anachronism it thus becomes.

I have never had much use for home-made wines, which, except when concocted, usually from family recipes, by country people, smack of amateurism and artiness, and even when offered to you in a Cotswold kitchen are often acid, sickly or immature. An island in which the grape does not naturally flourish is no place for wine-making, and in a better age, when a farm-house provided itself with liquor, it was the home-brew which was worth drinking, not the fruity solutions pulled from the parlour cupboard by the farmer's wife for her friends.

It is the mixtures and contrasts which can be obtained from spirits, the cocktails, punches and cups, which justify me in calling my cupboard under the stairs a 'bar'. Some of them are of ancient origin, some may be recent inventions of American barmen, but nearly all of them repay the work and care which go to their perfection.

Cups, now, on a summer day, can be the most exhilarating and cooling of drinks, but cups have been grossly abused by parsimonious hosts and hostesses who find in them a means of giving liquor, abundant in quantity, to a large number of poeple at small expense. A cup might be gratefully received at a garden-party, but in a crowded London flat at a time when one expects a cocktail or a glass of sherry it seems sweet and weak, while as a midnight drink it is often quite nauseating.

That does not detract from its merits at the right time. As elevenses on a hot Sunday morning, as a cooler between sets of tennis, as a picnic drink when wine would be spoilt by rough treatment and beer is apt to taste raw and gaseous, a cup is an excellent thing. Even old Saintsbury, that merciless purist in matters of wine, is reconciled to at least one cup. 'Champagne-

and moselle-cups,' he says in his classic *Notes on a Cellar Book*, 'seem to me to come under the double sentence more than once applied in these pages. If they are made of good wine they are wicked; if of bad, unpardonable. Indeed, on the whole, it seems to me that no cup comes up to cider-cup, for the simple reason that there you are not contaminating but corroborating. A very little fizzing water, a good dose of stout well-flavoured sherry, just a *pousse* of brandy, with lemon and borage, will make *the* drink for hot weather, and the drinker will escape some inconveniences formerly hinted at as attending the drinking of "apple wine" neat.'

One need not be ashamed to add ice-cubes to the jug if there is not time to chill it by standing. When that is done it is amusing to let a cherry or a few anchusa petals freeze in the ice-cubes as they form.

6

I am not a passionate lover of cocktails, though I do not believe that they are such destroyers of the palate and digestion as they are reputed to be. When mixed by an unpractised hand they seem to me either to be based too obviously on gin—a liquor for which I have no great love—or if based on rum or whisky to be fruity, sweet, almost sticky. But my own preference for a whisky-and-soda or a dry sherry must be regarded as almost eccentric today, for the cocktail has become a part of Western life, an American contribution to the culture even of France. It is only when lazily, carelessly or too frugally mixed that it degenerates, or becomes a soulless means of absorbing alcohol, a mere quick cut to inebriation. It can be an excellent appetizer, and if an interval is allowed between the last cocktail and the time for dinner, it will not spoil the enjoyment of wine. But swilled in long, quick succession, or even carried to the table, cocktails can be a vicious desecration.

As a medium of hospitality and entertainment, they are in the long run economical. Guests accustomed to the slipshod mixture of synthetic vermouth and gin with ice, which has been given them too often both in homes and bars, appreciate a carefully mixed cocktail, and in spite of the excessive taxation of spirits it will cost less than many other drinks. But no economy is possible in the initial stocking of a bar with both utensils and ingredients, and no substitutes should be accepted for either. One must have both a mixing-glass and a shaker, for a cocktail which should have been made in one and has been made in the other is a mess. Then a long mixing-spoon, a strainer and a row of small bottles with stoppers from which bitters etc. can be shaken drop by drop. These can be multiplied almost indefinitely and look amusingly ostentatious, but one each for Peach Bitters, Angostura Bitters, Orange Bitters, Curaçao, Absinthe, Grenadine, Sugar Syrup will be more than enough for any ordinary purpose. As for the ingredients themselves, a long row of bottles is necessary, though only the gin and vermouth will need frequent replacing. Pernod as a substitute for absinthe, brandy (and I find South African brandy good enough for its bastard function here), French and Italian vermouth, Bacardi, dry Sherry, lime-juice, Irish whisky, Plymouth gin, Jamaica rum are all fairly often demanded. Carried to the niceties of flavour and appearance, cocktails demand many more bottles, chiefly of liqueurs, among them Anisette, Curaçao, Green Chartreuse, Sloe Gin, Maraschino, Calvados, Dubonnet, Noyau, Fernet Branca and Benedictine. But these provide a variety which no ordinary mixer will want, unless for experiment. With them and sufficient ice, and a few fresh ingredients such as oranges, lemon and mint, there are few cocktails which cannot be achieved.

The secret of a successful cocktail is, I believe, a disappointingly simple one—it is to follow slavishly the instructions of the experienced mixer in matters of quantity and proportion, when making a known cocktail, even if you experiment at other times with new ingredients and contrasts. Since, for instance, a Side-Car is made from Cointreau and brandy in equal proportions, with half the same quantity of fresh lemon-juice, poured over half a shaker full of broken ice and well shaken, it is unwise to suppose that by pouring what remains of your brandy into a jug, squeezing a lemon and using some Maraschino because you are out of Cointreau, you will achieve a good drink. A drink you will get, cold, alcoholic, possibly commended by polite or undiscriminating guests, but it will not be a Side-Car. And so on. It is easy to mix good cocktails if you follow the book, but they are not often achieved by chance.

7

There are other cooling drinks to mix apart from cups and cocktails, and on a warm day in the garden one should not have to dream in vain of all the Fizzes and Coolers, the Cobblers and Flips, the Frappés, Highballs, Juleps, Sangarees, Slings, Sours and Shandies. Perhaps because my house is a garden house with two sets of French windows opening on a long terrace, with the bar only a few feet from the lawn, or perhaps because my first summer here was a warm one, or perhaps because I just like alcohol, I have learnt to make a good many long, cold and anything but spiritless drinks.

There are countless ways of making Sherry Cobbler, but I turn to India, where in our two centuries of soldiering and police work we had time and temptation to invent good cooling drinks. This recipe comes from a book published in Calcutta seventy years ago. Its anonymous author describes himself as 'A Thirty-five Years' Resident', and there is nothing emasculated or watery about his suggestion for what, among lesser authorities, is a rather harmless drink. 'Pour into a tumbler,' he says, and perhaps it is only my imagination which detects a certain gusto in the flat phrase—'Pour into a tumbler two wineglassfuls of sherry, half a wineglassful of rum, and half a wineglassful of maraschino; add half an orange sliced fine, and fill the tumbler with crushed ice; take the preparation through a reed, quill, or common straw.'

The best Fizz I know is this : Pour on to broken ice in the shaker the white of an egg, a dessert-spoonful of sugar syrup, the juice of half a lemon, a little good lime-juice—not the synthetic muck sometimes sold as lime-juice—a teaspoonful of absinthe, or if you have only Pernod a dessert-spoonful of this, and half a tumbler of gin. Shake violently for about three minutes and strain into tumblers, about three fingers to each. Then fill up from a siphon which has been chilled.

Of the Flips I avoid the Champagne one for Saintsbury's good reason that in mixed drinks the Champagne is killed and wasted. But Bitter Flip is excellent. Beat the yolks of two eggs thoroughly with a little castor sugar; chill this either by standing on ice or leaving in the frigidaire for a time. Then take a half-pint glass of bitter (*not* bottled beer) which has also been chilled and beat the two together very thoroughly. Grate a little nutmeg on this and put a sprig of rosemary in each glass.

The various Slings, all coming from the East, are not unlike the Fizzes, and are also mixed in the shaker, poured into tumblers till these are one-third to a half full, and filled up with cold soda-water or aerated minerals. A favourite, to which my stock of bottles will just stretch, is a Straits Sling, a drink which one imagines to have been consumed gratefully by characters in Mr. Somerset Maugham's short stories. Two shakes of Angostura and two of Peach Bitters, the juice of half a lemon or a little less, a table-spoonful of Cherry Brandy and one of Benedictine and two wineglassfuls of gin.

As for the Juleps, I begin to doubt whether any European can prepare them. When I remember a Mint Julep handed to me by an American woman in Buenos Aires, who said that no, she couldn't make it, but her aunt from Virginia who was staying with her could, I am almost convinced that it really needs a secret recipe. From books I have collected a round dozen, some which vary basically in method, and none of them promise anything like the Julep of the Southern States.

8

If the very names of these drinks are effervescent and thirst-quenching, those of the hot alcoholic potions for winter nights hum and crackle with warmth and cheer. Bishop and Punch, Nog and Negus, Toddy and Grog, comforting, friendly and nostalgic names to send one to bed warmed and smiling. Of Bishop it must be Saintsbury who speaks in a voice which we should revere: * 'It is, as I have found more people not know

---

* *Notes on a Cellar Book*, by George Saintsbury (Macmillan).

'The bar should be garish and prismatic'

than know in this ghastly thin-faced time of ours, simply mulled
port. You take a bottle of that noble liquor and put it in a
saucepan, adding as much or as little water as you can reconcile
to your taste and conscience, an orange cut in half (I believe some
people squeeze it slightly), and plenty of cloves (you may stick
them in the orange if you have a mind). Sugar or no sugar at
discretion, and with regard to the character of the wine. Put it
on the fire, and as soon as it is warm, and begins to steam, light it.
The flames will be of an imposingly infernal colour, quite
different from the light blue flicker of spirits or of claret mulled.
Before it has burned too long pour it into a bowl, and drink it
as hot as you like. It is an excellent liquor, and I have found it
quite popular with ladies.'

Negus I have made and drunk for a good many years, since its
exotic and at the same time quaint name attracted me in *Pickwick
Papers*. Cross-references to the *Oxford English Dictionary* and the
Dictionary of National Biography explain that it is named after a
Colonel Francis Negus, who is said to have invented it 'to avert
a political fracas, attention being diverted from political matters
at a party in Queen Anne's reign to a discussion of the merits of
wine and water'. It is a splendid drink to provide for a small
intimate party in winter—after Midnight Mass in the small hours
of Christmas morning, for instance—or for a ghost-story session
round a bright fire; but it is not a way of providing an alcoholic
beverage to a large number of people who expect hard liquor.
It is made by heating a bottle of red wine almost but not quite to
boiling point and pouring on an equal quantity of boiling water
in which a couple of dessert-spoonfuls of sugar have been dissolved.
Drop in a few cloves, some thin slices of lemon and a good grating
of nutmeg. Port wine is best, but any red wine will serve the
purpose. A measure of brandy is a worthwhile addition.

Mixing a good Punch is a less haphazard thing altogether, and
can be the occasion and not merely the accompaniment of a
party. It should, I think, be done under the eyes of those who
are to drink the resulting liquor, and without haste or fuss. A
punchbowl may be improvised, but a long-handled spoon is as
essential for this occasion as for supping with the devil. Every-

G

one interested in good living has a recipe for Punch, but I find
Mrs. Beeton's unrivalled, though she warns us in a prim footnote :
'It is more intoxicating in its effects than other alcoholic bever-
ages, especially so when composed, as is usually the case, of several
alcoholic liquids. Moreover the strength of the spirit being
partially disguised by the acid, sugar and flavouring ingredients,
not only makes this beverage more palatable than it would otherwise be, *but probably causes the partakers thereof to unconsciously
imbibe more alcohol than would be agreeable to them in another form.*'
The italics are mine; the split infinitive Mrs. Beeton's. After
this cautionary proviso, however, she proceeds to give details of a
Punch which would knock a horse sideways and to follow it with
another about twice as potent. Her first demands half a pint of
brandy and the same of rum, a pint of boiling water, two ounces
of sugar, a lemon, a pinch of ground cinnamon and one of grated
nutmeg. 'Remove the rind of the lemon by rubbing it with
some of the sugar. Put the whole of the sugar, the cinnamon,
cloves, brandy, rum and boiling water into a stewpan, heat
gently by the side of the fire, but do not let it approach boiling
point. Strain the lemon-juice into a punch bowl, add the hot
liquid, and serve at once.' The second recipe calmly lists a quart
of very old ale, a pint of boiling water, half a pint each of rum,
whisky and gin and the same minor ingredients and method of
preparation.

From these it will be seen that there is a good deal of scope for
individual taste, for inventiveness and for variety of occasion.
But it should be remembered that Punch is a mixture of spirits,
and wines should not be wasted on it.

As for Grog or Toddy, I mean no disrespect to them when I
say that they are nothing but whisky or rum with lemon, sugar
and hot water, but they are best made by dissolving the sugar in
the spirits, adding the water and finally dropping in the lemon-
slice. When these are made at my small bar they are drunk from
one of a row of giant rummers, not because the name has any
connection with rum, since it is derived from the German *Römer* or
Roman glass, but because, with their strength and heavy stems,
they can be held in the hand while the liquid is still too hot to drink.

9

Not very willingly I consider the subject of beer. It has degenerated so miserably in my life-time that I find now that bottled it is gaseous without being enlivening, and from the barrel it is often oily, flat and insipid. This may not be wholly the fault of the brewers, who are hedged in by restrictions, but they cannot be entirely blameless, I believe, since the decline in our national beverage began before the law-makers gained their strangle-hold. Lord knows what chemicals and colourings, what hygienic or money-saving processes are now employed, or what dilutions or medicinal infusions have been ordered; but the result as one buys it now is feeble stuff without much cheer or value in it. Nor is such lager beer as may be obtained in bottle to my taste, though I still dream of the beers of Germany and Holland before the war.

There are kept in my bar a dozen bottles of a much-advertised brand of light ale, but these are for undiscriminating men who seem to think that the sole alternatives which life has to offer in liquor are 'light' or 'bitter' and of these two dull liquids choose 'light'. It is frothy, tasteless stuff which must have degenerated sadly since Goethe died crying, 'Light, more light'. For myself, I can occasionally stomach a 'strong' ale which is sold at a shattering price by certain inns—drawn from the wood, of course, not bottled. Even this I find better mulled in winter or with a sprig of rosemary in it in summer. To mull ale I pour a quart of it into a saucepan kept for the purpose, add a heaped dessert-spoonful of brown sugar, four cloves, and a pinch of mace, cinnamon and nutmeg, and two of ground ginger. When it is nearly but not quite boiling I add a gill of South African or other ordinary brandy and serve it in rummers.

But I find little pleasure in the suburban cult of a public-bar atmosphere in the home which goes so far as to include darts or shove-ha'penny, games which are natural to a pub setting but affected and boring in the house. With this go tankards, stolen ash-trays, even clay pipes and table-skittles. They have no place in my modest bar, which does not try to be more professional in character than it is.

10

So the cupboard under the stairs has been made to provide in a good many varieties that most civilizing influence, good liquor. I am of those who believe that the peace of the world will be achieved by the benign persuasiveness of Russian vodka and our Scotch and American whisky more probably than by conferences or threats. For, as Wordsworth said, 'by our own spirits we are deified'.

Wine

I

HAVING presumed to use the phrase 'a civilized way of living' as my ambition in setting up house in the country and planning existence here, I should perhaps have come sooner to the vital subject of wine; for without wine, I am convinced, there would be for occidental men no civilized living and eventually no civilization. Wine is the very life-blood of our culture and has been since the darkest ages. It is wholly good and almost supernaturally healthy. Of all our benefits it is most certainly God's kindest gift, with God's smile in it, a little parental present with no conditions attached, no retribution, no reserve. It was not chance which made the First Miracle the turning of water into wine, and wine of a particularly heady quality, as we are authoritatively told. Moreover, the greatness of our race has declined as we have drunk less of it, just as it rose with its increase, and this is no coincidence.

To those who rule us, and to those who have done so for the past thirty-five years, it has been an Import, a frivolous luxury in which a few rich men indulge, which may be taxed with impunity or barred rigorously from entrance to the country if that helps some artificial balance of trade. It has been considered by successive Budget-makers the most superfluous of extravagances, a foreign fal-de-lal about which reactionaries like Chesterton and Belloc had a bee in their bonnets, a liquid of less consequence than eau-de-Cologne because instead of being sold by that earnest and useful chap the chemist it is retailed by outmoded and unpatriotic tradesmen called wine-merchants. Necessary? Perhaps 'medicinal' wines, as prescribed by the less conscientious doctors operating beyond the National Health Act, might at times be thought necessary to patients who were prepared to pay for them privately, but wines, as such, are politically rated as the very antithesis of necessity, and no man with a social conscience, we are told, should want to purchase them.

Wine-drinking except in the home and restaurant has been reduced to such an unhappy nadir in this country that a modern publican, asked what wines he has, will say promptly 'Port or Sherry', and offer you a thimbleful of a sweet cochineal-coloured chemical or a microscopic measure of a brown beverage which the Spanish call *vino dulce* and sell at a farthing a glass to any strong man who can stomach its liverish acerbity. For these you will be charged two shillings a time. I never see in fading letters on old inns the word 'Wines and Spirits' or 'Finest Quality Wines', without regret for the days, not more than four decades back, when such advertisements spoke truth. I remember in defence of Victorian England that a poor man might drink wine then, as Dickens shows us, while no prosperous household was without its cellar. In promoting its restoration in the only ways we can, by drinking wine and offering it to our friends, by studying a little of the vast lore which has come to surround it in the seventy centuries or more of its existence, by encouraging those who speak for it, we are carrying out a conspicuous moral obligation.

So even if I have to sell a picture or write an unwelcome article, or keep one or two opulent creditors waiting in order to achieve it, I shall manage to have a few bottles of wine in hand, to choose them with care, to drink them with pleasure.

2

There is, under this house, a cellar, or at least a space between the floor and the earth. It is accessible only by a trap-door which is now under the felt of the hall and it is less than five foot deep, but one day, I hope, I shall be able to turn it into the wine-cellar which it could easily be. I am almost tempted, in fact, to apply to whichever Board or Council or Committee considers applications from house-owners for permission to use their own money in improving their own property, and demand a licence to spend the necessary sum on adapting the present dark vacuum to the purpose of a wine-cellar. I would certainly do so if I could see the faces of the members of that Board or Committee when they heard of my request. 'A *wine*-cellar,' they would repeat in shocked and trembling, or loud and derisory, or high and angry, voices. 'What profligate voluptuary, what corrupt dipsomaniac, what egregious anarchist is this? When there are new testing-stations to be built for the Milk Marketing Board, new laboratories for the elementary schools, new offices for the Advisory Council to the Committee for the Study of the Promotion of Dietary Reform, does any man dare to suppose that we shall allow him to spend his money on the housing of *wine*? He must be out of touch with all reality, still living in the Middle Ages. Or a paid agent of Communism, exerting a subversive influence. Or a criminal dealing in the Black Market. Or simply a mad-man in need of constraint. His application is, of course, refused, and we recommend that he himself should be investigated.'

So my cellar is unmade and in the meantime the shelves of the bar, arranged in bins, keep all the wine that under existing taxation I can afford to buy.

3

Because I was not old enough to drink wine before the First World War, I have never known it drunk as a matter of course in England, and it occurs to me that it was for a similar reason that the English always had good taste in wine—as an import it was never quite taken for granted even in the years when, on the authority of Mrs. Beeton's price list, you could buy claret or burgundy for a shilling a bottle and Bollinger at six-and-six. For me it has had always a certain magic, and I have learnt to love and respect it not as a Frenchman does, by being brought up with it, but by never quite deeming it an everyday drink. I could, I suppose, write a vinous autobiography, bottles as chapter-headings, which would stretch from the Muscatel of my boyhood to the bottle of Cos d'Estournel which I drank with a shoulder of kid last week.

My father knew wine and drank it frequently, but usually with some pretext, for it had already become a luxury. Before I was twelve I was given a little with any meal at which it appeared, and at fourteen I knew a burgundy from a claret and a dry Champagne from a sweet one. Like boys today, but precociously in those years, I crept into bars when I was still in my early teens, and would drink Port at sixpence a glass if I had the sixpence. But when I was eighteen an old Swedish retired diplomat called Count Wachtmeister invited me to France for a summer as private tutor to his son, and I had my first opportunity for lapping among the vintages. In those two months I learnt the elements of something which I shall carry to the ugly, half-open front door of death—the unflagging gusto of one who can find riches in each new bottle.

I remember the queer liquor which I drank at table on the cargo-boat which took me to Buenos Aires as a boy of nineteen. It was shipped for the Spanish emigrants who were carried below, and it was so inky and acid that it could only be drunk with water and sugar. But there were some excellent local wines in Argentina, from the province of Mendoza, and what was more important, perhaps, there was a good everyday wine which I could afford to drink and which I always remember with gratitude. It was called Trapiche and it had that freshness and fragrance of a very fair claret.

Back in Kent I found that my parents had as neighbour a frail, white-bearded, stooping man who lived alone in an excessively ugly house and went to London every day. My father asked him to dinner, and he came bearing a bottle of Veuve Clicquot 1921, explaining that he had been a taster for the firm for many years and was given 'a few bottles a year' for his own use. Thereafter it became his pleasant custom to arrive unbidden at lunch or dinner-time, always with his precious burden. I shall not readily believe that there could be anything much better than that dry and delicate wine, and I have never since those days cared for lesser champagnes which have been recommended as 'passable'.

Long stays in the Rhineland in the early 'thirties taught me something of Hock, and I remember that bottle of unspecified *Schaumwein*, sparkling Moselle, which I bought in 1929 for my hosts in the little Alte Herrlichkeit hotel at Monschau, where I was living on the day when a telegram from England told me that at last a publisher had accepted a novel of mine. If Aladdin's djinn appeared at this moment in the uniform of a wine-waiter I would ask for a Hock from the Rhinegau; from Rudesheim, I think, because I remember that brightly-coloured little town so well; a Berg Orleans of 1945, I daresay, though I have never had the opportunity to taste it, but certainly a Hock, for I find the habit which Germans have of drinking their good wines at almost any time of day an endearing one, and I have enviously watched while a party entered a restaurant or bar and, sitting round a table, called for a bottle and another until perhaps two hours had passed, then ordered food, or left, or danced, or sang, or just drank another bottle.

It was in its own country, too, though not in its province, that I first drank Sherry with any discrimination, for I lived during 1932 in Barcelona. I could remember the Manzanilla which I had drunk eight years earlier in the vine-shaded *patio* of a Swiss hotel in a suburb of Buenos Aires; it had been served in large green glasses, shamefully frozen, but refreshing. None of our English authorities on wine have enough to say about Sherry; even Mr. André Simon, who speaks *ex cathedra* on the wines of France, is almost perfunctory, I find, when he deals with this amber nepenthe in which the salt winds of the Atlantic may still be sniffed and the sunshine of Andalucia. Saintsbury mentions none specifically but Tio Pepe, which in his time was less standardized as a reliable dry sherry for English bars. There is little guidance to be got, either, from English wine-merchants, and when I lived that year in Spain I had to make my untutored way among the Finos and Amontillados, the Vinos de Pasto, the Olorosos and Amorosos. But I have never lost my early delight in the faintly nutty dry sunniness of Manzanilla.

Tokay in Hungary, a good red wine called Colares in Portugal (but no port there, for it is made for the English market and un-obtainable, as we know it, in the country of its origin), Chianti both mediocre and superb in Italy, and all of them in England at rare times (rare because they were little cheaper than the great wines of France). These passed the years before 1939, and after

that, during my time in the army, there were only four short
periods during which I could drink wine at all. During the first
I was nominally in training at Winchester, and I would go with
young Eddie Bates, who afterwards became a fighter pilot and
was killed, to an hotel called the Southgate, which had neither
exhausted nor reserved its pre-war supplies, and we would recover
from arduous hours on the parade-ground by drinking our way
steadily through the Burgundies, from a different bin each night.
The second period was in Madagascar, where our political department suddenly discovered that it had the authority to release
what supplies there were. The fourth was in Goa, to which
strip of Portuguese Indian territory I went on leave in 1944, to
find it the only area in India supplied with wine. The Indian
hills, so happily placed to grow the vine, are without it through
religious prejudices both Brahminical and Mohammedan, so that
life in that hot and dusty climate is unsolaced by the good wines
that might have been grown there.

But in the third period, in South Africa, I really tasted, for there
is wine here which a Frenchman could not spurn, wine of a
quality which belies the narrow traditionalist who trusts no
vineyards but the European. The industry in the Cape Province
is three hundred years old, and it is interesting to find, so far from
Europe, a whole tradition of vintnery with its own names, its
vintage years, its distinctive achievements in body and bouquet,
all highly developed, but little appreciated beyond the country
which has produced them. The names range from Dutch to
English; some suggest hocks, some the good red wines which you
may buy so cheaply in the Union. Constantia and Wynberg,
Drakenstein and Malmesbury, Schoengesicht and Caledon.
They are not yet classical names, but I believe that they will be.

4

When I came home in 1946, it seemed at first that 'wine'
was a word no longer used, like 'gentleman', 'society' and
'patriotism'. The whole tradition of wine, if it persisted at all,
must be under hostile suspicion, I thought. During that summer
many pubs were closed for half the evening because they had no

beer to sell, so surely the luxurious wine-bibber must be out of official favour? He was, it now seems, not so much frowned on as forgotten; so rare, so almost extinct a bird that he was not worth plucking by the tax-gatherers. Wine escaped the harshest impositions of those days, and now, although it is still unduly expensive, its price is not out of proportion to other necessities which have been labelled luxury goods.

Indeed, it is argued by some sanguine souls that wine may be drunk as cheaply, almost, as beer. A bottle of wine, they contend, carefully decanted, will last a man for three meals and be as good at the third time as the first, whereas a pint bottle of light dinner ale costs one-and-sixpence, so that wine is a little, but not a great deal more expensive than beer. I should like to agree, but find that no bottle of wine lasts me three meals and none is as good after twenty-four hours in a decanter.

It is, however, possible for a man of moderate means to buy and lay down some pretty good Burgundy and Claret. He may attend one of the wine auctions at Restell's which were once closed to the layman, or he may buy at auction when a private cellar is being disposed of. Even if he must buy from a wine-merchant, there are 1949 table wines of great promise to be bought at 6/- to 7/- a bottle, or wine of later and more uncertain years for even less, if he wants to gamble. Then 1943, 1945, and 1947 were all good years, and I have seen in reliable merchants' lists wines of all of them at less than 8/- a bottle.

Sherry, too, is fairly plentiful, though at a price which would seem quite silly to the hospitable majority of fifty years ago, who kept a bottle for ever at hand to offer to every visitor. A fairly pleasing Manzanilla costs about 16/- a bottle, and a good Fino or Amontillado a guinea or more. There are some drinkable South African sherries which are cheaper, and there is, I am told, something called British Sherry; but sherry is a wine peculiar to one region of one country, and few other vineyards can produce more than a bilious imitation of it.

Port, too, though stupidly dear, is at least obtainable, and vintage ports of recent years shipped by Graham, Dow and other shippers can be bought for about a pound a bottle and should,

I suppose, be laid down even at this price. It is an Englishman's wine—perhaps the only one which owes its very existence to English taste—and I cannot see how anyone who respects our national principles of hospitality can be without it. In the dark recesses of my cupboard under the stairs, where the ceiling has sloped almost to floor level and one must stoop or kneel to reach what is in the little bins, as far as possible out of temptation's way, are a few bottles of 1942 vintage shipped by Quinta do Noval and a precious half-dozen of 1947 by Tuke Houldsworth. Among all the regrets which I hear voiced by people who failed to buy this or that 'when it was cheap', none are keener than mine that I did not as a young man inherit, buy, or come by a few dozen port from which I might, with quickened pulse, draw now.

In our manner of drinking it, port has been much abused, for it is no wine to swallow in great quantities, in the way of our ancestors. I remember only once seeing it used as a thirst-quencher, and that by an iconoclastic schoolmaster of mine who, far afield on a hot June day, demanded from a publican four measures of port in a tumbler, a draught which he swallowed in a moment. Nor is it a wine to dribble out into the silly little glasses which, I suppose, publicans have deliberately popularized for it. Nor yet is it an accompaniment to coffee and cigars. Best of all with cheese, I think, it is enlivened by dessert, particularly good nuts. It is the one wine which must be decanted. And, ironically enough, since it is the wine most frequently sold in bars, at its worst it is undrinkable, and even when mediocre is not worth drinking. A wine, in fact, of which only the best is good.

5

The wine-grower himself must think in terms of decades, and the buyer should at least presuppose a few years in which his cellar may escape atomic bombing. So although I am warned by men better qualified than I to foretell the world's future that to invest in such a thing as wine is transparent silliness, I have stocked my bins with a modest but promising collection which I carefully catalogue in a cellar-book. It is, as it is meant to be, a symbol, a rosy promise of good days to come, of happy occasions

which next year and the year after will bring to this house. The
sum of money it represents is not large, and has been the best-
spent money in my memory.

But there is not among my bottles, as there is in almost every
French house, a cask of *vin ordinaire* for rough drinking and cooking. The lack of an everyday wine at a price which makes it
freely usable has to be accepted, and there seems little hope of a
remedy. Wine-merchants do their best, and in the list in front
of me I see that under Claret there is a Fronsac at 7/-, under
Rhône wines a *rosé* at 8/-, under Burgundy a Beaujolais 1947 at
7/6, an unspecified white Bordeaux at 7/-, while from South
Africa there is a 'red wine' at 6/6 and a 'white wine' at 7/-.
From other lists I know of a Yugo-Slav wine of a Hock kind at
6/- and a Portuguese *tinto* at the same price. These are all very
well, but *vin ordinaire* should be cheap enough to use freely in
cooking and to make water or beer unnecessary on the table at
daily meals. Where is Mrs. Beeton's Burgundy at a shilling a
bottle? And what statistics or polemics can justify mulcting the
average wage-earner of a full day's pay for something which
should be neither difficult to buy nor very expensive—a bottle
of reasonably good Champagne to be kept for festivity or illness, for love-potion or pick-me-up, in all of which rôles it is
supreme?

The truth is that we are forced to fight for this very simple
human prerogative, the right to a glass of wine; but let it also be
admitted that the struggle may ultimately improve its taste in our
mouths. When I look at the rows of black bottle-ends in my
cupboard under the stairs and think what they have cost me in
effort, and know that my hard-won possession of them would be
quite widely considered self-pampering, I feel a certain pride
which may communicate itself to the wine. Pride, above all, in
being what is called anti-social, since society will only be saved
by those who are now named its enemies, those who will not run
with it headlong. But pride, too, in belonging to that great
company, the gayest and the best of humankind, who have
appreciated God's kindliest thought for them and have loved
wine. Pawkiness, pretentiousness, selfishness, misanthropy and

meanness are its enemies; but good-fellowship, content, charity and inspiration can scarcely live without it. No more can I.

6

After wine, brandy; an intense and passionate warmth to succeed the milder benison. It is, of course, a spirit distilled from wine, and although the word has been applied to liqueurs like Calvados—which used to be called Applejack Brandy in England —it is nothing else. It is with some unction that I write of brandy here, because in England there are some odd and almost universal misconceptions about it: that it is the English word for Cognac, that it is a sort of French whisky and, worst of all but increasingly common as we 'farther from the East must travel', that it is exclusively a medicine or a restorative kept for those prone to fainting attacks.

Nor is it universally realized that in France there are two distinct kinds of brandy: Cognac, which is distilled from the wines of the region round the town of that name, and Armagnac, which is distilled in the Department of Gers, south of the Bordeaux wine-country. But the Spaniards call their excellent brandy Coñac, and the commonest of them—Fundador, a bland and kindly spirit made by the ancient house of Domecq—merits the name. There are also reasonably good brandies distilled in South Africa, Australia and Portugal, while the Aguardiente of Argentina needs to be drunk to be believed. (It is not a true brandy.)

There is, in my cupboard under the stairs, one bottle—now, alas, transparent to within two inches of its base—which has no label, no tasselled cork, no gold foil, but stands, a brown and lonely column, among more festive fellows. It comes from a *cave* not twenty miles from Roquefort in the Landes, where I lived and worked through the spring of 1948, and it contains an Armagnac of such blandness and antiquity that only three Englishmen of my acquaintance have been invited to sniff and savour it, and they are a wine-taster, a wine-collector and C. P. Snow, who, not long from an Oxford common-room and with a slightly Pickwickian *bonhomie* and an honest taste in liquor,

seemed likely to (and indeed did) enjoy it. It came into my
hands that spring because of a dear, claret-faced Frenchman in the
village of Roquefort who asked me if I would like to drive out
with him to a *cave* he knew.

'For Cognac,' this M. Pedluque explained, 'there are great
distilleries owned by famous firms like Martell. But our
Armagnac is made by small independent distillers, none with
even national fame, certainly none known internationally. You
shall see.'

We drove through the sunlit morning to a remote village, and
from it by a mere cart-track to a group of barns with a modest
old stone house among them. It was like a sleepy farm—
scarcely visited, one would say—with a few chickens picking in
the yard, a dog not bothering to bark and no human being in
sight. But presently the proprietor, a little hirsute man who
looked like a peasant farmer, came out and, greeting us cordially,
took us into the long, cool cellar, where vast tuns were ranged
from end to end. We began to taste.

Was it a ritual, I wonder? Were all his visitors taken back
through the years in this way from the raw spirit of the previous
harvest to the war years, the 'thirties, the 'twenties, the years of the
First World War, the early days of the century, while the
Armagnac offered from each grew ever more creamy and easy
to swallow and it seemed that we had exhausted the last cask?

'You like it?' asked M. Pedluque rosily.

'I adore it,' I said without hesitation.

'But there is one more,' said the whiskery proprietor—from a
considerable distance, it seemed to me. 'It is some way from
here. We may perhaps go in your car?'

We might and did, bumping over a field to a little out-
building which stood alone.

'You see,' he said, 'when the Germans came we thought they
should not have certain barrels, and we brought them here and
put them under this stack of straw. This one, of which I am
going to give you a glass, was distilled by my grandfather in
the year I was born, 1881.'

There are limits to the verbal ecstasies I will allow myself, even in the matter of Armagnac. Let me say only that it was the best brandy I have tasted. It was, it is, supreme. But the proprietor would only sell me one bottle of it, and soon the last royal measure of it will be gone.

7

It was as we sat in the kitchen after that transaction, I remember, that we discussed the important question of glasses. M. Pedluque and I had brought with us two other men professionally interested, for I had met a few days previously at a vinous occasion in the Bordeaux country Rupert Denny, the wine correspondent of a London daily newspaper, and a Frenchman, also a Chevalier de Tastevin.

'From what kind of glass,' I asked the proprietor, 'should your finest brandy be drunk?'

The discussion which followed was lively and discursive, but led to agreement among all on a few cogent points. The big balloon brandy-glass was condemned. It had been originally invented for tourists, it wasted fine liquor, it could not conveniently be warmed when held in one hand, and there was really no reason for it except that it was showy and had become popular. On the other hand, its shape, if not its size, was as it should be. A brandy-glass should swell out and then rise to a smaller circle at the rim. It should have a stem so that its bowl rests in the palm and the brandy is kept at blood heat. It should not be too thick nor yet so paper-thin that it cannot be trusted. A miniature balloon-glass, in fact, about three and a half inches in height, which may be slightly warmed before such brandy as that old Armagnac is poured into it. With such authority to guide me, I purchased in France a dozen of these glasses, which are common enough there but almost unobtainable in England, and they stand on a shelf of the bar now.

For other wines no great variety is needed. Before the war it was possible to buy at Woolworths and at sixpence or less apiece all the glasses that one needed, and I still have a set of long-stemmed hock-glasses which are used universally in Germany. More graceful for Hock are those tall glasses, their rims no more than two inches in diameter, which taper down in a straight line to a point at the foot and are often engraved with the traditional grape and vine-leaf design. These are delightful to a wine-drinker as sentimental as I, for by them are recalled the Christmas Annual pictures of hunting men or highwaymen, squires or parsons, who lift them to the light and wink at their golden contents as they stand in breeches and flowered waistcoats before log fires. I have three of these, but that is a good number for the drinking of a single bottle.

For Champagne nothing is better than the wide bowl on a fairly long stem, such as in England has become the convention, though in France it is seen less often. Sherry likes a fairly wide glass, not a mean little thing with a narrow top. Nothing is worse than claret or burgundy poured out in driblets into glasses too small for them.

For beer I keep a variety of receptacles, some curious. I find that pewter, however scrupulously cleaned, fouls the beer and gives it a harsh, metallic taste; but tankards of glass look well, and are conveniently hung on the fronts of shelves. Best of all, for me, is a *stein*, the heavy earthenware mug holding a pint which is universal in Munich, though a rummer, which looks as though it will hold no more than a pint, but often accommodates a quart or more, may be filled for a thirsty guest. A good cocktail is better for a wide, bell-shaped glass like a miniature champagne-glass, and for liqueurs I like those narrow, fluted glasses which look like exotic flowers when they are filled.

Glasses, it seems to me, are of real importance, and their shape, thickness, size and colour need careful consideration. And although in wayside inns abroad I have been given good wine which, in those circumstances, tasted none the worse for a thick, crude tumbler or even—in one case—a cracked cup, I believe that in England we are constrained by our dull climate to seek always the most fitting vessel for the wines we have to import.

8

There remains but one kind of drink in the cupboard under the stairs of which I have said nothing and shall say little—liqueurs.

H

These are baroque absurdities, mere alcoholic assorted sweet-meats with which to follow food and wine, and although they are reputed to please 'the ladies', this must have been a reputation gained when 'the ladies' were less experienced in such things than they are now, for all of my acquaintances emphatically prefer an honest brandy after dinner. But poured into fluted glasses, liqueurs make a pretty display, and for the two or three of them which I like to keep there is an imposing list from which to choose: Crême de Menthe, the supposed favourite of Edwardian whores; Cherry Brandy from Denmark glowing beside it; Danziger Goldwasser, with its fragments of gold leaf catching the light; Van der Hum, a manlier liqueur from South Africa; the monkish Benedictine and Chartreuse; Curaçao, which is distilled from Seville-orange peel; Maraschino, made from cherries, and Noyau, from plum-kernels; a sickly yellow liqueur which I once sipped in Switzerland called Cream of Bananas or something of the sort; Anisette and Kümmel, those two most herbal liqueurs; Grand Marnier, Kirsch and Quetsch. There is the harshly excellent Calvados, the brandy of Norman cider, and many liqueurs of local popularity which are rare in England. For me, though, they are ornaments of the cupboard under the stairs rather than drinks for frequent consumption, but because such small quantities are poured from their bottles, and those so rarely, the row of them once purchased costs little to maintain.

English Water-colours

I

W<small>HEN</small> I told H. E. Bates that I collect early English water-colours, he said, 'Yes, everyone starts with them', and glanced fondly at one of his French paintings. Because he is far from snooty and is almost as interested in art as in literature, I thought over the rather absent-minded remark and saw just what he meant. Many a collector has begun by buying a few little drawings by English artists because they can still be found at prices which are not prohibitive to a man of moderate means, because their merits are easy to recognize and because, within the limitations of their medium, they are perfect. Such a collector, once enslaved by the tyrannous passion for picture-buying which dominates so many human beings and takes no count of their circumstances, might begin after a time to ask for more depth, more body, more movement and significance in the pictures on his walls, and slowly his beloved water-colours would give place to oils, until he could speak of them as Bates did.

I have never been tempted to develop in this way. I recognize, of course, the severe restrictions in this medium, but I have also seen them transcended. I admit that none of the world's greatest artists could have been satisfied by painting in transparent colours on paper, but I maintain that some very fine artists wanted nothing more. And, apart from any question of the importance of water-colours as compared with that of oil-paintings, there are some practical advantages in collecting them—unless you happen to be one of the few dozen Englishmen whose inherited capital is large enough to provide pocket-money for a life-time. The collector of water-colours can have on his walls, without impoverishing himself to get them, some of the best work of some of the best English artists, modern and early; whereas the collector of oil-

107

paintings, unless by some freakish piece of luck, or unless he is phenomenally wealthy, will have only a few minor productions of the less sought-after.

I have collected early English water-colours since I came of age because—I recognize now—they are the only pictures of real quality which I can afford to collect. But also because I have come to like them, to prefer them, for my own walls, to anything else, to believe in them and the integrity of the men who painted them, to know them intimately both as a kind and individually.

2

I owe my initial interest in them to one man, much of my knowledge to two others, a curious trio when I think of them together.

At school I had two friends, brothers, Richard and Lincoln Brown, the sons of an American business man long resident in England. Richard was two years older than I, Lincoln five days younger. For our years at Tonbridge, Richard and I were inseparable, but later in London, when we were both living in rooms, it was with Lincoln that I stalked through the spring and summer of 1925, for Richard had gone to a theological college, from which he later emerged a Church of England parson.

Lincoln, unlike his brother, was born in England, but there was —and there still is, I think—something of the American *émigré* in his character. It would be unfair to use the word dilettante of him, even more unfair to call him an amateur, for he has attacked most of the arts with enthusiasm and sincerity, though his interest in each has burnt up too quickly. He trained his voice for a time, intending to dedicate it to the opera. He decided to be a publisher, and two books appeared under his imprint. Late in his thirties he resolved to go on the stage and took himself, then a married man with almost grown-up children, through a gruelling training at a school of dramatic art. But throughout this variety of short-lived careers he has kept one abiding interest which has never slackened—pictures.

I remember very clearly how he arrived one day at the house in Bryanston Street in an attic of which I lived, paying a kindly landlady twenty-five shillings a week for this room and a daily breakfast. I had not long been home from two years in South America and had not seen Lincoln since we left school. I was a *gauche* and provincial young man of twenty and he seemed to me almost unnaturally *soigné* and sophisticated. It was the year of 'Oxford bags' and little flat hats for men, and he wore them in an unexaggerated form. He had brilliant china-blue eyes, curling fair hair and a broad, good-natured mouth which belied the some-what faun-like pointedness of his features. He was very slim, and dressed, as it seemed to me, with the easy elegance of an artist concealing his art. I was at once captivated by his air of modest but confident omniscience. It seemed to me that here was a man who would be at home anywhere, whose taste and experience left no gaps.

One evening in Lincoln's room I began to examine the pictures. They appeared dim and colourless to me and one, a French church depicted in fluent detail, seemed a melancholy piece of decoration.

'That,' said Lincoln, 'is by Samuel Prout.'

He began to talk about water-colours, and before half an hour had passed I was a lost man. What he, the all-knowing and deeply experienced arbiter, did, must be done. Within a week I had purchased for a shilling at a stall in Hammersmith an ink drawing of Louis XI peering through a grille at a celebration of Mass, a strange sketchy impression signed by an artist called Eyre Crowe. I have long since lost it without regret, but it seemed an enviable possession then.

'Would you call it a master drawing?' I asked Lincoln, for I had heard him use the term.

He smiled.

'I should hardly call Eyre Crowe a master. But it's really quite good. *Quite* good.'

Thenceforward I was a collector.

3

The first water-colour of any importance which I bought was by Paul Sandby Munn (1773–1845), a godson of Paul

Sandby, and a fine painter in his own right. He was, like many of these old water-colour artists, the son of a painter. There was a David Cox Junior, a John Varley Junior, a T. L. Rowbotham Senior, T. M. Richardson father and son, while Reinagle, Charles Claude Pyne, Pugin, Prout, George Barret, Richard Parkes Bonington, Morland, to mention only a few, were all either the sons or fathers of artists less distinguished, and William Moore the portrait-painter had no fewer than fourteen sons, of whom Albert, Henry and John are all remembered as artists. Paul Sandby Munn was born when his distinguished godfather was fifty years old and already famous as a landscape artist and a Foundation Member of the Royal Acadamy. Since Sandby lived till he was eighty-four, he must have seen his god-son's success, but I can find no record of their relationship, or even of the friendship which probably existed between Paul Sandby and old Munn, who named his son so fully after the other. Of this Munn the father nothing seems to remain—even his Christian name is unrecorded, and the South Kensintgon Museum has no example of his work. I bought recently a little sepia-wash drawing, able but pointless, because in Victorian hand-writing on the back of it are the words 'Munn, Senr.'

Of Paul Sandby Munn little more is known, but a good deal of his work remains, and it is memorial enough. An excellent draughtsman, his landscapes are delicate and decorative rather than powerful, tending to conform to a pattern which includes a pale, breezy sky, some gentle outlines of hills, a farm, a stream, a bridge, grey, feathery trees and a recurrent group of little figures dressed in pink and blue—figures which are fittingly placed in the landscape. It is an agreeable scene which charmingly recalls the artist's period and his liking for Welsh foothills and English downland. It is the work of a highly talented man who knew his limitations.

But I was aware of none of this when I bought that first land-scape, and although I saw the faint pencilled signature 'P. S. Munn 1805', I had never heard the name, and was for the first time trusting my judgment of a painting. It was in 1928, I remember, and I had rented half a shop-front in Rochester from a strange old man called Cowper Terry, a descendant of William Cowper. Into this half-a-shop I put my own books and called myself an antiquarian bookseller, while in the other half old Terry tried to deal in antiques. He was the second of the men to whom I owe what I know of water-colours, a strange Dickensian figure whose dry parchment face I can see more plainly now than the faces of living people.

His story is not without pathos. He was a cashier in one of the local banks who volunteered for the Navy during the First World War and spent three or four years on minesweepers. He must then have been in his later forties, and the disruption in his life of scrupulous accountancy was such that, returning to the bank after the war, he was unable to tolerate the regimented life of a clerk and threw up his job, together with the pension which would have been due to him in a year or two. He then took a little, overhung, grubby shop in Rochester High Street and endeavoured to turn his knowledge and love of art and porcelain to advantage. Alas, knowledge and love are not the only qualities necessary to the hard and grasping life of a dealer, and this remote, gentle little man was soon edged into failure by hardier tradesmen. When I first knew him he was still living in furnished rooms, still playing tennis and bridge with his friends in that stuffy town, still retaining, out of reach of bullying buyers from London, his remarkable collection of Toby jugs. But as time went by and his small capital dwindled he moved into a little room at the back of his dingy shop, sold the last of his possessions and eked out a dwindling living by buying at auctions for another dealer. In the last years of his lonely life even his habits of personal cleanliness broke down, and he died a few years ago a penniless, dirty, under-nourished old creature who had lived squalidly in one inadequate room and had no relative even to receive news of his death.

In the year in which I shared his shop, however, old Terry was still an active and good-humoured man with unerring taste in pictures and a dozen good water-colours to sell. It was to him that I eagerly brought the portfolio which I had bought at a sale in Farningham, the portfolio which contained among amateur paintings and uninteresting prints the water-colour with 'P. S. Munn 1805' in delicate letters in its corner.

Old Terry knew.

'Well done,' he kept saying. 'Well done! It's a beauty. Munn—I know the name. We'll look him up. It *is* a beauty.'

So I think when I see it now hanging in the hall in the most honourable place I can give it. So I have thought these twenty-three years during which I have managed to keep it. So much do I still agree with old Terry's enthusiasm that I recently bought for more than it was worth a second picture by that rather too formal artist whose landscape started my collection.

4

It was soon followed by another. I had gone to an auction sale at Fawkham to buy some books when I saw on the wall something that was very obviously an early English water-colour, though a strange one. It depicted a dark cavern with walls of granite blocks lit only by a theatrical shaft of light which shot down from a gap in the roof and illuminated three figures in Greek peasant dress, one of whom smoked a yard-long pipe. In the entrance to this cave stood a Greek soldier with a rifle. It was painted with great cunning, a fine, eccentric piece of work. I took it down and found written on the back 'The Inside of Agamemnon's Tomb by H.W. Williams'. I bought it for two guineas.

This time old Terry knew the artist.

'Hugh William Williams,' he said; 'they call him Grecian Williams.'

Later we looked him up and found his life-story a teasingly interrogative one. He was born at sea in 1773, and while young settled in Edinburgh. At the time of the battle of Waterloo he was travelling in Italy and Greece, and in 1827–29 he published the book *Views in Greece*, which earned him his nickname. Then, 'towards the end of his life he married a lady of position and fortune'. This leaves me with a number of questions. Was he, as his name suggests, a Welshman by parentage? A sea-captain's son, or merely born to passengers coming home from the East?

'Hanging in the most honourable place'

How could he be calmly travelling and sketching in Greece during those critical years? Above all, who was the 'lady of position and fortune' whom he married when he was in his fifties, and what happened to her subsequently?

There are ten of his water-colours in the Victoria and Albert Museum, but every one is of a scene in the Highlands; no view of Greece is there. Mine was chance-collected, bought blind, as it were, and only because I recognized its competence and because it was sold cheaply. It is the most curious, if not one of the most beautiful that I have.

5

There was a long gap in my collecting then—if I may yet use the word collect—for I was abroad for a year or two, and when in England I had not even the little money necessary to buy a drawing. But in 1935 I met the third of the men from whom I learnt to know water-colours, and from that year onwards I have bought rabidly.

Norman Trace was of my own age, an ex-International Rugby player, a dealer in the fine arts. He had a shop in Cheltenham when I lived ten miles away, and we formed a business association which sent us over the country buying whenever I could take a day away from work. He was a ruddy, stalwart fellow with thick, reddish hair leaving a sharply outlined bald patch, and an Edwardian moustache. His knowledge of beautiful things was uncannily wide and deep; he was the son of a collector who had given him three or four years in the museums in England and abroad. He knew porcelain, pottery, furniture, glass, silver, carpets, textiles—almost everything that men buy in order to beautify their homes or to give themselves the importance of ownership. He could gauge the value of a piece of African carving, a Roman urn, a Chinese bronze, a Victorian musical box. But, above all, he was the best judge of a picture I have ever known, with flawless taste and judgment and merciless contempt for the mediocre.

We would sit by the open fireplace in my cottage at Salperton and talk sometimes till it was daylight. He could summon up

for me the dark ages of man's first endeavour to outline figures on
rock, or convince me of the rightness and significance of a modern
experimental picture.   He could discourse on the perfections of
Chinese art and make the life-story of Girtin seem an almost contemporary one.   This was not ostentatious knowledge; there
was nothing of the charlatan in Norman Trace.   He really knew
his stuff.

He encouraged me in my determination to collect water-
colours, recognizing, as I had done, that this is one of the few
ways for a poor man to possess the best in one kind.   And not
long after we had started to buy together he called me into a back
room of a house in which we were 'viewing' for a sale next day
and said, 'Buy that'.

I saw what at first in that dingy room and in a black frame and
dirty mount seemed a muddled water-colour drawing of ancient
sailing-ships and impressionistic figures.   Slowly I sorted it out:
the ruddy, threatening sky; the great archaic ships with sails set
and banners in the wind; the curious tower, which was in-
definably mythological rather than historical; the group in the
foreground with its laden camels so surely moving.   I realized
that it was magnificently painted, though it had nothing at all in
common with my pretty English sketches.

'Whose?' I asked.

Norman Trace sounded subdued.

'I don't know.   At least, I think I do.   I don't want to say
what I think.   You buy it.'

This fell to me for a negligible sum, and when I brought it
home I knew that there was something quite remarkable about it.
Norman Trace stared at it for nearly half-an-hour.   He was too
old a hand to be surprised that it should turn up in the back room
of an ugly little house in Cheltenham, for fine things perpetually
appear in the most unlikely places.   It was its very existence
which seemed to surprise him.

At last he told me.

'There's no doubt about it,' he said.   'There's no one else
possible.   It's a Delacroix.'

I have never needed confirmation of an opinion of his, but in this case it has been thrust upon me. He was right, and as I look at the little picture now, so much romance and beauty, so much movement and gorgeous colour and exuberance, I cannot see why Trace himself should have hesitated. It is slightly anomalous among my temperate English landscapes, this small, brilliant square. But it is, I suppose, the most significant thing I possess.

6

Another water-colour he found for me has importance of a different kind. English of the English, green and pleasant, in the true tradition, it is, I think, a good example of the work of that prince among the topographical artists, Michael 'Angelo' Rooker (1743–1801).

Another nickname, you observe, but this one was conferred on him by Paul Sandby, who was his master. He was the son of an engraver. His life-story is a simple one, recalled by all the writers on the early English water-colourists, but in most detail by C. E. Hughes,* who seems to have held his work in greater esteem than other critics. Rooker started to follow his father's profession, but trouble with his eyesight made him seek less finicky work, and he became scene-painter at the Haymarket, his name appearing on programmes as 'Signor Rookerini'. He made a number of sketching tours on foot in England. A disagreement with his employers at the Haymarket is supposed to have caused him such depression that he never recovered. He died in 1801.

His work shows the engraver's influence, and never became quite emancipated from the conventions of the topographical art of his time, but within its limits it is superb. He had the knack of suggesting a wealth of associations, so that you wonder as you look where his roads lead, who lives in his houses, what the men and women, so graceful and so beautifully grouped, are discussing as they stand there. He can light a landscape with the bright warmth of noon or soothe it with the peace of a summer evening. Above all, even if he paints a ruined abbey or a grey fortress, he can populate his buildings with unseen but strongly sensed

* *Early English Water-colours*, by C. E. Hughes.

inhabitants.   He is the most human of these landscape-painters—
his very hills and valleys wait for the footsteps of men.

His portrait by George Dance shows him as a lean-faced,
frowning fellow, thin-lipped, sharp-nosed, severe.   Yet he must
have loved his kind when he painted each benign scene, not as the
fortuitous face of nature, but as a haunt of men.

My own Rooker landscape is of Harrow-on-the-Hill, and is
dominated by an avenue of magnificent elm-trees in full leaf
under a June sun, the nearest of them drawn in such detail that the
very bark shines.   The scene, though the figures are sparse and
rustic in character, is not without plenty of life, for a workman
sits on a fallen tree-trunk in the foreground while his dog rests
his paws on the trunk beside him and his three horses graze at
hand;   two men fill a wheel-barrow from a heap of stones;
another lights his pipe as he leans against a tree in the middle
distance, while behind him a horseman trots and a woman and
child are walking.   It is late morning, one knows, and the green
slopes to the right are so warm that one would want to sit in the
shade of the trees there, while behind that high brick wall to the
left, one feels, gardeners are thirstily working.   It is so full of
atmosphere that one can almost hear the birds which are not even
painted, one can smell the cowslips and wild thyme which are
invisible.

Hughes calls Rooker the English counterpart of van der
Heyden, 'as a careful and accurate draughtsman who achieved
breadth of effect by an assemblage of minute details'.   I remembered his words recently when Mrs. Dorothy Hart showed
me her remarkable collection of van der Heydens, no fewer than
twenty-four of them.   Yet the Englishman, in spite of the transparent paint he used and his less courageous choice of subjects,
seems to me to have a conception of landscape more likeable and
more warmly felt than the Dutchman's.   The ineffable 'finish'
and mellowness of van der Heyden's work are instantly attractive
to the eye, but every landscape Rooker painted is seen over his
shoulder by mankind;   the footpaths on his hills have been
trodden out by countless dead pedestrians;   his walls are not
casual barriers but the careful work of men whose lives were of

importance to the painter when he sketched them; his sunlight was created by God for man's pleasure. I believe Rooker's place in English art to be with Turner, Constable and Morland rather than with Hearn and the other topographers most usually compared with him.

7

I made a few mistakes in the following years: a John Sell Cotman which wasn't and a highly dubious Cox. But just before I joined the army I found a pair of seascapes by that indefatigable marine-painter Thomas Bush Hardy (1842–97). For years, indeed since I had first been awed by Lincoln Brown's familiar references to the masters, I had heard this T. B. Hardy discussed and had seen a good many of his grey, threatening skies over ruddy-sailed fishing-smacks. Now I seized the chance to possess two of them and, since my belongings were already in store, left them with an accommodating publican for six years, until I was released from the army. Then I added a third and rather larger water-colour by the same artist.

8

It is since the war that I have turned these few water-colours, bought when chance allowed, into a sizeable collection.

There was, for instance, a windy little sketch by Thomas Barker, 'Barker of Bath', (1769–1847), which I bought from a Welshman in Margate, who told me that among other achievements he had succeeded in producing and selling in England tinned beer, on the American model, and actually opened a tin of it to prove his point. (It tasted like any bottled beer, I remember.) The water-colour was more interesting to me than the Welshman's brewing achievements, for it was a bold little sketch by an interesting artist. The sole figure in it is the focus of the scene, a tall woman in the clothes of a peasant of the eighteenth century standing under a blasted tree on a hilltop. In her right hand is a stick on which she rests, in her left a basket of green foliage. Her red cloak, yellow scarf and light blue blouse make her stand out against the pale colours of the mountain landscape, faint blues and greys and a washy green. The effect is desolate but powerful, the work of a man who could with surprisingly little brushwork interpret a wide scene. Barker was born at Pontypool in 1769 and died at Bath in 1847. He, too, was the son of an artist and the brother of another. My curiosity is roused by a bald statement in the *Catalogue of Water-Colour Paintings* in the Victoria and Albert Museum that his noblest effort is a huge fresco, *Inroad of the Turks upon Scio*, painted in 1825 on a wall of his house at Bath.

I bought then for a few pounds in Cumberland one autumn a small but highly characteristic water-colour by John Varley (1778–1842). I had always wanted a drawing by this artist for his robust and trusting personality. His long life of prolific production and unspoilt friendships with almost every English artist of his time, the stories told of his kindly disposition, his boundless energy, his generosity as a teacher, had attracted me to his name. I knew that most of the artists who followed him were indebted to him for instruction, assistance or advice, among them Linnell, Mulready, De Wint, Copley Fielding, F. O. Finch, W. Holman Hunt, Turner of Oxford and, most significantly, David Cox, who was his pupil. I knew that his work is of three periods, each in its way excellent, that he was a friend and admirer of William Blake, that he had an open-mouthed trust in the wonders of science and was a lifelong believer in astrology. I knew that he had to fight hard to live by his art and that he died at last in penury.

During the same visit to Cumberland I found a tinted sketch by Thomas Girtin (1775–1802), unluckily an early and rather trivial piece, but not lacking wholly in the daring and vigour which characterized much of his more important work. My sketch shows the ruined arch of an ecclesiastical building almost hidden by trees whose foliage is lively and lucid in a fairly strong wind, while the distance goes back to a far-away and stormy horizon.

Did not Turner, Girtin's contemporary and friend from boyhood, say that if poor Tom had lived he would have been the greatest of them all? He was twenty-seven when he died, and his portrait by John Opie shows him as a strong, sensual young man, with passionate dark eyes and a look of eager intentness. His potentialities seem to have been almost limitless. Even in the few years during which he painted he brought new life to English art. I would rather own an important water-colour by Girtin than any other English picture.

9

Once more before I left London I bought water-colours—this time a collection of eight by that interesting and dynamic artist whose name, given in baptism, was Hercules Brabazon Sharp, but who at the age of twenty-six changed it to Hercules Brabazon Brabazon (1821–1906). A rich man who rarely bothered to exhibit his work, he must have been damned as a dilettante by his contemporaries and yet, rich or not, he worked as hard as any of them. It was not until he was seventy-one years old, in 1892, that he allowed any sort of fame to come to him, but in that year there was a remarkable exhibition of his water-colours at the Goupil Gallery. Harrow and Trinity College, three years of study in Rome, tuition from A. D. Fripp and J. Hervé D'Egville (a fine water-colourist who died in 1880—an ancestor perhaps of our contemporary *Punch* artist?), travel with Ruskin and Arthur Severn, leisure and means which enabled him to sketch as he wished in Egypt, India, Italy, Spain—Brabazon had everything which was considered desirable for an artist of his day. He played the piano almost as well as he painted. He inherited great houses in Durham and Sussex. He lived to the age of eighty-five.

His work was almost revolutionary. It was as though he resolved to go farther than Turner, to adapt the methods of the French Impressionists to the tradition of the English water-colour. The results are often startling, sometimes a litttle too gorgeous, almost always highly effective. But for me his pictures do not wear well. Too modern to hang easily among the landscapes of the earlier men and yet not sufficiently iconoclastic to contrast excitingly with them, they do not seem quite strong enough to hold their own, and slowly the eight of them have found their way into the bedrooms, a sorry ascension.

10

Very clearly I saw that in the life I planned to make in Sussex
this inexpensive and rewarding form of picture-collecting would
have its place, but now, I resolved, the sketchy outline of a collection should be augmented. Somehow I would find a Paul
Sandby, a J. R. Cozens, a Peter de Wint, perhaps even a Constable, a Rowlandson, a Copley Fielding. These would give
shape and balance to the little collection as it stood, would enable
the beholder to trace developments. Collecting, I told myself,
should be less haphazard than mine had been. All very well to
buy what one could when there was an opportunity; it was time
now for some principle and pattern.

The town in which we inhabitants of Ticehurst do our shopping
is Tunbridge Wells. I have known it for most of my life, since
I cycled here as a boy from Tonbridge. Like Cheltenham and
Bath, it was long populated by the old and wealthy, by eccentrics
and valetudinarians, by retired officers of the army and navy, by
yellow-skinned men who had given their lives to the service of
what was then called 'their country' in the East. Like those other
towns, it has lost much of this character, and although not all its
large houses have been hacked up for flats and not all its pen-
sionaries forced by the dwindling value of the pound in which
they are paid to give up their homes, Tunbridge Wells, for good
or ill according to your views, is becoming more and more a
proletarian dormitory town, a shopping-place for excursionists
bound for the south coast and the new Americanized youth of the
English streets.

Still, here and there craftsmen in this one-time home of
quality in men and things persist in their crafts, here and there
shopkeepers refuse to stock *ersatz* and trumpery goods, here and
there are the courtesy and dignity which belonged to a more
virile and less hysterical age. It was almost too much to hope,
however, that there might remain extant in Tunbridge Wells a
master in the craft of picture-framing, a craft which has become
almost universally debased to the shoddiest carpentry.

In London I had failed to find one. There were plenty of

shops in which a frame of sorts could be made, so long as one did not demand anything but bare oak, because that alone avoided purchase tax, and so long as one did not expect a wash-line to surround a water-colour, or a mount to be correctly tinted for it. There were plenty of shops in which they could shove a shining black frame round a photograph and cut a piece of glass to fit it. There were some whose workmen could simplify the ornamentation of a Victorian plaster frame and smear it with cream to make it surround a modern painting. But I had never found one capable of framing a water-colour as it should be framed.

It was with incredulous delight, therefore, that I saw the first pictures which I had taken for framing to a shop called Walter's in Tunbridge Wells High Street. At last here was someone who knew his job. The mount toned with the colouring, and the wash lines were ruled to perfection, and colours had been used for them which brought up the tints in the little drawing. A plain frame had been made with a precision now rare, and the glass was flawless and not, as on a recent occasion in London, knotted at one point.

The proprietor chuckled over my congratulations and took me up to his workshops. He himself was in his seventies, and no longer did more than direct his business, but the men he employed had been with him for years and had served an arduous apprenticeship in a most intricate craft.

One after another I began to bring in the water-colours which needed re-framing, and with time they all received the right setting. Then one day, after I had become a long-familiar customer, old Walter said: 'You seem to like water-colours. Would you like to see what I've got?'

The sequel developed into fantasy. For fifty years or so the shopkeeper had been accumulating water-colours, buying them in auction among other pictures, pulling them out of frames bought for the glass in recent years, even being presented with them by customers who wished to re-use an old frame and did not want the picture in it. For fifty years an artist's print-chest had been the recipient of drawing after drawing, till the aggregation ran into thousands. No one had examined them for years. No one was much interested.

I

It took me half-a-dozen afternoons to go through the entire collection and to extract from it the water-colours which I wished to buy. But they were afternoons of such bright pleasure that I would gladly live them again. I do not know when I have been happier than while I scanned those ugly, those sometimes quite horrifying pictures, finding here and there one to re-examine, and at last bringing my selection down to the twenty or so which I wanted. It was absorbing and exhilarating both.

But alas for my determination to apply strict rules to my collection, to be ruthlessly selective of the artists represented! I had at the end of those six afternoons almost doubled the number of pictures I possessed. I had added a score of fine water-colours by men whose work is remembered and preserved, and one at least by a giant among them. I have never regretted buying them, and I recognize that they have given me a most catholic collection. But I am no nearer to being ruthlessly selective than I was when I bought my 'Grecian' Williams, knowing only that it was old and good.

II

First in importance is a David Cox (1783–1859). His reputation suffers, I think, by the rash or dishonest attribution of much mediocre work to him and even by the forgery of his signature on many a poor water-colour of his period. This has been made easier by the fact that so many of his early drawings were done to be purchased by print-sellers in their dozens, and all his life he continued to throw off innumerable sketches and water-colours which were often not up to his own standards.

A Birmingham blacksmith's son, he found his way to his profession with difficulty, and seems never to have ceased to wonder a little at his good fortune in being able to make a living from art. He worked for a maker of ornamental articles in Birmingham, became a scene-painter's assistant at the Birmingham Theatre and left it to go to London on Astley's invitation, though there is no evidence that he ever painted scenery at the Amphitheatre. His London lodgings were kept by a widow whose daughter, Mary Ragg, he afterwards married, living happily with his intelligent wife for thirty-seven years. John Varley gave him drawing lessons (free of charge when he found that young Cox was a professional artist), and he himself lived by teaching and painting landscapes first at Dulwich, then, after a year as art-master at Sandhurst, in Hereford for twelve years, then for another fourteen on Kennington Common, finally at Harborne, near his birthplace, where he died at the age of seventy-six. It sounds an unadventurous record, but his biographers have been able to show a modern reader something of the contented, industrious, humorous and exceedingly modest man who in his fifty-sixth year took lessons in painting in oils from an artist twenty years younger and who expressed no surprise that his fine drawings fetched so little money. He was never affluent, but from the first he realized the precariousness of art and, living modestly, was able to save money and enjoy prosperity in his later years. His portrait by Sir W. Gordon shows him as a handsome, healthy-looking, elderly man, shrewd, kind, thought-ful, with a hint of the eternal child which persists in many artists.

The water-colour drawing of his which I found among the miscellany at the back of Walter's shop is a fine example of his later work, a coastal scene on a day of wind, sun and rain with a single very Coxian pink-and-black female figure introduced with remarkable effect. It is painted on the coarse paper which he loved, spontaneously and probably swiftly, but with un-faltering care. The amount of brushwork is quite extraordinary, the effect is positively luminous. It is, in the old phrase, a hole-in-the-wall picture, radiant and exuberant. It laughs at the limitations of its medium and challenges a landscapist in any other to be more profound or poetic or more technically assured.

12

Nothing much seems to be known of William Payne. The Victoria and Albert Museum has a score or so of his water-colours, but its Catalogue cannot give his dates, noting only that he first exhibited in 1776 after teaching himself art and developing 'an original style'. He was still living, it appears, in 1830. The Epitome of the *Dictionary of National Biography* is more generous, saying that he 'increased the resources of water-colour art especially in the rendering of sunlight and atmosphere; invented Payne's grey'. C. E. Hughes, Charles Holme and Cosmo Monkhouse do no more than include his name in their lists.

Looking at the sketch of his which I found among that same vast store, I see just what the curt tribute in the *D.N.B.* means. It is a panoramic strip, 10 inches long by $2\frac{1}{4}$ high, with a tree in the right foreground from which one low branch spreads half-way across the top of the picture. There are four sizeable figures in its shade, all of them in whole or in part coloured in 'Payne's grey', as are the tree-trunk and much of the ground beneath it. Away to the left is a large house on a tree'd hill, and the centre of the picture is occupied by a herd of pack-donkeys being driven into the sunlight. The effect is really astonishing, for the man and woman driving the creatures are half blinded by the light, and a man looking at the picture today feels its almost uncomfortable warmth and radiance.

I am glad now that I have let chance shape my collection, for a scheme, even the most comprehensive, might not have included a drawing by Thomas Stothard (1755–1834). Born at the Black Horse, Long Acre, he died in Newman Street, having lived nowhere but in the London area. He was apprenticed to a designer of brocade patterns, and the exquisite delicacy and feminine grace of his work may owe something to this. He was, of course, one of the most talented book illustrators who have worked in this country, and the superb composition and fresh sweetness of his work are still a pattern.

There were several other fairly early drawings among the few I chose from the many in that print-chest. There was, for instance, a curious wash-drawing with figures and foreground features in Indian ink which is the work of that mad and tragic creature Robert Blemmel Schnebbelie, who was found dead of starvation in his room in London in 1849. This drawing of his is dour, even a little frightening: a dockyard scene at night in slate-grey and brown-grey, with hurrying figures under the stark outlines of unlit buildings.

More interesting technically is a drawing, heavy with body-colour, by John Marten, who, astonishingly, was exhibiting in 1822–34. It is strangely impressionistic in treatment: a scene on the Thames in which two boatloads of gaily dressed people are brilliantly indicated by bright dabs of colour and the trees have a tender delicacy which recalls Fragonard, and there is a late afternoon sky richly tinted and clouding to a violet haze on the horizon. It is so supremely well painted and so audacious for its time that it gives one new pride in our national school—for probably no one now has heard of this John Marten, except a few specialists who have preserved one water-colour of his at the Victoria and Albert and can say only that he 'lived at Canterbury and Hastings'. Work of this quality in France or Italy would have given him a name which would be familiar still.

A wider reputation is that of T. M. Richardson (1784–1848), but the example of his work which I found with the rest of these drawings, though painted in 1847, is strictly traditional, indeed belongs in spirit to the early romantic school. It has a somewhat faery, though no doubt identifiable, castle and trees of the assertive dark-trunked kind which Francis Nicholson and the rest of them loved to set in their craggy landscapes, while the figures, two old women, one seated on a rock, are dressed gaudily in scarlet and blue.

13

And there was, at last, a Samuel Prout (1783–1852). It was just a quarter of a century since I had seen that drawing of his in Lincoln Brown's Bayswater room, and I had always wanted to find another which I could afford to buy. It is characteristic and pleasant rather than an important example of Prout's work; the 'broken line' has been used with all his cunning and affection, but the subject is modest—an isolated fifteenth-century house by the side of still water, with one female and a negligible background of blue-toned distant trees. The house shows all his love of buildings, chipped, irregular and standing under the threat of decay. Smoke comes from a chimney, but its lattice windows seem permanently closed, and only in one dark room, one feels, are people moving. If all the colours were washed away, the soft brown-pink of the roof, the dusty green of some grass in the foreground, the house would be discernible in all its detail in the brown-ink sketch so adroitly made.

Samuel Prout, who was born in 1783 and died in 1852, was a life-long invalid through a severe sunstroke in his fifth year. His struggle was not against poverty, but against ill-health and his own conscious deficiencies. He defeated both, and though he never passed a week of his life without illness nor was able to paint in the open air for more than the briefest periods, he became what, perhaps, he remains—our greatest interpreter of architectural beauty.

Here, too, is a curiosity—a water-colour by that ex-coach-driver animal-painter, John Frederick Herring (1795–1865). 'Forge', it is called, a lively sketch in which a hairy young black-smith in a blue-and-white striped shirt gossips with a girl in pink over the nose of an interested grey horse. And here is Tenby, South Wales, seen from along the coast and from under clouds, though sunlight brightly lights up the harbour wall. This is by Henry Gastineau (1791–1875), a long-lived and industrious topographical artist of the first half of the last century. Then a little monochrome of Scarborough beach by an officer who left the navy to be an artist—H. B. Carter (1795–1863). And a stormy landscape with a windmill dominating it by George Vicat Cole (1833–1893), a follower of Constable.

But other early Victorians are more unexpected. John Varley's brother-in-law, William Mulready (1786–1863), was a versatile artist, and the little sketch of his which I found with the rest may have been done, as are many of his water-colours, as preliminaries to a full-dress oil-painting. If so, it can scarcely have been more telling and human in the finished version. With a few strokes of wash a woman in a mob cap is created, intent on threading a needle. It is strictly a period piece, yet there is no sentimentality or mawkish humour in it—a stark rather than a pretty portrait.

A landscape by Andrew Nichol (1804–86), an Irishman who taught art at Colombo University, is interesting as a piece of quite effective virtuosity, a waterfall and river in full pelt under cliffs of grey slag surmounted by silver birches. Another, by a third Irishman, Henry Albert Hartland (1840–1893), is called 'Near Inchegala, Ireland. A Damp Day', and is dated 1870. Hartland was yet another artist who broke into his profession through the craft of scene-painting. This is a somewhat over-atmospheric scene in which the mist settles on bound corn-sheaves.

The largest water-colour I have was also found in Walter's print-chest. It depicts Godesberg Castle in the Rhineland, ten miles of flat country behind it and a range of blue hills in the background, the whole under a sky in which every vaporous finger of cloud is clear against the soft blue distance. Detail? There could scarcely be more. The picture measures 20 inches by 30, and in it each individual stone with which the castle tower is built is outlined, each leaf of the trees at its base, each tree on the farthest hillside. Yet the picture succeeds. It is a co-ordinated and a significant whole; the heat-mist rises and the lazy clouds scarcely move, the rock surfaces are hot and the two women praying at a shrine are still and devout. The artist's name is John Dobbin, and the only example of his work in the Victoria and Albert Museum is also large and depicts the Court of Lions in the Alhambra. I am almost afraid to see in what detail that has been drawn.

A little sketch of cattle and ducks on a grey paper is by Harrison William Weir (1824–1906), a friend of Darwin and a naturalist as well as a fine animal-painter. And a sketch of a ruined church in London which might have been done on the morning after a recent air-raid is by Richard Henry Nibbs (1816–93).

Finally there are four water-colours by late Victorians which bring my collection as near to the present as I wish to come. First a conversation piece, depicting two women in the dress of the 'eighties playing chess before a Chinese screen while a third fondles a cat and watches them, is by Auguste Jules Bouvier, who was born in London of French parents in 1827 and died in St. John's Wood in 1881. It is almost impudently pretty.

Second, a water-colour drawing of Rouen by John Varley's

grandson, also called John, which is again too pretty and too slick to be quite admirable, though its tones are soft and appealing and its conception sound.

Then a very gorgeous cornfield and reapers with the North Downs (I think) behind them, by a spirited Victorian called Lewis Pinhorn Wood, on whom no reference book can inform me, though his water-colours are in the Victoria and Albert Museum.

Last, and as intrinsically interesting as any, a seashore at low tide by a one-time Newquay shop assistant, Albert Ernest Markes, who had only one seeing eye and that colour-blind, but who succeeded in making a living in Southend and along the flat shores of Belgium and Holland until his death in 1901 at the age of forty-six. He signed always 'Albert'. His ships in still water, his foreshore figures, his quiet pools and wet sand are so uncannily real that they can almost be smelt.

14

These water-colours, then, which have come to me not without luck but after a good many years of searching and study, give some notion of the splendid variety in the English school. But even now I have none of the artists I hoped to find, nor of Hearne, Turner, John Sell Cotman, W. H. Hunt, Bonington or Thomas Collier, each of whom should be in a representative collection. On the other hand, my water-colours have cost little in money (whatever they may have cost in time), and represent, if one chooses to consider them thus, a small but secure investment. At its lowest, the collecting of them has been a hobby, but as they have increased they have become a dominant interest.

It is only now, however, when they hang on walls built not long before they were painted, with light and space for their display, that they come into their own.

First Year in the Garden

I

A MONTH after the house had taken on some semblance of order, the ground from its windows down to the far acute angle of the garden's end was a depressing waste, littered with broken glass and china, ridged with the remains of concrete floors where those decaying sheds had stood, scarred by asphalt paths which were in the wrong places and trenched and burrowed where the high *Cupressus* hedges had shielded the windows from daylight. The former occupants had grown vegetables to within a few yards of the house, and a few desultory cabbage-stalks still stood there while baleful clusters of horse-radish broke the soil. Except for some Michaelmas daisies blooming bravely in the September mists, there was no colour visible.

The task of making a garden from this stony shambles seemed so formidable that I allowed a week or two to pass before doing more than formulate a plan. Clearly there was work for several men for months, and although the season of unemployment in the building industry was approaching, there was still the cost to reckon apprehensively. I had spent everything earned or soon to be earned on the interior of the house and frankly funked the expense of making a garden.

The essential was an overall plan. I had a triangle, the base of which was formed by the house, a base twenty-five yards long. The apex was nearly a hundred yards away, an acute angle indeed at which the roads forked. One side of the triangle, which faced south, was marked by a brick wall with oak palings on it rising to a height of nine feet. The other side, for forty yards, had a very high mixed hedge which divided it from the garden of my statutory-tenant-occupied cottage, and for the remaining thirty-five yards had a high brick wall forming the back of what had been the builders' timber shed.

I was determined that my plan should be simple, as open and uncomplicated as the house which overlooked it. In that great storehouse of horticultural information Bailey's *Hortus Second* * I came on this prim sentence: 'The home garden should be useful in the degree to which it expresses the sentiments of its maker or proprietor; a garden planned without regard to personality may not fulfil the requisite.' I do not know whether my personality is uncomplicated, but I certainly wanted no winding paths, no secret corners, no artificial woodland in this triangle of mine. On the other hand, I did want plenty of colour and scent and as much sense of space as its contours would allow.

First I had to resolve the question of division. How much space—if any—should be given to vegetables? A trained economist could, I suppose, answer this question firmly and to a square yard, neatly balancing the cost of labour, the sacrifice of space which might have been used for flowers, the cost of plants and seeds against the advantages and economy of having fresh vegetables. The results might be surprising. For me it had to be a question of inclination and taste. I wanted to grow those vegetables which are noticeably better when garden-grown and freshly picked, and I wanted to give up as little as possible of flower-garden for the sake of them.

The decision, then, was easy. The narrow end of the triangle was awkwardly placed and shaped in any case, and would serve well for vegetables. This gave me forty yards of only slightly narrowing ground to lay out as a garden proper.

Among my possessions when I moved to Ticehurst was a pair of wrought-iron gates. They came from Spain, and had been used in some old *patio*—interior gates with a bold design of loops. Two brick gate-posts were built for these with brick wings running back from them so that the whole stretched almost across the width of the garden, forming a division between the

---

* *Hortus Second: A Concise Dictionary of Gardening*, compiled by L. H. and Ethel Zoë Bailey (Macmillan).

flower-garden and the utilitarian regions beyond. So now my space was ready.

There could only be one way of laying out this area, at least only one which would satisfy my longing for simplicity and colour, and that can be described in a couple of lines. A herbaceous border down the wall facing south, a width of long grass in which to grow flowers suited to a wild garden down the side of the hedge which faced north, and between them open lawn. As simple as that.

2

When the rubble-and-stone foundations and tree-stumps had been cleared from the plot it was ready for a rotor plough. This would save weeks of digging and hoeing. A happy-go-lucky individual from a neighbouring village who owned one of these useful contrivances volunteered to do the job if I could persuade another improvident soul who owned a lorry to drive man and plough across country. This led to some pretty discussion over a number of pints of beer. Was it my job to arrange transport? When would both plough-owner and lorry-owner be free? What would be the cost of the ploughing and the cost of transport? Discussions raged and waned fitfully for a number of thirsty evenings, but reached a conclusion, as such discussions do, so abruptly that I was almost startled on the appointed day to see the plough commencing its rotations. Before nightfall my garden was a bumpy but recognizable plane and a start could be made with the levelling and rolling of what would one day be a lawn.

Looking out now, I realize that heaven has been kind, for down to the wrought-iron gates it stretches in a not too patchy, not too uneven green sheet, a decent lawn. Easy to forget now the hours of labour, my own and others', which have gone to the making of it, the rolling, the sowing, the bird-scaring, the rolling again, the weed-killing, the long war fought with a filthy adversary called coltsfoot, a pestiferous and persistent weed which I have defeated at last, the mowing, the watering and the weeding. It has cost as much in my time as would the writing of a novel, and as much in other people's as would a holiday abroad. But it is there, respectably smooth and green, and it has been created from the earth in which it grows, not laid on in rolls of turf from elsewhere. I am more proud of my industry in making it than if it had been an area of paper which I had covered with words instead of half-an-acre of soil spread with grass.

3

When I looked round the bare waste of ground which was to be cultivated, I saw only half a dozen growing things which I wanted to preserve. There were two clipped yews, one against the house and one, a taller and more elaborately patterned one, near the south wall in what would be the herbaceous border. There was another, an unclipped Irish yew, which grew magnificently to the height of the house and prevented the upper part of my garden from being overlooked from the windows of my cottage. And near it, also shielding the garden from these, was a fine sweet chestnut of excellent shape and colour. Down by the wrought-iron gates was one prolific pear-tree, and in the furthermost angle of the garden, a landmark as one approached Ticehurst by road, was a weeping ash.

That was all. Some peonies which might or might not grow when they had been moved, a few irises, some rather wilting Michaelmas daisies and there was the entire legacy of the previous garden. Yet I did not think that in this I was unlucky, for the trees were sufficient and well-placed and aided rather than impeded my plan.

The yew-tree near the south wall, for instance, gave me the shape I needed for the herbaceous border. It was clipped to a circle about nine feet in diameter, and I could bring the edge of the bed out to follow its circumference. This gave the whole border a plain but not monotonous outline, for after a straight edge for much of its length I brought it out again towards the wrought-iron gate in a corresponding sweep.

Thus, working in the chilly and moist weather of October and November, I succeeded in forming the outlines. But it was too late in the year to do more.

4

Or was it? G. B. Stern, paying a visit on a chilly day, thought not.

'You must', she said decisively, 'have a terrace.'

The word seemed full of grandeur and implications of quite impossible expense. Yet 'Peter' Stern's advice was not to be too carelessly ignored. Her own Berkshire cottage has a stream running beside its garden which, a mile back, has come through that of Kenneth Grahame's old home and is the very stream about which *The Wind in the Willows* was written. She has known how to make her whole garden but a wide terrace down to this delightful little water-way. And she sounded so very certain of herself.

'A terrace?' I repeated helplessly.

'Certainly. Your two French windows open on to—what? Lawn, I suppose. All right in summer. But you want somewhere to sit even then. Somewhere for meals. Somewhere dry in winter. Besides, it will set off the house. You *need* it along this long flat front, or back, or whatever it is.'

Uncomfortably I looked out on to the damp clay in which the grass seed was, I hoped, sprouting. Yes, blast her, Peter was right. A terrace of some sort was not an ornament, a luxury or an extravagance, it was a necessity.

'Only,' she went on uncompromisingly, 'don't be half-hearted about it. No good having a terrace if you don't make it wide enough. You want plenty of room.'

She was right again. There could be nothing worse than a little narrow strip on which chairs balanced uneasily. But with every word she spoke my estimate of the probable cost increased.

'And don't try to make it any shorter than the house,' Peter continued grimly. 'It would look quite absurd if it were not to run the whole length.'

It would. Quite absurd. But that meant a paved area of about seventy square yards.

'And what,' I asked, trying to control the asperity in my voice

—'what do you suggest as material for paving this terrace of yours? Gold, perhaps?'

'No,' said Peter Stern calmly. 'Bricks would be best. Old ones, preferably. And not laid in concrete. Not too trim and measured. A bit higgledy-piggledy.'

'That at least I can manage. The higgledy-piggledy part, I mean. Even if I can't get the bricks.'

'Can you? You won't find it so easy. There's nothing harder to simulate than untidiness. However, that's what you need.'

And that, I need scarcely admit, is what I have, though I still dare not caluclate how many of my unpaid debts would have been obliterated by now if I had not listened to the tempter when he chose dear Peter Stern as his mouthpiece. But that, I decided, would be the last expense before the spring.

5

Again, would it? It might have been if I had had no gardening enthusiasts among my friends. When Beverley Nichols came down he looked with favour on the general plan, but began at once to ask those awkward questions which lead to long accounts from nurserymen.

'Yes, yes,' he said. 'But what have you got *in*?'

'In what?' I asked, playing for time.

'In the garden. It's all very well to plot out your ground, but a garden is a place in which to grow things.'

'The spring . . .' I tried.

'Oh yes. For most things. But for trees and shrubs and so on it's now or never. At least, it's now or this time next year, with twelve months wasted.'

'But do I want any trees?' I asked doubtfully.

'Not many, but surely, if you're going to let that side of the garden run wild, you should have a couple of pines and perhaps a few silver birch. If you get them in now they'll have established themselves by next year.'

That sounded modest, and I decided to meet the expense some-how. Anxiously, I began to lead the way back to the house.

'Isn't that wall south?' Beverley was in no hurry for tea. 'It must be nearly a hundred yards long. There are gardeners who would give their right hands for that. I suppose you're taking advantage of it?'

'I had thought . . .'

'Then you had better think quickly. You're just in time to get your climbing and pillar roses in and some fruit at the kitchen garden end.'

Naturally. A south wall was certainly not to be wasted for a whole year. There could be no argument about it. Then, to my relief, Beverley moved towards the house.

'Let's get back to the fire,' I suggested heartily. But he was staring at my white walls.

'You *are* going to have wistaria on the house, aren't you?'

'Next year.'

'But it sometimes doesn't move for two years. It really should go in now. Then there's that blank space between the windows. What are you having there?'

'I hadn't really decided.'

'*Eucryphia pinnatafolia*,' said Beverley with authority. 'A gorgeous thing.'

'I must write that down,' I said desperately. 'I'll do it now before I forget. Let's go indoors.'

But he was staring at the blank white wall of my cottage. Its windowless cliff formed a right angle to the south end of the house.

'Clematis would do quite well there. And on that little piece of wall, honeysuckle, of course.'

'Of course,' I said.

There is a small courtyard running up to the kitchen window but overlooked by a window of my study. I pointed rather hysterically at it.

'I suppose you want something to climb there?' I suggested with what I thought rather crisp irony.

'Yes. Winter jasmine.'

I felt a little dizzy when I had made out orders for these. Eight roses—American Pillar, Allan Chandler, Lemon Pillar, Madame Edouard Herriot, Paul Scarlett, Albertine, Etoile de Hollande and, because I remembered it over the pergolas of my father's many gardens, Dorothy Perkins. Then the peach and nectarine and cordon pear-trees for the lower end of the wall—the espalier-trained peaches at 25/- each. And all the rest—including the imposingly named Eucryphia. They all arrived and were planted, and I had to admit that Beverley was right in persuading me not to miss a year's growth.

6

But one thing he had not mentioned, and I chuckled when I realized the omission's significance. Gardeners, I am sure, think beautiful thoughts and are far too much influenced by the flowers and birds and butterflies about them to be capable of the least tinge of invidiousness, but there *was* the undeniable fact that for years Beverley's most passionate horticultural ambition has been to grow rhododendrons, while for years he has been defeated by the soil of his large Surrey garden. Each year with new hope he tries, filling whole pits with peat and leaf-mould, creating beds of sandy loam and planting the bushes in them with infinite care. Each year their leaves turn brown and fall and his attempt is acknowledged a failure.

'It's simply that they won't grow in certain places, and flourish in others,' he explained to me before I had a garden. 'But it's maddening, because I would rather grow rhododendrons than anything else.'

Small wonder, then, that coming to see my house in the heart of one of the best rhododendron areas in England, he should have failed to suggest them for the wild side of my garden. But as I ordered the plants and shrubs he had proposed, I added a few rhododendrons—Doncaster, Daphne Millais, Pink Pearl, Bagshot Ruby, Duke of York, White Pearl, John Walter and Cynthia. They have flourished wonderfully, but I have noticed that no invitation to Beverley is accepted during April, May or June.

7

I would like somewhere in the future to make a formal garden as one enclosure in an area much larger than my present plot,

1. 'A small court-yard running up to the kitchen window'

'He must not be mistaken for a dog'

for there is certainly no room for rectilinear beds here. But although my general design was full of irregularities it could not be carried out without respect for one piece of geometry, one long, straight line as a basis. This line, I thought, must not be too obvious or too oppressive, yet if it did not exist there would be nothing to co-ordinate the whole.

The longest distance in the garden is from the very apex of the acute angle at its far end to the house wall. I discovered by experiment that a straight line drawn over that distance would strike the house in the middle of the hall window and continue straight through the hall to the centre of the fanlight of the front door. Fortunately I discovered this before the wrought-iron gates were up, so that the same line passed through their centre. Moreover, the two steps down from the newly-made terrace to the lawn were put where the same line would bisect them.

I know little of garden design as an art except that it is a poor sister of the grandiose landscape-gardening of the eighteenth century. Then, with the skyline as boundary, great parks were planned, trees planted, temples and gazebos built, to produce a view from the windows of a country house. Flowers were scarcely thought of in such a scene, and trees were but pieces of brushwork. Too often, in Victorian times, attempts were made to carry out such designs in little, to treat an acre of garden as though it were an entire panorama, and the result has been the wiggly and segmented plots which are still to be seen round some country houses.

The essential, it seemed to me, was to realize the limitations of one's ground. Had even my long triangle been surrounded by fields which sloped down from it to a far-away stream, or with woodlands which formed a background to its colouring, I might have been able to plan it so that it aped greater expanse or merged mysteriously into the landscape. But it was a long, walled spike of land between two roads, which, though it was miraculously not overlooked from any direction or from any window, was yet a garden in a village and not a garden in open country. It could be made secluded, picturesque, even beautiful. It could have character and a certain spaciousness. It could be given some of the slightly

K

lugubrious grace of an eighteenth-century garden. But it could not be made grand or imposing or apparently boundless.

So that its length was its first virtue, and if I exploited it to the full I could make the whole garden appear larger. The line was there—all the hundred yards of it—but its terminus needed pin-pointing, so that if one stood on the steps of the terrace one could follow its course to the limit.

It was the tree down there at the foot of the garden which gave me the idea I needed, the weeping ash with branches touching the ground. An urn! What could be more in the neo-classical tradition which created Palladian architecture and gave designs to the book-illustrators of the time? A tree weeping over an urn. It was almost too much of a copper engraving to illustrate an eighteenth-century elegy. It would be far from the house, a small, absurd vignette beyond the vegetables.

But urns, like most garden ornaments, have in the last few years become rare and costly, since dealers have realized belatedly their attraction for garden-planners. Although they exist usually in pairs, so that a single one might be less expensive, it would even so be beyond the means of a hard-working novelist who had just bought a house. It might, indeed, still be waiting at the head of my list of things wanted for the garden if I had not, on a certain day, made one of my periodical calls on my Romani friend Ned Skelton, whose scrap-and-metal yard is five miles from my house.

I saw it at once. A stone urn of good proportions, its lid rising to an acorn.

'How much?' I asked Ned.

'It only came in today,' he replied with a hint of regret in his voice. 'Still, you can have it for a quid.'

So there it stands, a mournful symbol beside a weeping tree, making, for some reason, a most cheerful rococo picture when it is viewed from the house. It completes the long, straight imaginary line from which all my planning radiates.

8

It is only one of the ornaments in my garden. I am aware of the need for caution in introducing these, and feel as embarrassed as anyone else at the sight of coloured goblins on toadstools of painted clay or bird-baths on pillars of shaped concrete or cement sundials.   I am not too fond of lead figures unless they are earlier and less sentimental than those depicting Kate Greenaway children, ogling cupids or Dante and Beatrice which became popular fifty years ago.   Still, judiciously used, a few bits of old nonsense can be appropriate and unaffected.

For instance, a head of Antinous which looks down from a carved bracket on the high blank wall of my cottage.   That wall has to be broken, for it has no window through which my ground can be overlooked, but is a twenty-foot square of white weather-boarding.   The head admirably breaks that monotonous sheet, while the clematis planted beneath it grows to surround it.

Then, in the dusty yard of a Peckham antique dealer's shop, I found a terra-cotta toy—a small nude boy stooping over an inverted bowl in which the hours are marked, while a leaden blade bisects it, a curious form of sundial from Italy.   I found no place for this at first, but I knew that it could be used without ostentation somewhere.   Finally, on a little plain stone bracket on the wall facing my study window I fixed a stone head, a strange relic of Chaucerian England which I bought in Upton-on-Severn years ago.   It has weathered the rains of five centuries, but still the pleated hood and goat's beard are distinguishable, and its eyes stare blankly across the little court outside the window. These are sufficient.   They seem rooted in the place, and have a pleasant air of being timeworn and irremovable, though none of them was here when I came a year ago.

9

One other task I accomplished during that autumn, this a highly utilitarian and yet not unromantic one—the beginning of a large and varied herb-garden of culinary herbs.   It has spread now almost embarrassingly, for most of these plants are only kept in their place with difficulty, so eager are they to increase at the expense of their neighbours.   But it has repaid a hundredfold the trouble and expense which went to its beginnings, for all through that summer and autumn it meant that salads, cups, stews, omelettes, forcemeat—indeed almost every dish—has been improved, freshened, made more savoury. I am a shameless proselytizer over this; I think that every garden should have a place where these delectable and appetizing things grow. Mine, perhaps, is too comprehensive, even redundant, but that is a good fault. Sage, thyme and mint, the trio too often unsupported, are not enough. Here is my collection, not in order of importance, but as it happens to be planted.

First is Savory, which gives a smoky, slightly bitter flavour and is invaluable in too rich or luscious dishes. Then that all-important herb Lovage, which looks like a large celery plant and has a smell and taste like concentrated celery. It must be used rather sparingly in omelettes and stews, but should not be omitted from the *Bouquet garni*, that little bundle of sprigs of herbs which is tied with cotton and dropped into so many dishes to be recovered before they are served. Its stalks can be blanched and cooked and added to Russian salad and, I read, confectioners use it, though no one seems to know what for. The only confectioner I asked said simply that he had never heard of it, but as caraway seeds represented the limit of his enterprise, this was not indicative.

Then Marjoram, an ancient and aromatic herb with countless uses and a sort of brother-in-arms to the onion. Whenever onion is being used, a few leaves of marjoram or a sprinkle of it dried will contrast and bring out both flavours. Tansy has a dangerously powerful smell and taste, rich and gingery, but a suspicion of it improves certain dishes, and a sprig of it goes well in shandy-gaff. Pennyroyal makes a tisane of faintly peppermint flavour and can also be used in stews. It grows along the ground, and has to be watched or it will creep all over the herb-garden.

Fennel is quite indispensable if you want to make coarse fish edible. It has leaves which look feathery but are oily, and it grows to four feet or more. It is a flavouring not to be used too often or too heavily, for it can become sickening, but with care and pepper it does its work. Tarragon has a somewhat similar flavour, but suggests aniseed rather than liquorice. Chopped fine it can be sprinkled over salads instead of chives. Like most of these herbs, once established it thrives, but the root I planted in

October made no appearance until the following August, when it suddenly shot up into a healthy growth.

I have two or three roots of Burnet, a deliciously fresh herb which smells and tastes like cucumber. It can be put to any of the herb uses, but is almost an essential in a Cup. Rampion I have planted but cannot yet recommend for any special purpose, since all it has done so far is to bloom. It has small, campanula-like flowers and looks charming among the more useful herbs. Its correct name, I find, is *Campanula Rapunculus*, and Baily says 'its first-year roots and radical leaves sometimes used as salad'. Caraway is another herb which seems to enjoy its growth in my garden but has done nothing so far to justify its existence, for it has not flowered in its first year to produce its aromatic seeds.

Then Sorrel. 'Why grow it in your garden,' someone asked me, 'when so much of it can be found wild?' But not when one wants it. Sorrel makes a sharp and astringent purée which, with some of the more oleaginous kinds of meat which one eats nowadays—calf's foot and sheep's head, for instance—is a saving grace.

So to some of the commoner herbs, more frequently recognized as essential. There are, I believe, a dozen or so kinds of Mint, of which I find three too many, for it is impossible to distinguish these when they are in use. Chive is as necessary to many dishes as parsley, and cut fine with a pair of scissors can garnish almost anything which likes a fresh, clean flavour of onions rather than a steamy, cooked one. Thyme is redolent of summer and by its scent recreates the sunny hillsides, the open downs. Lemon Thyme is no less pungent and lives up to its name. Sage I grow also in two varieties, indistinguishable when cooked.

Rue suggests Ophelia, but has some more practical purposes. Its leaves have a spicy fragrance which rises faintly from the stewpot and enlivens the flattest dish. As usual, Shakespeare has said it—'there's rosemary and rue; these keep Seeming and savour all the winter long'. Hyssop is another powerful seasoning, with a fresh-air, heady scent that is good in a *bouquet garni* but rather too heavy for an omelette. Rosemary has countless uses: a sprig in beer, its leaves chopped in a salad, a few of them whole in jam, and all the other herbal purposes. Chervil can be used as a parsley variant (though Parsley itself must be kept in plenty) and is as essential in many fish dishes. Borage looks pleasant in Cups, and although I grow Garlic, I find the small bulbs which are all that form in England less satisfactory than the fine white Italian ones to be bought in any greengrocer's shop.

At the end of the herb-garden is a Bay-tree, which flourishes less than proverbially, and a bush of Southernwood, which is also and paradoxically called both Ladslove and Old Man. It has no culinary use, but a strong, pleasant smell when its feathery leaves are crushed. Coriander I grow for its seeds, which are used in curries, and Camomile for its flowers, but this latter not in the herb-garden.

To these I have added this year Angelica, Skirret, Balm, Clary, Basil, Catmint, Dill, Comfrey and Purslane, and I think that in herbs for the kitchen the collection is almost complete. It has already given me and my household and guests great satisfaction and interest. It is just the sort of thing I longed to do when, from the grey miasma of Doughty Street, years ago it seems, I contemplated living in the country.

Second Year in the Garden

IT takes a gardener of more passionate enthusiasm than mine to work outside in the winter, and the place remained bleak and colourless until a freakish afternoon of warm sunlight in March. The lawn was already established enough to be trodden, and there was evidently too much of its unbroken surface to be proportionate with the whole. Anxious though I was to avoid bits and pieces, squares and crescents, little beds and narrow paths between them, I recognized that something must be done to vary that stretch of lawn—something which would increase its apparent size rather than otherwise. That March afternoon I decided, on an impulse born of the sunlight, to create that variation.

Covetousness sent me astray. On a December afternoon I had walked round the fields and woods which surround Pashley Manor, a house of pleasantly mixed architecture on the outskirts of Ticehurst, and coming in through the garden had been shown a square of camomile lawn surrounded by aromatic herbs. Even on that cold and misty day, when colour had gone from the garden and scents were part of a scarcely-remembered summertime, our feet on the coarse little plants which made up the lawn caused a rich smell of pear-drops, a fragrance altogether unwintry, to rise to our nostrils. The lawn looked trim and green and its lazy name sounded attractive.

'Awfully easy to make,' I was told. 'You simply put in camomile plants every three inches or so, and you can buy them by the hundreds.'

Why not, then, I thought on that March day, a camomile path? The more the plant is trodden the better it grows. A camomile path round a central bed. Simple, not too commonplace, attractive. The central bed? Roses, of course. There were no bush roses in the garden, and that was an ugly omission for England. The whole thing thus took shape. The little, worn, terra-cotta sundial in the centre, conventional but not arty, a score of roses round it in a bed about twelve feet in diameter, round that a sunken path of camomile, with aubretia falling from the lawn level down the small banks to the path.

To work, then. With springtime energy and enthusiasm, Joseph and I marked out our outer circle, raised the turf which had already formed and dug down eighteen inches for our path. With planks across the lawn for the barrow wheel we carted away the soil we had excavated and threw it over the area which was to be the herbaceous border. The rose-bed was therefore on a slope from the sundial in the centre downwards to its circumference. It was all very promising.

Within a week or so the whole plan was, in its initial stages, complete. The camomile had been ordered and planted. The roses chosen—two each of Crimson Glory, Vandal and Golden Dawn making an inner circle and two each of Etoile de Hollande, Golden Mainze, Mrs. E. Laxton, Betty Uprichard, Mrs. G. A. van Rossem and President Hoover forming an outer one. The small fat terra-cotta boy leant over his inverted bowl of time, set according to horology more ancient than Single or Double Summer Time. Aubretia was planted round the outer rim in the confidence that it would finish blooming before the roses came to clash with its mauve and purple. Dwarf alyssum was ordered to make a white sheet on the ground between the roses. The central bed promised well.

Knowing gardeners will have perceived the fallacy. That sunken path became a pool in rainy weather, and it was almost impossible to cut the camomile down to form a grass-like path because it had a small bank rising on one side of it and the gentler slope of the rose-bed on the other. This winter, in fact, it has been re-modelled. The camomile now makes a small lawn round the sundial and the rose-beds are like the sloping backs of two capital D's on each side. A load of earth was necessary to fill in our dip and to raise the rose-beds slightly above lawn level.

'The essential was an overall plan'

2

Still, as one looked down the garden from the house the walls of the garage and timber-shed were of a rather new and ugly brick colour. On the end of this building is an outside stairway to the potting-shed, and there is something attractive about this stairway with its simple handrail, something which, for reasons on which a delving psychiatrist could doubtless enlarge, recalls to me Brittany and Provence and Spain—all places where white buildings stand in sunlight. Moreover, I noticed that in the afternoon, as the sun came round to the west, shadows were cast on this shed which were homely and deeply peaceful. So I decided that its walls should be white.

A month previously a decent young man of our village who had a good record both as a citizen and a soldier had been brought up before a local Bench because he had omitted to mention that while he was drawing the dole he had done a few days' house-painting for me. An anonymous letter-writer—that cowardly pest of rural life—had informed some official in the local labour exchange, and the official, not daring to ignore the contemptible screed, had made his enquiries and caused a summons to be taken out. I was asked to give evidence that the young man had in fact worked for so many hours, so that I spent an infuriating morning in a local Court. I had expected that because this was his first appearance he would be bound over, or at the most lightly fined, but to my astonishment he was sent to prison for a month. Such a sentence seemed and still seems to be an almost certain way of making a criminal out of a useful member of the community. The young man fully recognized and regretted his slip and pleaded guilty, but for a first offence, and at that a small technical one, he was put among criminals for three or four weeks. That sort of malice or stupidity by a local Bench should be argument enough to support the growing body of opinion which demands the abolition of jurisdiction by amateurs and its replacement by the proved and practised work of stipendiary magistrates. It was a disgustingly vindictive sentence which failed to undermine the young man's character only because he happened to be neither stupid nor volatile, and he has since been given a good job by an employer who recognizes this.

It chanced that it was during the week of his return to his family from Brixton that I made up my mind to have the shed whitened, and he gladly undertook to do the job while he awaited full employment. It is a shining tribute to his energy, and the placid shadows play on its surface in the afternoons to make me think of France and to remind Joseph of India.

3

'Wild garden' sounds a pretentious name for the strip of ground, no more than six yards wide, which runs down the south side of the lawn, but it is a convenient one and accurate in description, even if it implies a larger area. Its possibilities are as interesting as those of the herbaceous border, for so many wild flowers look delightful in a garden.

When William Robinson, perhaps the greatest gardener we have known, quarrelled with his Irish employer and let the frost into his greenhouses to kill his tropical plants, he fled to England and was employed at the Royal Botanic Society's garden in Regent's Park. Very soon he was put in charge of the garden of English wild flowers there, and nine years later he published his *The Wild Garden or Our Groves and Shrubberies Made Beautiful.* To the end of his life—and he died in 1935, at the age of ninety-seven—Robinson kept his interest in wild gardening. It seems to me one of the happiest of occupations, though more exacting than the growing of garden flowers in the fertile earth of a border.

As we cleared up various parts of the garden, all daffodil and narcissus bulbs were put in that strip of grass, and several hundred bluebell bulbs which were found near the house. But before they had bloomed the grass was thick with primroses, for during half a dozen afternoons of early spring I had gone with Joseph into nearby woods and brought home the young plants before they bloomed. There are those who criticize this raiding of wild places as unethical and selfish, and I agree at once if the stricture is applied to those who dig roots from roadside banks or from places where the flowers would be seen and enjoyed. But to fill a basket with primrose roots from hidden places in the woods where nobody would see their blooms, and transfer them to a garden where they will be appreciated, seems both right and sensible. They flourish in the most extraordinary way, a small plant increasing in a week or two until it bears twenty or thirty flowers.

Where they grow in the woods there may also be found wild orchids, those magenta or mauve flowers which grow from tuberous roots and have spotted leaves. Then bluebells, which, brought to cultivation in a garden, seem to strengthen their stalks and deepen their colour. With them are some common cowslips from the fields—one of the few plants whose scent is still perceptible to one standing over it. Wild violets grow beside them in the grass, and, with the daffodils and narcissi, bring the wild garden through to its second glorious period—that of fox-gloves and ferns. On the other side of the lawn the herbaceous border begins to blaze with colour, while here under the silver birches the foxgloves are more casual but no less attractive, and the ferns, with their impossible names and feminine curls, push up through the grass in clusters.

At the house end of the wild garden the rhododendrons were magnificent in colour and the size of their blooms, but they are slow-growing for their first year, and I find myself impatient for the time when their branches will meet and they will grow up-ward in a huge variegated pile. In front of them are irises and anemones—the latter seem never to stop blooming, not copiously but persistently. At this end, too, is a patch of polyanthus.

After the foxgloves comes a colourless month or two, but this matters little, because the ferns still flourish, grass covers the bare earth, and the herbaceous border opposite is at its best. Then the clumps of montbretia turn orange and the autumn crocuses come up through the grass, and at the back are a few tall spikes of goldenrod.

This little wild garden needs a good deal of attention, its grass being scythed whenever there is an opportunity between periods of bloom and its weeds dug out from among the grass-roots. But it seems to me richly worth it, for I have scarcely begun to exploit the possibilities of growing certain worthwhile plants from the hedges or to put in cultivated plants which are improved by a grass bed.

4

Even a garden as modest as mine could not be cultivated without some skilled labour, and I began to enquire for one of those useful beings, commoner in towns than villages, who used to be called 'jobbing gardeners'. Hard things have been said of them—that with a day or a few hours here or there they can take no interest in any garden; that they concentrate on light work and advise against everything which entails the honest use of a spade; that they give the minimum of time to each employer and in any case regard with contempt a man who 'just wants his garden kept tidy'. My father, whose life knew all the financial vicissitudes which a stockbroker can experience, never failed, in the darkest periods, to find enough money to employ a full-time gardener, and it was only at the homes of maiden aunts with villas in St. Leonards-on-Sea or Barnes that I had seen the arrival, on one morning a week, of elderly and fretful men in baize aprons who came to 'do the garden'.

It was not quite such a one that I sought now. I wanted to work myself, indeed to give as much time as I could to exercise so healthy and creative; but there were many things that neither I nor Joseph could do, from lack either of knowledge or experience, of energy or tools, or because some jobs in a garden seem frankly tedious, or because we had not enough time. So I wanted a man for one day a week.

There is only one place in a village like Ticehurst in which to make fruitful enquiries—the village pub. If you want to buy a lawn-mower or sell a perambulator, if you want advice about bee-keeping or help in horse-buying, if you want your window cleaned or your cat doctored, furnished rooms for a week or the loan of a bicycle, your action is the same; simple and speedy. You go into the public bar on a busy evening and put out your enquiry. It is possible that the person you seek is not present, that he or she 'uses' another pub or is a teetotaler, but someone there will be able to direct you or arrange a meeting. Unless you have that dire thing, a 'bad name in the place', you will get what you want.

It was thus that I heard of Stanbridge, who appears in my garden with clock-like regularity every Wednesday morning, arriving with the cabbage or tomato plants he promised to bring and working steadily till five, when he manages to convey an air of regret that he must go home. A man of the Kent and Sussex border, uncertain to which county his allegiance is owed, he is the son of a head gardener of the old school, for before the Seacox Heath estate was sold to the Russian Embassy to be used, it seems, as a rest centre for overworked diplomats, he was head gardener there, and Stanbridge himself worked under him, one of a dozen men. Indeed, Stanbridge still 'does a day', as he calls it, for Lord Goschen, the previous owner, who now lives in one of the estate cottages.

His father's maxims he remembers faithfully, though the older man died some years ago. 'Never rush,' his father warned him. 'You can't get anything done in a hurry,' while more technical advice on planting and pruning, manuring and spacing, is remembered and quoted with affection. Having tact born of frankness and an interest in growing things rather than in people, Stanbridge can control my wilder enthusiasms and impatiences. 'Not till October,' he will say of some project, or 'I should think half a dozen, not a dozen, would be enough of those.'

His abiding fear is of things which 'you can never get rid of'.

'Montbretia?' he once said in a hostile voice. 'I don't like that stuff. Once you put it in you can never get rid of it.'

'But I shan't want to get rid of it,' I pointed out.

Stanbridge shook his head and looked severely at the wild garden.

'Never get rid of it, once you put it in,' he warned again, in the voice of a Roman augur.

But he is not against experiment and above all he belies one slander against his kind, for he is truly interested in the garden he is helping to make. I am sure of this, not only from the tour of inspection he makes at the beginning of his weekly visit, ex-

amining each new appearance and development, but from the
way in which he speaks of the other four gardens to which he
ministers. 'Mrs. Walford put those in a few years ago,' he says
dubiously of my Regalia lilies, 'now she's got too many of them.'
Or, when he is examining with disappointment my pale sweet
peas which bloom on short curling stalks—'You ought to see Mrs.
Benatar's. She put them in last autumn.' Or I am asked to
envy Lord Goschen's dahlias or to commiserate with a Mr.
Akers-Douglas (whose name is a household word since Stanbridge came, but whom I do not know except by horticultural
report), in the fearful shrivelling which has befallen his new
asparagus bed. One thing we all have in common, we employers
of Stanbridge for the five separate days of his varied week :
we all suffer from not being able to get rid of things we have
planted in the teeth of his warnings. 'Once you put that stuff
in you might as well stop trying to grow anything else, because
you'll *never* be rid of it !'

But there are advantages in being one of this scattered quintet,
for between us there is mutual aid, tacitly organized by Stanbridge, which benefits us all. Certain plants of mine have spent
critical months in the greenhouse of another one-day employer
of Stanbridge, while 'thinnings' from me have been planted in a
neighbouring village, and cabbage plants for the winter supply of
each of us are sown and raised somewhere else. All is managed
without fuss or petty calculation, for Stanbridge has an admirable
sense of justice.

5

As soon as Stanbridge started his weekly visits we came to the
urgent task of making the long herbaceous border. I wanted
this to be as full as possible of perennials, but I realized the extravagance and wastefulness of trying to achieve this in the first
year, since each of them would so much increase that their roots
would need dividing in the autumn. I resolved, therefore,
to put in one or two, or at the most half-a-dozen, of the perennials
I wanted and to fill in the gaps with annuals raised from seed—
a fairly obvious procedure, I imagine.

My preference was for the traditional. I could not, for instance, imagine the bed without hollyhocks, those gay giants which grin and nod in cottage gardens as well as against the grey stone walls of large and ancient houses. There is an intriguing mystery about hollyhocks. They have an air of belonging to old English gardens, yet I can find no reference to them by poets who have listed flowers in their works, and even John Clare does not recall them in his *Cottage Garden*. Bacon in his essay *On Gardens*, which does not forget many species popular in his day, speaks of 'hollyoaks', and as the *Oxford Dictionary* finds the word hollyhock of dubious origin, this may be its derivation. That boring old versifier Austin Dobson has the line 'flaunts the flaring hollyhock', Robert Bridges is content to call them 'high-grown' and A. C. Benson says that the 'red-rosetted' hollyhocks 'toss their pale stalks in upstart pride', which is a harsh criticism of so homely a flower. I planted a dozen or two of them in groups against the wall, midway between the climbing roses, and they promised well until rust attacked their leaves so that they have bloomed rather rudely on long, naked stems. Next year their leaves shall be treated with sulphur, and even now I am removing all the pustuled leaves of the new clumps, and shall watch them again in spring.

Lupins, of course, delphiniums and anchusas (the tall kind of the latter called Morning Glory)—these were inevitable. I found another very tall plant—Rudbeckia Herbstone—to stand at the back of the bed, and some aquilegia farther forward. It was annoying to keep my order down to six of these latter, for columbine is so truly in the tradition of the old English garden, and in its first year is not very assertive, but again I comforted myself with thoughts of the future. For the tail end of the season Korean chrysanthemums and Michaelmas daisies—I was surprised to find them called asters—but no campanula, for it is one of the two common flowers which I dislike, the other being the geranium. I think every honest gardener must have a few dislikes among the flowers, but not many will admit them. Then three Gaillardias, six Phlox, some Pyrethrums and Canterbury Bells, and I felt that the foundations were there.

But I had forgotten to provide enough flowers for cutting, and found one rose-pink and two white varieties of Spiræa. Then, after putting in some clumps of Helenium which a friend, dividing these in his border, had given me, I turned to bulbs and tubers.

Ideally, I suppose, none of them should be grown in a herbaceous border, but, with less than an acre of ground to plan, there is no room for separate iris borders and peony beds. With each of these I waited to see how those left in the garden would flourish, and was rewarded by heavy peony blooms and a few quite good irises. But I put in five groups of Gladiolus, five corms to each, Rose de Lima, Acca Laurentia, Snow Princess, Crimson Glow, Mrs. Mark's Memory. They have brought me into one of those horticultural divisions of opinion which seem to rage round several common plants. This one concerns the corms in winter. Should they be left in the ground, with the risk of their being killed by a hard frost? Should they be dug and kept in the potting-shed, where they may wither and die? Or should one be resigned to losing the old corms and prepared to replace them each spring? I know experienced advocates for each of these courses, and, since this is a sheltered garden, I have decided on the first.

There are other bulbs and tubers which I grew this year experimentally. For instance, an astonishing monster called Galtonia, or the Cape Hyacinth, which has flourished rather pushingly in a corner of the garden, sending up blooms which rise to four feet and look like overgrown white hyacinths. When I planted it I knew little or nothing about Tigridia, the Mexican Tiger-Flower, except that its blooms lasted only a day and were renewed through August and September. It has turned out to be a most charming and exotic thing with three petal segments and a freckled throat. Alstroemeria has only managed to produce some little flowerless shoots this year, but I am promised that it will show its fiery colours next. And Asclepia tuberosa seems a rather dull bit of orange unless it means to develop some unexpected size and quality in the future.

1. 'One of those useful beings who used to be called jobbing gardeners'

'A terrace of ome sort was a necessity'

6

It became, then, a choice of annuals.

'Except for a few petunias,' said a neighbouring gardener airily, 'I have stopped growing annuals.   Can't get the labour.'

That is reasonable, I suppose, but it would deprive me of two of the keenest pleasures of gardening—sowing and planting out. I would not wish to lose those early summer afternoons when the seedlings seem far enough advanced to be independent, when they can be made to form groups and clusters and with every moment of work one feels the promise in them.

I chose them the first year in an almost haphazard way at the seedsman's, only ensuring that I had plenty of clarkia and godetia to form a rough border.   This would have worked out very well if these two had not so flourished in my soil that they grew to a height of three feet and hid things behind them which should have been taller.   I sowed Love-Lies-Bleeding, which no one seems to know by its proper name, *Amaranthus caudatus*, because it can be used with quite astonishing effect as a cut flower and because I like its tasselled absurdity.   Larkspur, which is nothing after all but an annual delphinium, I have found a great success, a showy, delicate, persistent flower which lasts through September. Love-in-a-Mist (*Nigella damascena*) comes late and shows its blue stars rather briefly, but cornflowers, planted out in large, close groups, grow here to three feet or more, and continue to bloom rampantly for three months, while Iceland poppies last nearly as long.   Linum I found to be a most brilliant little scarlet flower which broke the line of clarkia effectively and lasts well, while marigolds of various kinds, wherever their dangerous colour does not clash with neighbours, are gay and useful for vases.   But of all the annuals the petunias bloomed for the longest time and most profusely here, and their velvet texture and trumpet shape are a lasting delight.

But this year I have been more ambitious.   'In our travels through the country', begins airily a passage in the Seed Catalogue of Messrs. Thompson and Morgan of Ipswich, 'we have seen so very few Hardy Annual flowers grown that we are forced

L

to the conclusion that this interesting, beautiful and easily grown class of plants is not known or appreciated as it ought to be.' Nurserymen's prose is always a delight, but this sentence conjures up an unusual picture. Do Mr. Thompson and Mr. Morgan, on their 'travels through the country', pause to peep over hedges in search of Hardy Annuals? Are they forever disappointed?

'Not a nasturtium!' says Mr. Thompson, viewing a front garden in Surrey or Somerset.

'Plenty of biennials,' admits Mr. Morgan, 'but not a sign of *Rhondanthe manglesii*!'

So they return to Ipswich and add this pleading note to their catalogue. It continues: 'There are really a number of most beautiful annual plants, the seed of which can be purchased for a few pence, and if sown in March or April in the open garden, will make a grand display over an extended period. We would like to call attention to a few little known hardy annuals such as *Collinsia, Collomia, Dianthus sinensis, Nemophila, Œnothera Drummondii* and *Phacelia*.' They do not call my attention in vain, and in addition I am trying *Xeranthemum annuum, Viscaria, Saponaria vaccaria, Nicandra* and *Limnanthes Douglassii*. It seems to me that one of the few advantages of a small garden is that it gives one the time to grow annuals. Long vistas, vast herbaceous borders and lawns need so much labour that no one owning them nowadays is left with time for sowing and pricking out these pleasant flowers. But my few square yards of flower-bed encourage it.

7

The terrace—I still hesitate over the word which smells of the House of Commons, of stuffy roads in seaside towns or of the vanished grandeur of large houses, but I can find no other name for my oblong of old bricks—the terrace has justified itself this summer. A lucky purchase was some Lloyd Loom garden furniture, and I have had it sprayed with paint in Mediterranean colours: brilliant reds, yellows, blues. Between the brick floor and the house wall a narrow bed has been left, and this year it has been planted with silver-pink antirrhinums, for no better reason than that I remembered how effective they were fifteen years ago when I planted them in similar beds along the front of a Cotswold cottage. Among the bricks themselves I want to grow a few spreading things—not too many—and have started with some roots of rock-thyme which Richard Church gave me from the fine garden of his converted oast-houses at Goudhurst, six miles away. He also gave me a piece of some close-growing pepper-mint which is spreading less exuberantly, but which has a per-ceptible scent, a reminder that one has to turn to herbs now if one wants to smell as well as see the flowers. In my father's gardens almost everything had its own perfume, and mignonette and heliotrope could be sensed from across the lawn on summer evenings, while the rose-garden was almost oppressive. Nearly all the scents have gone now because—I am told—there have been such improvements in the size, colour and variety of flowers. Only a few red roses have kept it, nasturtiums still have their sweet-and-sour smell, violets and primroses because they are uncultivated, and there is a very faint odour from the antir-rhinums. Otherwise, at least in my garden, it is only from the leaves of herbs that there is any fragrance. I wonder if this cultivation of colour and size compensates for the scented gardens of only a few decades ago.

8

'But where, you ask, where were the vegetables?'—So Miss Sylvia Townsend Warner writes, adding the retort—'They were not.' The triangular strip set apart for them was still a waste when Stanbridge started to spend Wednesdays in the gar-den. He soon changed that. Like most of his calling, he could coax vegetables from the ground with as much interest and affection as he gave to flowers.

When I had to decide what summer vegetables should be grown, though, I realized that it could not be a cut-and-dried matter. I suppose that every gardener with limited ground faces this problem each year and solves it according to his tastes, his ground, his experience, and the relative prices of vegetables in the local shops. I gave some thought to it, and propound my solution not because I think it remarkably wise, but because it may suggest something worth consideration.

First came the herb-garden, which by the spring was flourishing, then four rows of strawberries (of two different kinds), from which I did not expect to pick during the first summer. Strawberries seemed to me to fulfil every requirement; they are still our finest native fruit, their price never really slumps, and they are excellent for jam-making. I begrudge none of the space given to them or to the vegetable which grows near them and which, again, had to be planted with a second year and the future in mind—asparagus. The price of this most exquisite of summer luxuries rises each year, and for anyone who likes it—that is to say, anyone whose palate is not numb or immature—an asparagus bed in the garden seems a necessity.

Potatoes, in such a plot as mine, are only grown so that for the first few weeks of the new potato season we have our own. By the middle of September in this district we can buy them at ten shillings a hundredweight and it would be folly to use ground for them, but while the shops are still selling curious species from Algeria or Italy or the Channel Islands at eightpence a pound, it is economical to dig one's own, and they have a sapidity and freshness unknown to field-grown potatoes which have been in transit for weeks, or even to English potatoes from the shops. I grow Arran Pilot, a delicately flavoured white potato which forms early.

Two kinds of peas seem demanded, very small and very large. The large are excellent cooked in the English way, in water with a sprig of mint, and the small as *petits pois*. I prefer French beans to scarlet runners, and grow them in the proportion of three rows to one, bearing in mind the simplicity of preserving them for the winter. Then lettuces, beetroot, spring onions, radishes, broad beans—all the usual summer vegetables, but only a row, or at the most two, of each.

It is the more uncommon things which are the most interesting. The Cardoon, for instance. This excellent vegetable is easily grown and has a number of uses. Its heads are smaller than those of the globe artichoke, though they resemble these and are as good to eat. The central spine of its large silver leaves can be blanched and eaten, and the leaves themselves are valuable in flower decoration.

Then Capsicums. These have to be forced for part of their lives, but can be put out when they are an inch or two in height, and with any luck will produce a few sizeable pods in the open before the first frosts. They are delicious stuffed or used in many Spanish dishes. I believe that many kinds of Capsicum could be grown in England, and intend to experiment with the ordinary Indian green pepper, the seeds of which are sent to Joseph from India.

Sweet or Indian corn is easy enough to grow, but depends on a fine August and September for its success, so that in this part of the world it is at its best only two years in three. Red pickling cabbage flourishes, though, and is worth growing for *sauerkraut*. Tomatoes, of course—and I find that we need at least two dozen plants for all the purposes of pickling and chutney-making. Equally necessary are those delicious vegetables so oddly called Jerusalem artichokes, which are not artichokes and have no connection with Jerusalem, but have earned the name through a corruption of their Italian name, Girasole. This tuber is, in fact, a member of the sunflower family, *Helianthus tuberosus*, but tastes none the worse for that. It can be planted in any old corner, and will almost certainly do well. I would not be without it, though Stanbridge viewed its introduction with misgiving, clearly foreseeing the impossibility of ever getting rid of it.

As the summer vegetables have finished, Stanbridge has been practically waiting with a miscellany of greens for the winter, had indeed planted some of them between the rows of French beans before we had picked the last of these. But he doesn't approve strongly of my scheme for a few rows of tulips among the vegetables, though I tell him that I regard these as being suitable primarily for cutting and do not want them in the flower-garden.

As for fruit, I have no room, unhappily, for currant or gooseberry bushes or even raspberry canes. But there are the peaches, nectarines, greengages and cordon pears on the south wall, while facing them are two loganberries, two Edward Langley black-

berries, one apple and one Morello cherry-tree. An old and
faithful pear-tree is one legacy from the previous occupants of
the house which remains to bear plenteous fruit of great size and
good colour, but fruit which will not keep in store.

As a matter of economics, I think my vegetable garden saves
me on an average ten shillings a week and takes less than half a
day each week of Stanbridge's time, though it absorbs a few hours
of mine.   The simple balance of this is outweighed, however, by
the immense advantage of having fresh vegetables and of being
able to preserve a number of them.   Not to mention the satisfaction, known only to a garden-owner, of picking and eating
things he has grown himself.

9

'I pity that man who has completed everything in his
garden.'   Mr. Geoffrey Taylor in his brilliant little book about
Loudon, Robinson and Reginald Farrer * quotes this scrap of
wisdom from Alexander Pope, the first writer to make a famous
garden.   Most gardeners nowadays must be pitied not for com-
pleting everything but for not being able to achieve enough.
How can any man whose earnings are limited by income tax to a
mean standard figure, who is not allowed the disposal at his own
choice of more than a small fraction of what is paid to him,
afford to go beyond growing a few flowers and vegetables, and
that only if he himself has the time and vigour to do so?   There
will be no more great English gardens, and this national heritage
will be abandoned with many others, for good or ill, according
to your view of life. The 'cottage garden', however, will
persist, as it has done for a good many centuries, and the 'villa
garden', reduced in size and scope, will not be wholly lost.

Such a plot as mine need not be neglected while I can work
in it, but even in a garden of less than an acre many developments
will remain for ever unrealized.   Pope's pity would not be given
us today, although, with the £8,000 which he netted untaxed
from his translations of the *Iliad* and *Odyssey* cleverly invested,
he might spare a wry smile of sympathy for men who try to

* *Some Nineteenth-century Gardeners* (Skeffington, 1951).

make a garden now.   Still, in an age of planning, we may yet be permitted to have schemes, to imagine what might be done if the world should miraculously grow sane.   And I have plenty.

There is, for instance, the thirty-foot-long timber shed which runs down the length of the vegetable garden This consists of a ten-foot-high wall and a corrugated-iron roof twelve foot wide sloping down to an open side.   The high brick wall faces south, and the whole thing could be converted to a quite magnificent glass-house at a not exorbitant cost.   'Who loves a garden loves a greenhouse, too,' said Cowper, and I can find no fault in the assertion.

Then the terrace is two feet higher than the lawn, and of course demands a low wall to support it, over which plants could fall and against which grow.   The whole length of south wall is now high enough to prevent pedestrians and motorists from over-looking my garden, but passengers on the upper deck of the bus which passes every hour or so are able to peer down.   A row of lime-trees, espalier'd along the top of the wall, would prevent this and keep no sunshine from the garden.   And, of course, like most of us who read nurserymen's catalogues, I never come to the Hardy Aquatics and Nymphæa without certain ambitious notions of my own.

The best cure for such unsatisfying reverie is an hour's weeding, a kind of 'development' for which the means are never lacking, and which restores my pleasure in the garden as it is and as it will be next year.   A keen pleasure for which alone I should have been willing to leave all that London had to offer.   Indeed, I sometimes wonder how I can have remained four years there without a garden.

A Man in the Kitchen

I

THE First World War is reputed to have brought about the emancipation of women. The Second has given one kind of freedom to men. They need no longer be slaves to the dietary whims of their wives and housekeepers. They are not at the mercy of beautiful women who cannot cook. They have earned the right to pull on an apron and get down to the complexities of flavour, colour, consistency, contrast and surprise which are the prerogatives of a good cook.

In other words, where the pre-war male, faced with the refusal or inability of moody womenfolk to prepare a meal for him, had to go hungry or find the nearest restaurant, the New Man can roll up his sleeves, take down his tins and bottles, draw from the frigidaire and produce a dinner for himself as good as rationing will allow.

He has earned this freedom in the hard way, fighting for his ascent from the lowliest dish-washing and potato-peeling to the making of tea, then on to the dizzy heights of coffee-brewing, till he dared to seize the frying-pan, the casserole, and finally the chafing-dish. But it has been an inevitable progression. Once Woman, in a moment of wartime fatigue perhaps, called on Man to dry while she washed up, once she ceded him the right to stand over the sink, her sole authority was in jeopardy, and she might have realized that it would be only a question of time before her monopoly was over.

It was, of course, the discovery that he could do the first humble things well which gave Man the courage and confidence to go on. What he had believed to be the mysteries of the kitchen, secrets almost as occult and feminine as childbirth, were soon revealed to him as matters of common sense, judgment

and only occasionally of flair. He found he could polish a glass.
He realized that one who could peel potatoes could shred spinach.
He found that to put a roast in the oven long enough was no
harder than to fry a rasher of bacon. So he proceeded triumphantly to the ultimate mysteries. He was able to say that
anything his wife could do he could do.

If it had stopped there it would have been a small sociological
development during this last decade, but no more. Under
modern conditions (we should have noted), in which there
are no more domestic servants, the male is doing his share of the
preparation of meals. He does not expect his wife to do everything in the house, and has ceased to consider the apron and
feather duster symbols of servitude or effeminacy. That would
have been the extent of the change.

But no. Man is an adventurer. In this, as in all human
enterprise, from the making of the first stone weapons to the
discovery of relativity, it is he who has dreamed, rebelled and
dared, and Woman who has been the true conservative, satisfied
with what she knew and discouraging all search beyond the
horizon. It was Adam, I am sure, who went exploring round
Eden, while Eve's highest hope of new achievement was in a
novel shade of fig-leaves.

So, entering this new world of roasting and braising, of
blanching and grating, Man was soon dissatisfied with the elementary principles which in England have so long been the
stock-in-trade of the female cook, and began to ask restless
questions and to be stirred by such inspiring dreams as sent
Columbus westward and Darwin to the south, incited the
Montgolfier brothers and encouraged Mozart. The questions
came first. Must roast chicken, man wondered, always be
accompanied by this nauseating pulp which is one of the three or
four sauces known to the English cook? Can mutton be enlivened by nothing except the tinted and sweetened and chemi-
cally flavoured gelatine which is sold as red-currant jelly, or else
by crude malt vinegar in which a teaspoonful of desiccated mint
has been half soaked? Is this leathery parody of one of the few
good and original English dishes, the Yorkshire pudding, for ever

to be cooked when a small block of recently frozen topside is dried and heated in a gas oven before it is called roast beef? Above all, is the greatest of all cereals, rice, which, as the staple food of half the world's population, can be served in several thousand delicious and varied ways, to be relegated to one of two hideous purposes—either as the accompaniment of twice-cooked meat over which curry-powder and sultanas have been sprinkled, or, sickly with milk and sugar in a glutinous mess called a rice pudding?

'Those obstinate questionings of sense and outward things', those 'blank misgivings of a creature moving about in worlds not realised', began to trouble the head of the neophyte male as he dawdled among his new culinary handicrafts, but when he put them to his mate she was, it must be roundly stated, very far from trembling 'like a guilty thing surprised'.

'So you don't like my cooking?' she said, with characteristic evasion of the issue. 'You find it monotonous and unimaginative? Let me tell you that I give you what my mother gave my father, and if it was good enough for him it is good enough for you. What could be better, I should like to know, than the boiled mutton and caper sauce—*caper sauce*, mind you—followed by spotted dog, which you had for lunch? They've only had half-a-dozen jars of capers at the grocer's since the war, and I got one of them. As for the spotted dog, I suppose you think it's easy to get currants and suet? You just don't appreciate what's good, that's your trouble. Unimaginative! Perhaps you expect me to be producing all those messed-up foreign dishes? If that's so you've got another think coming to you. I was top of the cookery class at school, and no one has ever made a better toad-in-the-hole than I do. So if you're not satisfied, you'd better improve on it yourself!'

And that is just what her man has been doing during these last years. With some quite astonishing results. For, as usual, he has wanted to run before he could walk. It is one of his eternal characteristics, endearing or infuriating according to the occasion and the persons concerned. He has begun creating sauces and soufflés before he could turn his hand to a steak-and-kidney pudding. He will make a potato *cassolette*, a delicious elaboration

of potatoes *Duchesse*—themselves a variation of mashed potatoes
—before he can serve that excellent thing, a potato perfectly roast
in the dripping of a joint, its whiteness caked with a quarter of
an inch of crisp and golden crackling He wants to cook sweetbreads *à la Dubarry*, knowing precisely how to make his Hollandaise sauce for this, before he can guess what to do with the
common tripe which his wife is far more likely to obtain when she
goes shopping. But with all these leaps into advanced cookery,
these immature invasions of the *haute cuisine* by a creature whose
fingers are still white from his first pastry-mixing, Man's new
ambitions have had their effect on English cooking. At least he
has brought it out into the open, so that from being a closed shop
for women, with secrets never discussed except among housewives, it is now a keenly debated subject in mixed company.

This may not be due wholly to man's infiltration. Shortages,
expedients, substitutes are everyone's concern. But the new
tendency towards open discussion has produced a general stimula-
tion.

Last winter, for instance, when in rural areas we were forced to
subsist largely on the white and, on the whole, not very succulent
flesh of rabbits, you might hear in our local pub a discussion
among two or three married couples of the underfed middle
classes, a discussion which would have been unheard-of in such
a group a mere decade ago.

'We,' announces a sturdy estate agent whose fresh-water fish
from our river cooked *à la mode de Touraine* is as generally
appreciated as his wife's *apfelstrudel*—'we put the rabbit in a
marinade for forty-eight hours. Red wine, garlic and vinegar.
Then fry it in oil.'

'Sounds all right,' says a local J.P. who has spent some years in
the East. 'Prefer it curried myself. Or in a *pulao*.'

'Personally,' says a doctor's wife, who evidently knows her
onions, 'I find that you can't beat a casserole. But it's just no
good if you can't get mushrooms. Then I serve it on *croûtons*
of fried bread.'

'What,' asks a schoolmaster, 'about the good old white-
sauce-and-onion way?'

'*En blanquette*,' someone corrects him severely.

'Not the slightest good', propounds a stockbroker, 'unless you've got cream and eggs. Might as well eat it raw, otherwise.'

This harsh rejoinder silences the schoolmaster and allows a much-travelled lady to say that she brought a recipe from Sicily according to which rabbit was given a sweet-and-sour sauce, but that she preferred it done as she had tried it in Spain, with rice and pimentos. And not until we have discussed it in aspic, grilled, in a fricassée, marbled, devilled and as a *soufflé* do we turn to an appraisal of the chances of our local football team.

A revolution? I begin to hope so. It is only during the last century that English people have earned a world-wide reputation for their astonishing ability to live on food which other races find inedible. In the eighteenth century, for instance, we cooked as well as most people. Our decline has come during the time of our greatest prosperity and while all foods were plentiful and cheap. We are always at our best in adversity, by natural ingenuity able to overcome the gravest difficulties imposed by shortage. We are being forced now to use inventiveness, and the results may be far-reaching.

2

Already a man who likes cooking escapes the various kinds of abuse which would have belaboured him a few decades ago. He is not considered a Macaroni, a 'Frenchified bounder', a 'dish-washer' or a pansy because he undertakes one of the most severe and gruelling of tasks. This escape from opprobrium is not, I must own, a matter on which I congratulate myself, because I have never been troubled by sensitiveness to popular opinion and have studied cooking for many years because it has interested me, because I liked good food both in principle and practice, because an ability to produce it has meant, in many places and circumstances, giving pleasure to other people as well as to myself, and because I like cooks, finding them nearly always good fellows or kindly women.

The Countess Morphy, an inspired writer on this subject, which has, incidentally, been grossly neglected by creative writers in most countries, once gave a party to celebrate the publication of her book *Recipes of All Nations*,* and because most of the guests were the chefs of the great London restaurants and had to be in their kitchens to supervise the preparations for dinner, it took place at four o'clock in the afternoon—a curious time to drink champagne.   There was the Cavaliere This and the Maître That—impressive names and even more impressive personalities. I want no better company than these witty, thoroughly virile and courteous men whose faces radiated gusto and charm.   They praised that remarkable book, not as polite guests, but with spirited discussion of its many merits and few omissions.   They were at the head of their profession, but I have seen their characteristics in most men and women who devote their lives to this exigent calling.   'Cookery is become an art, a noble science : Cooks are gentlemen,' said Robert Burton three hundred and thirty years ago.

Like all good art, cooking is sometimes for art's sake.   The perfect dish can be appreciated critically but not voraciously enjoyed by the man who has just created it, and others to whom it is offered do not always realize that they are tasting history. But this need be no deterrent.   Once achieved it is for all time, and although, like a difficult musical composition, it may lack interpreters skilled enough to reproduce it, it has been added to the still limited store of human invention.   It is, in fact, worth while, as is the most slavish following of a good recipe.   All proficient or imaginative cooking is worth while, and discussion of it rarely means wasted time.   So let's go to the kitchen.

3

Faced now with this vast and vital subject, I realize that the aspects of it which are within the scope of this book are fortunately limited by my general scheme and purpose.   Fortunately, because although I can think of no book (except a novel) which I would rather write than a cookery book, I am not engaged on one

---

* *Recipes of All Nations*, compiled and edited by Countess Morphy (Herbert Joseph).

now. I am attempting to describe the home I have made and the life I wish to lead in it, and to protest at the obstacles raised against this and against all civilized living by the barbarian regimentalists of our age. I am not without hope that some of the results described or expedients advocated may provoke a few others to dissatisfaction with the second-rate in materials and method, or may entertain those whose knowledge of these things is wider than mine. But it is not my purpose to set down a collection of recipes on the one hand or to hold forth on general principles on the other. (General principles of this, as of most other arts and sciences, are excessively dull.) Rather I want to describe, with no arrogant assertions about their pre-eminence, a few of the things done in the kitchen of this house. Some of these will be commonplace to any experienced cook, some are mere makeshifts until better days, some have been learnt abroad or discovered by trial and error and may be new to English cooks, some may appeal to few tastes and be the result of personal prejudice; yet all, I hope, will help to demonstrate a certain way of life and show a respect for the art of good living and a faith in the bounty of God.

Food has taken on an almost symbolic importance in the years since the war with Germany ended, for in the Welfare State a man's menu is virtually written for him by authority. The planners employed by Government departments throw him, like keepers in the Zoological Gardens feeding wild beasts, the scraps of this or that provender which they have purchased in bulk to suit either the exigencies of their trade programmes or the postulations of their theorists on the subject of calories and proteins, carbohydrates and vitamins. Attempts have been made to stuff down our throats pieces of the filthy carcases of whales which have the nauseous and retching savour of bad meat steeped in fish oil. A tinned and tasteless substance of piscine origin has been vociferously recommended to us under the name of Snoek, and Australia has been enabled to solve a vermin problem of Hamelin proportions by sending us the frozen corpses of a million or two rabbits which arrive in solid blocks of ice. We are forced to eat muddy-coloured bread, a humiliation which is exacerbated by the assurance that it is 'good for us', and a man's natural need and liking for meat have been exploited and insulted by drums of tinted and faintly meat-flavoured cereals sold under such names as Ham Loaf, Beef Roll, Luncheon Meat, Pork Sausage Meat.   A whole generation is growing to manhood which would scarcely recognize unadulterated or untinned food if this were offered.   The results have not been quite as the planners supposed.   The various food substitutes have been accepted because many town-dwellers could find no alternatives, but scarcity and lack of variety have produced a new interest and ingenuity in both finding and preparing food, while the indignation of the housewife has never been lulled by the dulcet persuasions of successive Food Ministers or women politicians.   It has, indeed, become the duty of a good citizen to challenge this Cromwellian philistinism with every artifice he can devise, to determine that the generosity of God shall not be flouted by the smug theorizing of bureaucrats, and to defend that most elementary of human rights, the right to enjoy good food.

What follows, then, is a discussion of methods, discoveries, delights, failures and achievements in one English house; a house in which food is considered important enough to warrant much thought, patience and imagination.   A house, moreover, in which compromise in this matter is barred and in which Government-sponsored amphibious tinned mucilage is held in contempt, in which the preparation of eatable dishes is openly discussed and their consumption frankly enjoyed, but in which gluttony is no more esteemed than drunkenness.

4

In the matter of calefaction the ideal is impossible, but this does not mean that one method is as good as another.   The French use charcoal, the finest fuel for all kinds of cookery except roasting, for which our own wood-fire-and-turnspit method of two centuries ago is unbeatable. But these must be abandoned now in any modest home, because of the vast labour and expense entailed, though I cannot but think that a restaurateur who used them would be rewarded by discriminating customers.   For a house like mine the choice is between the Victorian kitchen range and the gas or electric cooker, but not the so-called 'stored-heat' cooker, which is economical in fuel and impressive in appearance but cooks in hermetically sealed ovens in which all crispness is lost and from which food emerges in steamed sogginess, permeated by stale savours, since the steam from previous dishes has left its film to be revaporized.

We use chiefly gas, but there is an electric cooker standing beside the gas range for use a as reserve or in case of reduced gas pressure. Gas has the obvious advantage of quick and precise regulation. But for grilling we have a superbly infernal machine, imported from Switzerland because in this country it is not yet on the market—an infra-red grill. This is already in use in many famous restaurants and hotels on the Continent, where the greatest cooks, after sceptical and scrupulous experiment, have accepted it not only because it will cook several hundred steaks an hour but because it cooks them better than any kind of heat previously known to man.

By habit a believer in traditional methods, an upholder of the charcoal fire as a cooking agent, I had every prejudice against this innovation, but I am sure now that for grilling steaks and certain other kinds of meat there is nothing better.

The trade concerned, however, seems either to hold a contrary opinion or to be unaware of the thing's popularity in America and Europe. It cost me £12 to convert this small grill to English voltage, and the electrician who achieved this maintains that it is one of two in use in the country, and that both are in this small backward rural area; Clive Brook, who lives a mile or two away, has the other, which he brought from the States.

As for implements and cooking-pans, these are conventional enough, though I dearly love a good gadget. The various Moulin shredders, mincers, grinders, pulverizers and choppers have an honoured place, and a crescent-shaped drainer which clips on to the frying-pan becomes a necessity after it has been used once or twice. An ornamental cutter which shapes starry circles from cucumber or beetroot slices makes salads more inviting in appearance. A sieve with a kind of steely-strong silk gauze is a vast improvement on the old wire kind, which rusted. And there is in a corner of the pantry a special chopping-block and hatchet for bones; this means far greater value for soups from even the whitest bones. The frigidaire is gas Electrolux, which has the virtue of silence. Equipment otherwise is that of most kitchens—adequate and carefully cleaned and stored, but not spectacularly varied.

It is the cupboard containing condiments, spices and so on, the cupboard near the stove and table to which the cook has ready access, which is stocked more lavishly, for here no economy either of space or expense is possible. First are the dried herbs for use in winter, of almost every kind grown in the herb-garden. They have not, of course, more than a ghost of their summer quality and scent, but can still be used with effect in soups, stews, omelettes, sauces, forcemeat, with vegetables or as garnishes. The English cook was satisfied too long with mint, sage and parsley, but now begins to return to the essential garlic. For too long if a bay-leaf was used at all it was to flavour a milk pudding or blancmange, and though Mrs. Beeton was not sparing in her suggestions for herbs of all kinds in sauces and stuffings, she was less mindful of them in stews and soups. Some of the glass jars of dried herbs in my kitchen are very rarely taken down, let me admit, but others are in almost daily employment, and there is merit in their very variety. They do not, however, compensate for the fresh herbs which are picked almost daily in summer for one purpose or another, and in winter there can be only a poor skeleton of a *bouquet garni*. Most cookery books talk with more or less conviction of the *bouquet garni*, but often forget it in individual recipes. It should be gathered in the herb-garden for its special purpose; there can be no fixed rule for its constituents. Parsley, thyme, bay-leaf, marjoram and basil are fairly regular inmates; chervil, chives, celery, tarragon are variants; fennel must be added for certain fish dishes, and lovage gives a stronger tang of celery than celery itself. Indeed, most of the aromatic herbs except tansy and pennyroyal have been included in one or another since my herb-garden has flourished. These are sometimes wrapped in leek leaves, and always used with economy. And in

M

the winter, when all we have are bottles of their dried and desiccated leaves, a pinch of each of those which would have been chosen for the *bouquet garni* has to serve its turn.

Next on the shelf come spices and condiments. It is not easy to realize now how much our search for spices has changed the world's history, how much it has inspired discovery and colonization in days when our need for all that was meant by spice was strong enough to send whole flotillas to the East and West. Since those brave and discerning days our understanding and use of spices degenerated, till in most kitchens they came to mean a shake from a tin labelled 'mixed spices', a couple of cloves in stewed apple or a grating of nutmeg on a junket. But they are becoming appreciated again, and it is cheering to find that even the most obscure of them are obtainable from grocers. Black peppercorns and a coarse grater for them; mace, which is the grated outer shell of the nutmeg but is more dimly aromatic; the nutmeg itself grated freshly for each purpose; stem ginger and ground ginger; allspice, which is the powdered berry of one tree and not a mixture of spices; cinnamon both in its bark form and ground; mustard and mustard seeds; turmeric, vanilla pods, coriander seeds, pepper and cayenne pepper; cloves and ground cloves, paprika, celery salt, caraway seeds and cardamom. There is no extravagance in making a collection of these, for each little tin will last for a very long time, and there are no satisfactory substitutes.

As important as any of these but most difficult to keep inexpensively in supply is wine. How envious one grows of the French housewife who can use a red or white wine for cooking which costs her a few pence a litre. But there is no escaping this necessity, and although a coarse draught cider may sometimes be discreetly used where a white wine is demanded, a bottle of red wine remains essential.

Food

IT would be a cynical exaggeration to say that the task of the good cook in these mid-century years is to make the inedible palatable, but his success does depend on ingenuity and courage in the face of conditions. He does not want to know how to cook a baron of beef, but how to make such food as he can obtain fit for consumption. I like to believe that in my house I can ask a friend to dinner at short notice and be able to feed him without a visit to the black market and without having to apologize for the meal which I offer him.

It is possible, for instance, to start such a meal, however unanticipated, with *hors d'œuvre*, and if there has been time to consider the matter these need not consist of the dreary collection of cold vegetables steeped in ready-made salad cream, tinned sardines, a sort of maize porridge sold in tins as 'sweet corn' and a couple of cold sliced sausages left over from breakfast. Nor need the choice of them slavishly follow precedent. There is, for instance, chopped ham, not derived either from a ham sent from abroad in a food parcel or from those tasteless and jellified hams sold in tins at about a fiver a time. Grocers who supply bacon cannot cut it from the last few inches of the knuckle, and are permitted by the regulations which rule their lives to dispose of these few inches. Questioned frequently enough about a customer's 'turn' for a 'knuckle end', a grocer will occasionally supply one of these, which will serve as a joint of boiled bacon. Thereafter its rather dry lean may be diced and spiced for *hors d'œuvre*, or potted and served with toast as a *pâté*—an excellent beginning to any meal.

Or, when the butcher who seems to like parting with a head no more than did Herod, eventually yields to persuasions, so that a sheep's head is delivered, the tongue sliced fills another of the *hors d'œuvre* dishes. The last scraps from the bones of a chicken or any other bird before it is relegated to the stock-pot will serve for another. It is possible, moreover, to buy a good salami sausage, though most of the English-made sausages being offered just now are quite abominable.

Because I find all tinned fish anathema, except the honest little Portuguese sardine, and would rather have none on my table than bottled mussels, Russian crabmeat, tinned pilchards and tunny or —and these were actually imported from America by one of our food-buying commissions or some such body—*tinned oysters*, I will only have such fish in a *hors d'œuvre* as may be in the house or purchasable on the day it will be eaten. But soused herrings are easy to prepare by making a marinade of a glass of white wine and half of vinegar, half a teaspoonful of salt, a sliced onion, one clove of garlic, some peppercorns, a small sprig each of chervil and tarragon, a bay-leaf, some cloves and enough water to make this meet the purpose of a marinade, but less than the quantity of wine and vinegar. This is boiled for a quarter of an hour, then poured boiling over the herrings, which are left to cool and stand in it for a night.

Cold hard-boiled eggs cut in rings will fill another dish, and root vegetables previously cooked, diced and mixed with mayonnaise another. Radishes, celery, beetroot, shredded capsicums or sliced cucumber or tomatoes in olive oil sprinkled with red pepper, French beans, gherkins, chicory—almost any vegetable cleverly treated makes a variation.

With a taste for *hors d'œuvre*, or for a guest who believes with André Simon that '*Hors d'œuvre* are a survival of the social spirit of the ancient Chinese and of the epicurean philosophy of the Romans', one may improvise endlessly within these limits. Yet perhaps one should remember sometimes the custom in many French families of serving as *hors d'œuvre* one cold dish, a tomato salad rich in olive oil and sprinkled with chive, an artichoke, *pâté-de-foie* or a slice of melon.

Many *hors d'œuvre*, and indeed all cold-fish dishes, deserve an authentic mayonnaise. This is one of the simplest of all good things and yet one of the most frequently mismanaged. It has only three main concomitants, and can be made in ten or at the most fifteen minutes, yet for every one occasion on which I have had an eatable mayonnaise, wither in private houses or restaurants, there have been a dozen on which I have been given some sickly substitute.

The making of it is a pleasant little chore to which one should settle down placidly with a pudding-basin and a wooden spoon (*not* an egg-whisk or similar contrivance), while about one on the table are two eggs and ready measured quantities of oil and vinegar (half a pint of oil to a dessertspoonful of vinegar), salt, pepper, mustard and, if it is obtainable, some cream. The vinegar should have been boiled and allowed to cool. The yolks (only) of two eggs are dropped into the basin and salt, pepper and a good pinch of mustard added. The oil, which must be true olive oil, should not be cold but at the temperature of the room or even faintly warmer. When the eggs have been stirred up, a trickle of oil is allowed to fall on them and stirred in rhythmically with the wooden spoon. Very slowly and steadily this is continued drop by drop, with now and again a few drops of vinegar. Soon the mixture will thicken almost into a paste, and if it is too thick, a little more vinegar is added. At last the cream is poured in while the mixture is still being stirred. This will produce a mayonnaise which cannot be improved by any addition, though there are perverted gluttons who add a sprinkle of fine sugar, and more excusable gourmets who rub the basin with garlic. It will make any *hors d'œuvre*, any cold fish or any salad about twice as good as it would have been without its rich saffron colour and creamy consistency.

If you are troubled by a poltergeist who causes you to curdle things and you find your mayonnaise—for that matter your Béarnaise or Hollandaise sauce—curdling, there is a remedy which seems to me to have something of the supernatural about it with which to defeat your hobgoblin. You drop a little very hot water in one particular point in the mixture as though you wanted to bore through it. You start stirring very quickly with a wooden spoon-handle round this point, then slowly increase your circles till you take in the whole mixture. This will miraculously restore its creaminess. And never put mayonnaise in a frigidaire, by the way.

2

I tend to grow pietistic on the subject of soups, to insist on a severe orthodoxy and to writhe with prejudice against dissent. Good soups, like good cocktails, are rarely achieved fortuitously and never without the observance of certain principles. Nor are the great standard soups made by guesswork, by compromise or by substitution. *Minestrone* is not any vegetable soup with cheese sprinkled over it; *bortsch* is not the water in which beetroot has been boiled garnished with a spoonful of cream; Scotch broth is not diced vegetables boiled with a handful of pearl barley, nor does mulligatawny soup consist of stock and curry-powder. Broth-like liquids can, of course, be made from almost any scraps of meat or vegetable, and with enough flavouring of herbs or spices, or enough admixture of 'thickening' preparations and colouring, may deceive the undiscriminating. But soup is a great nourisher; it can be, and in many poor European homes is, a meal in itself, from which the very name of supper derives. It is not a means of using up stale and miscellaneous food-scraps.

It is easy enough to find recipes for soups. Miss Nell Heaton * has some clever ones, though as usual, with all her originality and common sense, her recipes seem to me to be based on her deep knowledge of dietetics rather than on respect for the *haute cuisine*. Mrs. Beeton has about a hundred and forty of them. The Countess Morphy gives several from most countries. They are so varied that whatever stock may be available, whatever materials at hand, there will be a choice of a dozen soups to be made, and a dozen garnishes. No need to give these recipes, but let me roll on my tongue the names of some of the classic soups which we have made here without deviating in any detail from the traditional precepts.

First, of course, the *Pot-au-Feu*, the stockpot soup of all French families. Perhaps the fact that it needs stewing-beef accounts

---

* *The Complete Cook*, by Nell Heaton (Faber and Faber).

now for its rarity in England, since what we once knew as stewing-beef is sold now in curious 'joints' for the rations of small families; but beef-bones, which are also an essential, may still be bought fairly easily and a passable *Pot-au-Feu* made with them.

Bouillabaisse is a fish-stew rather than a soup and in any case essentially a local dish, seeming out of place even a hundred miles inland from Marseilles. But one need not go north of the Tweed for a good Scotch Broth if one has mutton stock and leeks and the other necessary vegetables, nor cross the Channel for *Julienne* and *Jardinière*—those stand-bys of the French *pension* and hotel—nor go to India for mulligatawny, which does not owe its name to an Irishman, but to Joseph's language, Tamil, in which *milagu* means pepper and *tannir* water. The often-forgotten essentials in this soup are a couple of apples and some coconut, though none of its ingredients should be neglected.

Cocky-Leeky, another from Scotland, must have chicken stock, and it is folly to try to make that glorious spring soup *Printanière* without green peas, French beans, lettuce *and* asparagus, though with these and a good stock it is excellent.

The herb-garden's supply of sorrel is essential for many of these, but for none more than the various rabbit soups. *Purée à la Palestine* is made from Jerusalem artichokes, and is one of the best of white soups, with Cream of Celery as a close competitor. These are both popular in my house, perhaps because they need *croûtons* of fried bread, and Mrs. Rummery, who has an economical mind, delights in using the last of a superseded loaf. Green-pea soup is another *purée* of which it may be remembered that a little added spinach gives it a good colour and that the stock must be derived from pork or bacon bones. And there is the classic *Bonne Femme*.

Minestrone can be as good in England as in Italy if one takes the trouble to get the little kidney-beans which are so important to it and some of the Parmesan cheese which is being sold again now. Onion soup is best made the Spanish way, with the onions fried before they are put in the stock. All the German and Austrian cabbage-soups are good, and demonstrate that caraway seeds are useful for other things than cakes. So is *Weinsuppe*, in many forms, from the same countries.

As for *Bortsch*, on this I follow very literally the instructions of Countess Morphy, though they entail a good deal of work. I am still not swept away by enthusiasm for a soup which seems to owe its fame to its colour and the dab of sour cream which contrasts with it. Eel soup, one of the best and easiest of fish soups, is made in several ways, but always served thick and white and garnished with a few capers. The American Clam Chowder, which is one of the best dishes to come from the Northern continent, can only be made here in order to use up those tinned oysters which were imported a few years ago by Government buyers, just as a poor sort of crab *bisque* can be made from Russian crabmeat. They will be recognizable as something in the tradition, but very little more.

3

The omelette is an excessively shy French creature which eludes most English cooks, and I have no secret process, no wonderful tip learnt from an old woman in Normandy, no elixir and no certainty of success. I do not dilute the beaten eggs with water, as I have been recommended to do, nor with milk, though if there is a dessertspoonful of honest cream in the house I add it. I use a very small scrap of butter to fry it in and have a flexible knife in hand while it cooks. I am lucky in having a special frying-pan for this which I bought in France before the war. It has such low sides to it that one may scrape under or fold the omelette at will. Finally, it is only for an *omelette aux fines herbes* that anything except salt and pepper goes *into* the egg when it is mixed, even cheese being coarsely grated and folded inside it rather than beaten in.

The only other egg dish with which I introduce a meal is that excellent little French *entrée, œufs en cocotte*.

4

So to the large and entrancing topic of fish, doubly important now that, six years after the end of war, a half-witted system of bulk-buying and futile games of argument with the Argentines have reduced our Government to the status of a lap-dog sniffing for scraps of meat from the tables of other nations. We must depend on fish to give us several meals a week, and since in its richer kinds, such as salmon, its price becomes exorbitant, we must do what we can with the commoner species.

There is a cardinal rule about the cooking of fish which is scrupulously observed in the kitchen here, and which I would like to see posted in every place where fish is prepared, particularly in hospitals and hotels. It is that fish, the natural element of which is water, should never in any circumstances be boiled in it. The only exception to this rule is for prawns and shrimps, and they should be cooked when possible in sea-water. Boiling or even steaming fish is an inexcusable misuse of it which destroys the flavour and the natural fats and oils in the flesh of the fish, which reduces even further to tasteless pulp a food which (in most cases nowadays) has already been frozen and thawed perhaps more than once, which so degrades the art of cookery that one who, for instance, boils or steams a piece of fine Scotch salmon should be put in charge of a washing-machine or a steam-engine rather than entrusted with the delicate and important processes of cookery. Even English writers on cookery speak cheerily of 'boiling' fish in water and describe pans in which the crime can conveniently be committed.

There are certain fish which may be poached, but that is another matter. For these a fish-kettle with a wire tray must be used and the fish laid in a *court-bouillon*—a stock specially prepared for it. Like the countless marinades which are used by cooks, the *court-bouillon* is often made according to individual taste or an ancient family recipe. In this the fish is not boiled, but very gently poached, the liquid only trembling with heat. Or it may be put in a casserole in an oven slow enough to keep in on the point of boiling. We use several kinds of *court-bouillon* for different purposes. The first is for salmon, and consists of a few pints of indeterminate fish stock, a wineglassful of vinegar, some salt if necessary, a couple of shredded carrots and a sliced onion, a big and varied *bouquet garni*, some peppercorns and a bay-leaf. This is boiled for an hour, then, strained or not, is cooled to be ready for the fish. For large fresh-water fish there is a far more highly seasoned version of this with nutmeg and other spices, a little garlic, some shallots and if possible some white wine. For 'white' fish like turbot or brill, three of water to one of milk, and one of white wine, salt, pepper, a little cinnamon and a bay-leaf. This latter should not be strained before the fish is put in it. With these three all 'boiling' is avoided, and the results are incomparably better than those blocks of white fish which appear, smothered in parsley sauce, on too many restaurant tables.

We in England have the most delicious and varied fish round our coasts, and it is sad to think that to many, perhaps to a majority of the population, 'fish' means a sliver of dog-fish or skate with sodden batter round it cooked in nauseous oil and wrapped with potatoes in a thumbed newspaper, or else, at home, fried herrings or boiled kippers. A method of cooking as simple as *à la meunière* or *doré* for our exquisite lemon and Dover soles or for fillets of plaice seems rarely to be attempted, while a *gratin* is thought to be something luxurious and difficult. As for sauces, an ancient stigma is still on them—they are 'Frenchified messes' or 'foreign clap-trap', unless made by putting anchovy essence or chopped parsley into a paste of flour and water.

Madame Prunier * gives forty-two sauces for fish, from the familiar *Béchamel* or 'white sauce' to such lucullan delicacies as *Sauce Newburg*. What could be easier to make than *Sauce Escoffier*, which, she says, is mayonnaise with grated horseradish and chopped chervil and parsley in it? Or more voluptuous than *Sauce Diplomate*? Some of them are rendered impossible for us by shortages of one commodity or another, but there are plenty which can be made without great difficulty or expense. Moreover, the same admirable instructress gives twenty garnishes, and though perhaps her *Joinville* (mushrooms, truffles, crayfish, prawns) may sound a trifle ambitious, her *Chauchat*, consisting of slices of hot boiled potato arranged to overlap one another in a ring round the dish with cheese sauce over them, is perfectly practicable and delicious. What is more, she has no fewer than thirty savoury butters.

These may help a dull fish, but only imaginative cooking will

* *Madame Prunier's Fish Cookery Book*, translated and edited by Ambrose Heath (Nicholson and Watson).

make it palatable. Cod, for instance, can provide a meal if its steaks are stuffed with forcemeat or if it is used instead of salmon to make that rich dish a *coulibiac*. Those unnamed fish fillets which are sold at not much more than a shilling a pound are satisfying and palatable when you bake them *à la Portugaise*, with onion, garlic, tomatoes, marjoram and parsley, and no more than one glass from a bottle of white wine, the rest of which you may drink *en mangeant*. And the freshwater fish which so many anglers about here throw back, believing them inedible, can be made worthy of any taste if they are treated with sympathy. Even bream, fried in butter and served with a horse-radish sauce, becomes pleasant, while carp, eaten with red butter after it has been basted with burning brandy, is something to remember. Pike, perch, tench are worth preparing and eating, while trout can be better than almost any salt-water fish. Nor need eels be supposed the prerogative of London shops, in which they are sold 'jellied'.

But the favourite fish in my kitchen is the fleshy, satisfying yet exquisitely flavoursome scallop. It is not outrageously expensive, and cooked in any of a dozen ways and served in its own shell it makes an excellent introduction to a dinner, a sort of hot *hors d'œuvre* or fish course which is almost universally liked. The shell, too, may be used for many small savoury dishes afterwards.

5

If Madame Prunier is my authority on fish, it is to Major Hugh Pollard * that I turn for suggestions in the matter of cooking game. And game in many varieties and conditions is important in the countryman's larder.

The grand scheme which I had for life in this house, life which was to be the apotheosis of all my experience and imagination, had one little aspect, a mere fanciful snapshot, which I meant to make real. Remembering some appetizing descriptions, in the last chapters of *Lorna Doone*, of a farmer's food supplies in a part of England which could become isolated in winter, I saw the great iron hooks which hang from the beams in my larder not suspending a couple of geese, a hare and half a dozen hams, but

* *The Sportsman's Cookery Book*, by Major Hugh Pollard (Country Life).

at least not unoccupied in the winter months. And with some luck and much generosity from my friends this came to pass. There were at various times a ham brought by John Hitchcock from the United States after a mission there on the irrelevant subject of nickel, and a haunch of venison sent to me by a land-owner lucky enough to be able to play Robin Hood in his own grounds. Moreover, there was a succession of rabbits, hares, and wildfowl from my curious friend Cocker and his earthy associates.

Cocker lives in a house beside a wood in one of the loneliest rifts of country around our village. Cocker works as a builder for certain hours of the week, but his real life begins, I think, when, with a mongrel bitch at his heels, he goes with his friend Perce into unknown country, carrying a box containing two ferrets, the 'old 'un' and the one which Cocker is training (he is always training a ferret), a couple of guns, a dozen nets and a spade. Then the two of them are happy as few human beings can be for an hour, a day, or if there really are elysian hunting-grounds, for ever. I cannot give them their full names here because I have never heard them; they are invariably and to all men 'Perce' and 'Cocker' and Cocker's brother 'Boy'. Satur-day, Sunday, week-end in and out from September to March, will see them, muddy to the ears, listening at a rabbit bury (as it is called hereabouts), digging for a ferret which has gone to earth, watching the sky with furtive glances, listening for 'that old cock pheasant that I saw yesterday when I hadn't got my gun', or trudging home with the bag. Cocker was born to dogs and birds and the earth; he knows all wild things and loves the chase of them. A ruddy, not over-talkative young man, he is less at home among human beings than with the creatures of the woods, but I have never known one so clearly predestined to a certain kind of life. He will marry—indeed, his excursions now are abbreviated by the need to 'go courting'—he will settle in a council house, perhaps, while he continues to work as a builder. But he will never know sounds dearer than the thud of a shot pheasant to earth, the squeal of a rabbit as the ferret bears down on it, the flap of wild wings.

To Cocker I owe many a good bird and a supply of rabbits

which continued steadily through last winter. But to Major Hugh Pollard I owe the knowledge of eighteen ways of cooking rabbit which have helped to make that supply a blessing, during the almost meatless weeks. And if ever a creature needed care and variety in cooking it is this little 'beast of warren' which can be sickly and insipid or almost as crisp and savoury as pheasant.

I have, then, learnt something about cooking rabbits since I came to live at Ticehurst. I have consulted all the oracles, from the early cookery books of the sixteenth and seventeenth centuries to Francatelli, Escoffier and the moderns. I have experimented with strange concomitants like prunes and almonds, and pestered friendly cooks for information. From all this I have drawn certain conclusions. First I would debar from the kitchen any rabbit which has been frozen, chilled, or brought from abroad. Such a thing is not fit for human consumption even in England, where things are eaten which would turn the stomach of an African primitive. Next I would generalize boldly and say that any tough rabbit, or any one intended for roasting or frying, should be marinaded for at least twenty-four hours. And last I conclude that cooks must have seen the necessity for variety in this matter, for apart from endless further modifications there are eight distinct ways of cooking a rabbit: he can be stewed, roasted, fried, in casserole, jugged, curried, cooked in a pie, or, in the gypsy manner, made into a steamed pudding.

All these methods are worth examination. I for one see no chance of meat in such plenty that we shall be able to forget the rabbit and the cooking of him. Stewed he can be with onions, white wine, and a good large *bouquet garni* of herbs which should contain thyme and lovage. Or with red wine, if the onions are fried and a dark stock used. Or *Paysanne*. Or in milk and mushrooms. Or with onion sauce. Or with tomatoes.

If he is to be fried, he can be served golden brown or he can be removed when nearly cooked, covered in egg and breadcrumb, browned and served like chicken Maryland. If roast, he must be stuffed with forcemeat in which thyme is the chief flavouring and served with a brown sauce made with sherry. Or he can be roast with a stuffing of tarragon and breadcrumb. Again, if he is to be in casserole, it will be with the usual flavourings, including several herbs, with the almost inevitable thyme predominant. Then a glass of red or of white wine can be added or one of brandy if you like a certain fierceness in the flavour. Or he may be done *à la mode de Touraine*, for which the liquor in which he is cooked is pressed through a sieve, re-flavoured, whitened, thickened, given a cheese flavour and poured again over him.

For hare I know no better way than the sovereign dish, jugged hare, but it is incomplete without forcemeat balls in which grated lemon rind is strong enough to be tasted when they have been cooked. Red-currant jelly is usually served with this, but we make a thyme jelly which is even better adapted, for thyme, that scent of summer fields, is the natural garnish for hare or rabbit.

A good many birds have hung in my larder here : pigeons which can only satisfactorily be cooked *en casserole*; wild duck, but never again the fishy shovellers or any bird that is skinned rather than plucked; golden plover, which is best cooked in a casserole and served under a blanket of Madeira sauce; and the excellent woodcock which must be roast as pheasant.

If I could find the way to do it, I would like to have an aviary of field buntings (ortolans) such as I remember in the garden of a little inn in the Landes, that region of forest fires and pine-trees in the south-west of France. The proprietress was—and I use the term advisedly—a great artist and cooked things over her charcoal stove in the general sitting-room, things which I had not forgotten in all the years since I ate them. There was no plumbing to speak of in her little house, and the sanitation was provided in a shed twenty yards away, but she kept her stock of live ortolans and cooked them for her favoured customers. They must be eaten whole, she said, head, beak and all. How gratifying it would be to breed those tender little birds as chickens are bred for eating. But how impossible.

6

There is a kind of game which Cocker cannot bring me, but which occasionally makes its presence noticeable in the larder, the most romantic of foods and, carefully prepared, one of the best—venison. The trouble about it now is that it is sold without any indication of its kind, and it needs an experienced marketer to know whether his joint is from the fallow deer of our parks or the roe or red deer of Scotland and Ireland, or whether it is roe imported from the Continent. The red deer certainly gives the finest venison, though none are to be despised.

I hang for ten days at least any joint which I know to have been freshly killed, and then put it in a marinade for another two or three, for dryness and toughness are its dangers. Before hanging it should be rubbed with ground ginger, and tansy leaves may be tied inside the butter-muslin with which it should be surrounded. It is at its best when roast, but if in spite of marinading it is tough it can be braised in a casserole. To a good stock should be added onions, carrots, chopped celery, lovage, thyme, bay-leaves, cloves, peppercorns and a tumbler of red wine. It will take two to three hours, and should be served, like roast venison, with red-currant or marjoram jelly. The reindeer which occasionally appears in shops may be cooked in the same way, though it should be soaked for several hours in water with salt, lemon-juice and vinegar in it.

What convolutions does history perform! We are back to the days when only rich men (who nowadays buy black-market meat at savage prices or dine in restaurants at even more out-rageous ones) can afford to eat more than particles of beef and mutton, and we must go 'chasing the wild deer and following the roe' through the nearest shopping-centre.

But there is game being offered as a sop to the housewife Cerberus which the most broad-minded lover of foods cannot tolerate. Such is the squirrel. It may be that, as its propagandists maintain, it was the favourite food of the early American settlers; it is still just a bushy-tailed rat to me. It may even be that I would not recognize it as other than rabbit if it was put before me, any more than I should know horsemeat in certain forms if it was called beef. It is in the knowledge that the nausea lies, and the hooks in my larder will not, until the famine of the future is brought on us by the progressive idiocy of bureaucracy, have 'tree-rats' (as they are called in India) hanging from them.

7

Of the domestic fowl I have not much to say, though I would like to argue with the epicures about the one garnish which appears in English homes and restaurants whenever there is a roast bird—bread sauce. It can be excellent. Cruel things have been written of it by critics, and foreigners have asked plaintively why we serve this tasteless pap with roast chicken or pheasant, but that is chiefly because bread sauce is often badly made. Carefully done, the bread rubbed through a sieve to ensure fineness, a thin white stock used, a grating each of onion and nutmeg, a clove, some butter and enough of salt and pepper, and you have something that may justly be called a relish, while a little cream will give it distinction.

Mrs. Beeton gives sixty ways of cooking a chicken, and there must be a hundred more, all with valid differences, but for the kind of pterodactyl which is sold in shops, at times with some honesty as a 'boiling fowl', at times more ambiguously, there is nothing to do but stew it, so Suprême de Volaille, with mushrooms deputizing for truffles, not infrequently appears in my home.

In Madagascar during the war I must have been offered the ceremonial and symbolic chicken—with which the villagers receive strangers—more than a score of times, and have watched it roasted on a spit over a slow wood-fire almost as many, though I was once given it garnished with grilled bananas. I have eaten in Chinese restaurants those morsels of long-dried white flesh, which might have come from the bones of almost any bird or beast, cooked with almonds or pineable. I have enjoyed chicken Maryland; in Norway I have eaten the bird braised in pure butter and in Hungary swimming in red paprika sauce. There seems to be no temperate country in which the ugly little creature does not flourish, and most nations have evolved their own ways of treating it. Our standard method—stuffed, roast and served with bread sauce—demands a fine young bird, but with that is as good as any of them.

Less can be said for our roast turkey, with its great cuts of insipid white meat; or for our roast goose, which brings out in

'The dining-room, formerly the kitchen'

that bird its worst qualities—the greasiness and solidity of its lean flesh. The French stuff the turkey with truffles and stew it with red wine and even brandy, while the goose, though spit-roasted by many peoples, would scarcely be left in a gas oven and basted only with its own unflavoured fat anywhere but in England.

Duck is better able to stand tough treatment, though even this I prefer in the French *dodine* or in a casserole, unless it is a young Aylesbury duckling in high summer, when our English way of roasting with green peas and apple sauce suits it well. I have twice eaten roast peacock, once in Gloucestershire—a young one of my own which had been wounded by a fox and had to be killed—and one in Central India, where we used secretly to pot at them with service revolvers, along the roadsides south of Delhi, in spite of their protection under Hindu law. It is not a remarkable bird—indeed, its flesh is rather heavy and savourless—but it looks well served with a few of its tail feathers.

8

There are certain pieces of meat, once almost unsaleable, which have become now the prized trophies in the daily marathon run by marketers to the butcher's shop and the butcher's heart. One of these is a sheep's head, and when I first ate the glutinous and gristly meat from it I decided at once that ways must be found of making it palatable, since it is one of the precious extras allowed unrationed to the victory-flushed people of England in these years of plenty which have followed the privations of war.

Indeed, it is not so bad. It must be left in brine for a night before it is stewed (with the brains removed to make a white sauce) for two or three hours in a good stock with a positive bundle of a *bouquet garni*, two or three cloves of garlic chopped up, two sliced onions, peppercorns, cloves, salt, pepper and a small piece of stem ginger. About an hour before serving, some rice, diced carrots, turnips, and more onions should be added. When it is ready it is laid on the pastry-board and all the meat is transferred in well-shaped slices to a very large open dish, surrounded with the rice strained and if possible garnished with red pimentos. Enough of the thick white sauce, with the brains and parsley in it,

N

to cover all the meat is then poured over. A *purée* of sorrel-leaves made with butter and a little vinegar is served with it. As a dish it would not be much esteemed in vanquished countries untroubled by welfare and rearmament, but here in England I do not refuse my butcher's offer of a sheep's head.

Or even of an ox heart, though this is a tougher proposition, from which Mrs. Beeton recoils, so that no recipe appears among the four thousand in her book. What can be done with this solid block of ungrained meat? I know of nothing but the obvious— parboil, then stuff and roast it, cut it in slices and pour over it a rich Madeira or a strong caper sauce, the latter with chopped herbs in it. A sheep's heart, a more manageable thing, may be treated in the same way.

There are other oddities and scraps of offal which may be cajoled from the butcher, and it is on these, in my house, that our ingenuity is concentrated, rather than on the cooking of what is now called, in contrast and awe, 'butcher's meat'. Though no such vast supply as might be provided by a calf's head has yet been released to me, I have not lost hope of ox-cheeks, which I have eaten braised, or ox-palates, which are also excellent in casserole, or even calves' ears, which would be interesting to try, anyway. I have been privileged to buy an ox-tail, which makes a fine *goulash* if none of the ingredients of that good Hungarian dish are neglected. Sweetbreads, too, have been supplied in moments of mad generosity by my butcher, and when these have been blanched (a process not to be hurried or skimped) they are cooked *à la Suprême*, with the contents of one of those very small tins of button mushrooms which are so much more useful for cooking than the cultivated mushrooms sold by greengrocers.

From the sheep, in addition to the head, I have had kidneys, and on one occasion enough for a *sauté* with a glass of sherry in the brown sauce, but more often a pair or 'one to each ration book', as the butcher's roundsman gaily terms it, when one of our somewhat barbaric but none the less inviting national dishes is made from them—grilled kidney with bacon for breakfast. I have never had the courage to ask for sheep's tails, for although I am not deeply concerned about local opinion, I will not actively seek the reputation of a werewolf, but if my butcher sees this and cares to send half a dozen along some time, I should like to try them cooked according to the recipe which Mrs. Beeton, nothing if not comprehensive, provides. Nor have I been reduced to sheep's trotters, though I do not see why they should not be eatable, cooked either *en ragoût* or *vinaigrette*.

A farmer is allowed, by an excessively lenient law which will no doubt be repealed as soon as legislators realize that it brings a little happiness to people, to kill one, or it may even be two, calves a year. When he does this, in a district in which all ears are to the ground, those of his acquaintance who are first to hear the news may, by deflating the motor-tyres of their rivals and racing dangerously through the lanes, be in time to persuade him to sell at a ruinous price one of those scrawny joints of veal which remind one, even when they are skinned and hung, that the calf killed was so immature that he was lanky and almost bloodless. Still it is meat, and 'off the ration' and—if it is of interest to you— within the law, and there are ways of making it eatable. The *blanquette* is hard to beat if it is really well made, though it can be insipid. I not only insist on lemon-juice in the sauce, but add grated lemon-rind, and make a surround of rice cooked in the veal stock and garnished with red pimentos. Some fairly violent concomitant must be used with veal in any form if it is to be good, a strongly herbal forcemeat, a highly piquant sauce, a sorrel *purée*, or something equally potent and sharp. Even the excellent *Wiener Schnitzel* is made with plenty of seasoning on the thin slice of veal which is to be cooked in egg and breadcrumbs and afterwards garnished with a shaving of lemon, olive, anchovy and finely chopped hard-boiled egg.

There is one last hope for the meat-eater when the butcher shrugs, or even, as sometimes happens in our region, apologizes. (Our butchers are not really full of evil intention and may be honest men, but so much do we discuss them locally, bragging of this one's bounty, grumbling of that one's niggardliness, that we all find ourselves playing general post among them, shifting our patronage from one to another at frequent intervals, prompted by greed, hope, invidiousness or disgust. I remember telephoning one of them with a suggestion that I should register with him, and hearing him proudly claim that above all he was fair, he treated all his customers alike. I instantly went elsewhere, of course.) There is one other recourse when butcher and farmer have failed : it is to find someone who keeps goats.

More than once there has hung in my stables a kid recently brought from the slaughterer. It remains there until a friendly and expert craftsman with a butcher's knife arrives and divides it into joints which can be kept in the frigidaire. There need be no hesitation or uncertainty about kid's meat; it is excellent—indistinguishable, in fact, from very good lamb. In India the mutton which is universally sold, and on which English residents have lived for two hundred years, is not mutton at all, but goat's meat; while all over Europe it is sold and eaten, sometimes under its own name, sometimes as mutton. In England it has never been much wanted, because until these seven lean years mutton and lamb were plentiful and cheap and goats kept chiefly as pets. Now that they are milked and bred for milking, the young billy is often not wanted, and may be killed by humane killer without a single permit or stamp, without a page torn from the ration book or an application form filled in.

It is godsent as a basis for meals, even enabling one to do that once simple thing—ask one's friends to dinner. Sometimes I have told my guests what they are eating with such zest, sometimes left them to envious wonder over my prodigal supply of mutton. It is satisfying, too, to have the whole animal—kidneys, heart, liver and lights—to dispose of at one's own discretion.

As for preparation, it must be remembered that kid's meat may be lean and dry, so that a rather oily marinade will help it. Otherwise it can be treated as one would treat prime lamb.

The shavings and fragments of meat which are called 'the ration' are so insignificant as to need little inventiveness in the cooking of them. But there is a dish eaten in Germany which solves the problem of what to do with that curious wedge of beef called 'stewing-steak', which is not large enough to stew or tender enough to eat as steak. This dish is known as Beefsteak Tartar, and the appropriateness of the name in a country once

conquered by barbarian Mongols will be evident. I may say
that I am alone in my house in liking or even countenancing it,
and that it produces shudders from many who see it made, so
that if I want it I have to prepare it myself. I put the uncooked
meat through the mincer, then mix pepper and salt with it and
shape it to the form of a large, round, flat fish-cake. This is set in
the centre of a dish, and on top of it the yolk of a raw egg. These
are surrounded with slices of raw onion, tomato, gherkin,
cucumber and, if you like, a little grated carrot. The whole is
sprinkled with cayenne pepper. A delicious and invigorating
dish, particularly recommended to the anæmic.

9

I approve, in principle, the custom in French *bourgeois* cookery
of making a separate course of one vegetable, prepared in one of
the splendid ways familiar to everyone who has eaten abroad, but
I am deterred by a veto instilled in childhood. My anxious
parents, who must have spent many dreary hours in the pursuit
of domestic servants, would impress on us that we must not
'make extra washing-up', and I suppose their apprehensions
remain. But how much better can vegetables be appreciated
when they are eaten alone—*petits pois* cooked with a lettuce and
onion, the liquor thickened with a beaten egg; cauliflour *à la
crême*, which has for me memories of a long day's walking in
Brittany crowned by a dinner in which it figured as a course;
artichokes served cold, with peppered olive oil in which to dip
each leaf till the centre is reached and the heart devoured; broad
beans *à la Poulette* or French beans *alla crema*; cabbage *au gratin*
or stuffed aubergine; mushrooms in almost any form or a spinach
soufflé. Still, even when they are to be served on the side of a
plate with meat on it, vegetables need not have all the flavour and
nourishment boiled from them while the house fills with the
odour of school kitchens, but may be braised or broiled or, at the
worst, steamed, while their natural flavour is heightened rather
than spoiled by certain additions. Here, for instance, is a way we
treat that potentially dull thing, the green cabbage. This costs
little more and takes no longer than boiling it to such a mushy

condition that it can be, and frequently is, cut into cubes before it is served.   A rasher of bacon is cut into fine strips and fried in a little fat in a saucepan with a finely chopped onion.   The cabbage is shredded, and with no more moisture than clings to it after washing, dropped in the saucepan.   The whole is sprinkled with a few cumin seeds or aniseeds, salt, pepper and sometimes a pinch of curry powder.   This is stirred and cooked over a slow fire until the stalks are tender.   The result is very much cabbage and not in the least a mixture of foreign flavours, but it makes the vegetable presentable and pleasant to eat.

I am no partisan of the salad as it is popular in the United States, a gallimaufry of vegetables and fruits arranged to please the eye rather than the palate.   A salad served on a crescent plate with game or meat must be, for me, of the simplest kind, consisting of those crisply curling, bitter lettuce or endive leaves so popular in France, with no more dressing than a well-stirred mixture of oil, vinegar, salt and pepper.   Or chicory and beetroot.   Or cucumber.   Or tomato.   Or even a salad *deux pommes*—potato and apple.   Or any suitable vegetable simply prepared with perhaps a shredding of chive or tarragon over it.   But those elaborate mixtures containing hard-boiled eggs, walnuts, pears, bananas, lettuce, beetroots, tomatoes, plums, potatoes, and any cold vegetables left over from lunch, with some grated cheese and a few flower-petals over them, seem to me to defeat themselves, to grow limp and stale before they are prepared and served, to be appropriate to no part of a meal and to produce an effect on the consumer which would be more pleasantly, quickly and economically achieved by a small dose of Epsom salts.   However, their popularity grows with their list of ingredients, so that mine is a voice crying in the wilderness.

10

Nowhere is the food known to us as 'sweets', or in less exalted homes as 'pudding' or even 'afters', treated with the earnestness that goes to its production in England.   But that is nothing to be ashamed of, for I know French gourmets who, even after experience of most of our national dishes, still ask for a '*boudin anglais*'.

In my home this matter is left entirely to Mrs. Rummery, who, like most English housewives, is adept in it. My only intervention has been to insist that no mis-named ice-cream shall be purchased ready mixed from any shop or itinerant vendor and that no so-called custard shall be made from powders or similar preparations, so that if there are not eggs for custard-making there is no custard. Some English steamed puddings are first-rate, though only a glutton could tackle them after a sufficient meal.

It would be interesting to revive one or two of the seventeenth- and eighteenth-century sweet dishes, the sorbets and junkets of those plenteous times, or even some of the grandiose *bombes* and *timbales* of the Victorian age, the *soufflés*, creams, *babas* and flans of Edwardian England; but it would, I am afraid, be no more than interesting, and the lack of materials for them is one that causes least concern to me. An occasional English pudding, an open tart with sliced apple glazed with sugar, fruit in syrup bottled at home, a rum or sweet omelette, an apple charlotte or something light on which white of egg has been toasted to a meringue consistency—these with what fruit may be obtainable are our only dessert, and appear only rarely.

But there are one or two kinds of cheese purchasable which are worth pursuit. One of the anomalies of life under our rationing system is that while soap-like imported cheese which is only fit for cooking is doled out by the square inch, the eatable cheeses— our own Stilton, ripe Camembert, Brie, Gruyère, Port Salut, Roquefort—are all in more or less free supply, so that it is possible to do that extravagant but kindly thing, to offer to a guest a choice of cheeses on a board or stone slab. If only there were good bread to eat with them!

II

To end this verbose menu, a word about coffee. It was in a detective novel* that I found the most sweeping but profound truth on this controversial subject—'There only seems to me one essential thing about making coffee and that is to put in enough coffee'. It is best, of course, to roast one's own beans by almost

* *Neck and Neck*, by Leo Bruce (Gollancz).

burning them in the oven, or even allowing them to begin to
burn a little, if one likes them well roasted. It is best to grind
only the quantity needed at the time. It may even be best to use
a percolator, or a filter, or one of those alchemist's contrivances
more proper to the laboratory than the kitchen, consisting of
glass containers over a spirit lamp. None of these things will
save you if you stint the coffee.

In my home it is made on the same principle as tea—simple
infusion. For a pint of coffee a large earthenware pot is warmed
and dried before six generous tablespoonfuls of coffee are dropped
in with a pinch of salt. Then boiling water is poured on and the
jug is left to stand for five minutes in a warm place. This produces that rim of amber foam round each cup which is a mark of
strength and virtue.

12

As the house is something of a repository for things collected in
travel, so I have wanted its cooking to reflect the art of many
nations, to recall gastronomical adventures in far places and to take
advantage of what I have learnt from foreign cooks. But because
I have an Indian secretary who, among other talents, is adept in
his country's highly nutritious and incalculably ancient cuisine,
it is to India that I most often turn in the matter of exotic foods.

There are certain vetos and provisos about it, however, which
make it rather troublesome to prepare and serve, which preclude
it from the menu of ordinary occasions. Apart from the difficulty
of procuring everything necessary to its preparation, it cannot be
offered without warning to guests who may be unable to enjoy
or even stomach it. No wine, indeed no alcoholic drink, can
well be served with it. Its proper accompaniment is iced water;
it kills any fine liquor, and is not itself improved by draughts of
cider, beer or mineral water. And although it may perfectly
well be eaten with knife and fork, it is at its best eaten with the
hand. Thus in my home, though on most occasions we eat
curry as we might eat stew—at the dining-table with forks—for
a ceremonial Indian meal to which Ram Gopal or some other
appreciative Indian has been invited, we squat on low stools or

sit cross-legged on the floor and eat with our fingers. This gives us relaxation, and a happy sense of fitness, but to an unprepared guest would seem affected to a degree, comic, barbaric, uncomfortable, unnecessary.

But the most severe limitation of Indian food is that it cannot be mixed with any other. A meal must be either Indian or European and to serve, say, uncurried vegetables or ordinary bread, when the basis of the meal is a curry, is to produce something hybrid, indigestible and uncouth.

Nor is curry, let me stress, ever made as a means of finishing up cooked food. Little wonder that it is unpopular or misunderstood in England, when it has been so abused. The first condition for a good curry is that there should be something fresh of which to make it, and that this something should be worth the trouble and time necessary. An Indian would rather make a curry of new vegetables with no meat at all than use the cooked scraps left on a bone or the pickings from an unfinished chicken. Almost anything fresh can be curried; every edible fish or fowl, meat of all kinds, vegetables, even eggs. In India I have eaten curried lobster, and curried quail. But not old boots or once-cooked meat. If anyone in England wishes to take a few of yesterday's leavings and cook them with sultanas or other dried fruit and pieces of apple, then pour over them a thick sauce made with curry-powder and serve them with boiled rice, I can see no valid reason why he or she should not do so, provided the result is not mistaken for curry.

Joseph Sussainathan, my secretary, who comes of a South Indian family which has been Catholic for a good many generations, has been brought up to certain traditions and customs in the matter of food which may be of religious origin, but food for him is not complicated by Brahminical taboos and ceremonies. He learnt to cook from his mother. In an Indian town like Belgaum, in which he lived as a boy, the people celebrate the feast days of their own religion by entertaining their friends. Muslims, Hindus and Christians all have their times of generous provision for others, and Joseph remembers how, as each Christmas came, his mother kept open house for twelve days, her chicken *pulao* and a delicious sweetmeat called *halwar* being eaten with rapture by a long succession of callers. Although he maintains that most Indian men, as well as all Indian women, know enough of cooking to manage in an emergency, and assures me that his skill is quite commonplace, I judge the matter perhaps with western eyes and believe that he was born to it. He has that assurance and calm, that audacity mingled with a respect for orthodoxy, that imagination and recognition of the importance of detail and appearance, which are characteristics of good cooks everywhere.

I have watched him make curries, listed the concomitants, copied his way of boiling rice, but neither I nor, I believe, any European can quite achieve what he achieves. There is something occult, slightly magical, about all oriental cooking which eludes us, and although I mean to describe his methods precisely here, because they will at least enable the interested reader to improve on usual English methods of curry-making, I do so without assurance that the results obtained from them by European cooks will be as good as they hope.

A curry is, very simply, food cooked with a number of herbs and spices. These, ready blended, are sold in England as 'curry powder', and some of them, like Vencatachellum's, are quite good. But no so-called curry powder or ready-made paste is to be compared with the ingredients freshly ground and made into a paste by the cook according to his individual taste and the special needs of the food which is to be prepared. When he has all the necessities at hand, Joseph grinds and prepares them as coffee is freshly ground for each occasion, but at times he is reduced by some shortage to the use of ready-made curry powder, which he adapts to his needs by additions.

The constituents vary in different parts of India and in the hands of different individuals, and certain of them are not essential. The list that follows is a comprehensive one, but I have given no precise quantities, since the proportions vary for each purpose. The first four are used in larger quantities than the rest. All these things can be bought from Indian retailers in London.

Dry chillies.

This is the first essential of a curry.

Turmeric.

    This is the colouring agent which produces the bright sunlit
      yellow.

Coriander seeds.

    We grow our own and dry them in October.

Cumin seeds.	Peppercorns.	Cardamom seeds.
Cloves.	Mustard seeds.	Fennel.
Cinnamon.	Mace.	Poppy seeds.

With these are ground and reduced to paste, two cloves of
garlic, and into the curry at a later stage are put a couple of bay-
leaves and a squeeze of tamarind or, failing that, of lemon. But
in the meantime we have these ground to powder and moistened
with water to make a thick, golden-brown paste.

Joseph always starts cooking in the same way: by putting a
chopped onion or two into a saucepan with some fat. If he were
in India this fat would be *ghee*—very pure clarified butter—here
it may be lard, dripping or oil. When the onions are browning
he puts in his curry paste and lets it remain with the onions for a
while before adding the meat or vegetables, or whatever may be
the projected basis of the curry.

In India a pulp made by pounding the flesh of a green coconut
would be added, and Joseph ingeniously extracts a sort of milk
from desiccated coconut and uses this when the curry needs
moistening. With fish curry he uses some of the dried coconut,
adding it at the same time as his paste. This gives to the dreary
fillets of cod which are often the only fish purchasable hereabouts,
a most agreeable vitality and flavour. He has another way of
obtaining, in the absence of coconut, the consistency required:
it is by adding tomatoes peeled and pulped, or tomato pulp which
is made from our own tomatoes and bottled in sufficient quantities to last through the year.

Meanwhile the rice is put on. If it is to be plain boiled rice the
procedure is a simple one. First the rice is washed two or three
times in cold water to rid it of rice-dust and loose starch. Then
it is put in a very large saucepan of water with about half a level
teaspoonful of salt to each cup of rice. There are Indian cooks
who maintain that this water should be boiling when the rice goes

in, there are others who say it should be cold and brought to the boil, and there are those like Joseph who believe that this is an academic point and that the rice is not in the end affected by it. The important thing is that there should be plenty of water, that it should boil with the rice in it, then be left to simmer for the time necessary to cook the rice. Herein lies the element of magic. It is impossible to state the precise time needed, yet all depends on that. Rice cooked for two minutes too little will be hard and indigestible, that cooked for the same period too long will be soggy and mushed. The Indian cook knows to a moment when to remove it, but can only say in explanation that he takes it off 'when it is cooked'. The time will vary with the kind of rice used, and, I begin to believe, with the shape of the saucepan, the state of the weather or the position of the moon. But it will be somewhere between twelve and sixteen minutes.

Thereafter it is strained, and should be ready to serve, but if it is in the least sticky, if its flakes do not fall singly from the hand like crisp snow, it should be washed through with cold water and left in the cullender in the oven to get warm again.

In the first year or two after the war, when rice was unobtainable, we were put to some curious shifts. My literary agents in New York and Buenos Aires were told that if they could not sell the American or Spanish rights of my books, at least they could send me rice, and responded generously, but even then supplies would run out from time to time and we would have to depend on *chapatis*. This unleavened bread Joseph makes simply by mixing a rather dry dough of salted wholemeal flour and water, rolling it thin, cutting it to circles the size of side-plates, and cooks by laying them, floured, in a dry frying-pan over a medium gas-ring. Or *paratas*, which are the same except that they are buttered before being put in the frying-pan, so that they are richer and more golden. Both are excellent, and can be eaten even when there is already rice with curry. It is also possible to purchase in England packets of *popadom*—wafers made of a very fine flour which are fried to a fragile crispness.

In the matter of chutneys Joseph is apt to show an indifference disappointing to English people, who are accustomed to consider them as the most important part of an Indian meal. He has no use for that sweet and sticky jam made from mangos, preferring simple chutneys of our own providing. Rings of raw onion sprinkled with red pepper, or onions, tomatoes and capsicums chopped and mixed with chilli sauce, are all that he thinks improve a meat curry, though for vegetable curries he makes a paste by pounding green chillies, coconut, mint, lemon, garlic and salt, moistening it with vinegar. He will countenance a sour pickle made of green mango and chillies which may sometimes be bought in England, but has no use for our own green-tomato or other chutneys.

Making the great Mogul dish, *biriani*, can be an infinitely complicated process, and in its finest forms it is made from traditional recipes only known to certain Muslim cooks. A *biriani* for a wedding, for instance, would need a whole day and several cooks, who would start with a long conference to apportion the various tasks. Joseph makes a much-simplified form of it which he prefers to call by the less pretentious name of a chicken *pulao*. For this he starts by frying onions in plenty of butter, adding his spices and herbs, which are cumulatively called *masala*, then adding the chicken, which has been parboiled and jointed. When this is golden-brown, the rice, damp from washing, is put in and left to simmer till it has absorbed the butter. Then stock, or the liquor in which the chicken has been boiled, is added in exactly the quantity which will be absorbed by the rice when the whole dish is cooked. This will be found to be about two cupfuls of stock to one of uncooked rice. Finally some seedless raisins, blanched almonds, cloves, cardamoms, peppercorns, cinnamon and enough turmeric to colour the rice, are stirred in. The dish can be garnished with shreds of onion crisply fried, or finely chopped hard-boiled egg, or both.

Indians do not as a rule regard any kind of sweet as part of a meal, though they eat fruit after curry. Joseph makes one Tamilian sweet called *korkas*, a kind of waffle for which he uses a special implement brought from his own country.

The Store-cupboard

I

IF good cooking is inspired by pride more than by greed, so, let us admit, are the lesser arts, scarcely more than hobbies, of preserving, bottling, drying and pickling. Shelves in the still-room or larder lined with bottles and jars in which the fruits of summer are stored for winter use—this is a common ambition, and promotes more business with syrup and vinegar than does a mere need for the things when they are out of season. But pride in such a store is legitimate, for it cannot be made without a great deal of hard work and lively interest. No one bored by such things could achieve them through a sense of duty or an aching to economize.

Our proudest achievement came almost by chance. The sweet-chestnut tree in the garden showered down so many firm little chestnuts that we decided to experiment with them. No cookery book in my long row of these had a recipe for chestnuts in syrup, however, even Mrs. Beeton being content with candied chestnuts. Everyone could tell me how to make *marrons glacés*, but no one gave details of this far more useful confection. When I had examined more books old and new and found that they were silent on the subject, I grew interested and enquired at the shops which sold *marrons* in syrup at about a guinea a jar. These, it appeared, came from France, no English firm troubling with them. The demand in any case was 'very limited', as well it might be at that price.

I soon found that our own little chestnuts were unsuitable, being small and fragile. The large foreign chestnuts which were sold last winter at a shilling a pound lent themselves far better to the purpose. A good deal of trial and error was necessary before I discovered that they could only be blanched if they were boiled for five or ten minutes then left in the same water while the first of them were pulled out of their jackets and dropped into a bowl of cold water and lemon-juice to wait their turn. Any that were broken in the process of blanching were at once discarded to be used in other ways.

The actual preparation is simple enough. The chestnuts are put into preserving jars, which are then filled with a syrup of medium thickness coloured a rich brown by burnt sugar. These are then put in a rather low oven and left simmering for an hour, or even longer. They are almost filled up from a saucepan of spare syrup kept boiling for the purpose and a little rum and a few drops of vanilla added to each bottle before they are screwed down. They will keep, to my knowledge, for eighteen months; indeed, they improve with keeping.

When a dozen jars of them stood on the store-cupboard shelf, uniform in size and colour, they seemed to demand as a label something more auspicious than the strip of stamp paper which is usually stuck on jampots. Just at that time I had to review a new and inspiring book by Miss Nell Heaton* in which I found a plea for the extravagance of a specially printed label. 'It is every bit as justifiable as a booklover's bookplate,' she says comfortingly. It happened that a few weeks earlier an itinerant artist had done a black-and-white sketch of the house, as trim and detailed as an architect's blue print, and I had a block made of this to form the heading of a small label. This has been a matter of childish but lively satisfaction to me as the store of bottled and pickled things has grown. It suggests professionalism—an ideal in such matters.

2

An unpromising material is rhubarb, its stringy stems, sharp with acid, seeming to demand quantities of precious sugar out of all proportion to its value. Stanbridge quotes an old saying —'Spring cabbage and rhubarb at Whitsun', but neither sounds more than mildly interesting, and I find that after eating fresh rhubarb once or twice in the spring I grow impatient for less common fruits. But rhubarb in winter—that's another matter.

* *A Calendar of Country Receipts*, by Nell Heaton (Faber and Faber).

Somehow the sticks which seem scentless and ordinary in sunlight take on qualities of fragrance and sweetness in November and December, or grace a flaky tart in January, or make a wickedly unseasonable Fool in February. So we put up a dozen bottles, cutting the stems on a marked board to obtain uniform length, and not forgetting a few drops of cochineal in the syrup.

Again it is to Miss Nell Heaton that I owe the only rhubarb jam of distinction as yet, I believe, compounded—rhubarb and angelica jam. This, a year or more after making, is quite remarkably pungent and vinous, a sort of liqueur of jams not to be spread meanly on bread and butter, but served in great dollops with some sweet, or piled on a wafer biscuit.

Other fruits which are bottled and lined up like the Brigade of Guards in my store cupboard are all more or less conventional, and conventionally done. Pears from the garden which will not keep in the fruit loft are peeled, bisected and cooked for twenty minutes in their bottles and in their syrup. A drop of colouring helps these to blush attractively and a little brandy in each bottle is a worth-while addition. Gooseberries in the same way, each one pricked with a pin before bottling to prevent them from shrinking to the appearance of wrinkled brown raisins. But bottled strawberries shall never again be attempted here, for if successful they are but wet and over-sweet parodies of their delicious selves, a messy, syrupy stew which would have been better as jam, while if unsuccessful, as is nearly always the case, they shrivel to the size of raspberries and rise to the top of the bottle, where they huddle in a sad little shoal, floating on a pint of useless pink syrup.

Strawberry jam—that luscious nursery favourite for which the most sour and peppery adult keeps a weakness—is not hard to make after a fashion, but tricky if the colour and consistency are to be right. There is a temptation, I suppose, to use grocer's pectin for this, but I am yet to be convinced that it is necessary or in any way an improver of any preserve.

Raspberry jam is the easiest and most rewarding of them all, needing only two commodities: the fruit itself and sugar. Loganberry is sharper in taste and duller in colour, but a useful contrast. Blackcurrant jam can be better than most and 'sets' with commendable ease. Blackberry jelly, though of saccharine sweetness, is a favourite always with very young visitors, and since most of our stock is in any case for them, and for some of their elders who admit to liking jam, our own consumption being negligible, a few pots of it are in the store-cupboard.

Commercial jam-makers nowadays are either much more clever or much more conscientious than of old, for the products sold by the best firms have a remarkable verisimilitude. Still, little though I eat of either, I can instantly distinguish the commercial variety from the home-made, and wonder whether it is not the much-vaunted pectin which is responsible. This conspicuous distinction makes the easy work of jam-making worth while, since visitors from London, I notice, though in their homes contemptuous of such lollipop confections, eat them with enthusiasm in the country house in which they have been made.

3

For my own taste there is a better use for the meagre dole of sugar which, from the glutted plenty of the West Indies, is all that is allowed to us. This is in the making of jellies to be eaten with various kinds of meat, game and poultry. We have this custom in common with the Germans and Eastern Europeans, and not with the French, to whom it seems somewhat bizarre and uncouth to eat red-currant jelly with mutton or hare. I must confess I do not find it so, and have carried the principle even farther than convention warrants by having a few jars each of marjoram and thyme jelly made in addition to red-currant and mint. Thyme jelly gives a summer savour to hare and rabbit, while marjoram jelly can be used wherever red-currant was customary. It is not easy, however, to make these with their leaf fragments spread evenly through the jelly, and in any case a good deal of green colouring is necessary. Apples may be used as the jelly-forming agent.

They suggest in turn the pickles and chutneys and sauces which are so much more important than jams. There is a green tomato chutney made by stewing slowly for two-and-a-half hours in vinegar the tomatoes which have failed to ripen at the end of the

o

season, say three pounds of them sliced with two ounces of salt, half a pound each of sugar, chopped onion and apple, spices, pepper, some red chillies, the juice of a lemon, some bruised ginger and six ounces of mixed seeded raisins, sultanas and currants with a few drops of green colouring. We make a dozen pounds of this, and use them all.

Much the same ingredients can be cooked rather longer, then passed through a sieve, and the fine pulp thus obtained reboiled with more vinegar for an excellent green-tomato sauce, appreciably better than the various tomato sauces turned out by the pickle factories.

Of chutneys there are of course such countless varieties that we make new kinds each year, though the sweeter, sicklier, fruitier kinds are avoided.

The 'straight' pickling of several vegetables which are useful in winter is done in rather larger quantities. Beetroot, for instance, which makes a salad with the refreshing witloofs of chicory plants which we draw from the roots in a dark shed in winter, needs only to be boiled, diced, covered with cold spiced vinegar and brought to the boil in preserving bottles to seal. Red and white cabbages for *sauerkraut* seem almost an essential, especially since one can easily obtain the little springy sausages sold as Vienna sausages, with which it can be eaten. The cabbage is shredded and pressed down between layers of salt and caraway seeds and left for three or four weeks. Nasturtium seeds pickled are rather better than capers, though gathering them while they are still green and fresh is a long and tiresome job.

French beans provide a quandary. Kept in a jar between layers of common salt and soaked overnight before use they retain their flavour, but look drab and yellow, while bottled in brine with a little sugar they keep their appearance but lose their taste. We plump for the former method.

4

Herbs which are to be dried for the winter must be gathered before they bloom. The best time is on a dry morning before the sun has been long on them. They should be dried in the sun, I suppose, but we use a rather deceitful method which I am sure would not be much approved by Gerard. They are laid on newspapers on the shelves above the tank in the airing-cupboard and in a day or two rubbed through a coarse sieve. But herbs and flowers for *pot-pourri* must be dried in the open, then sprayed with various oils and essences—neroli, rose, lavender, musk, cinnamon cloves. Orris root is sprinkled in, and a handful of rock-salt. This mixture, in a few jars, keeps the whole house fragrant, and when one enters it on a winter's evening, when the anthracite stove has been alight all day, the scent is almost over-powering. 'Popery', my fiercely Protestant aunt thought was the spelling of the name, 'because it was such a mixture', she used to add grimly.

5

Clearly much of this bottling and pickling is uneconomical, especially if the cost of one's time is assessed at all flatteringly. It is done here because it is interesting, a country pastime if you like, a relaxation after the strain of too much writing. Since the days when this house was newly built most of the processes of a still-room have become commercialized, so that a great deal of time can be saved by purchasing by the bottle or tin the things now made in it with such affectionate care. They will not be so good when mass-produced in factories, but they will not in all cases be different enough to justify the labour. Bottled gooseberries, for instance, do not vary much in quality. Merely sentimental considerations—that these things have been done just so in English kitchens for centuries, that disappearing arts should be kept in being, that ancient formulæ are used—are more than ever irrelevant. Only one thing justifies it all : the pleasure one takes both in the tasks themselves and their results. For me it is considerable.

Books

I

I WOULD make no strong objection to a definition of 'home' as the place in which one's books are kept, and not the least of my reasons for coming to live in the country was that here I could collect unhampered by restrictions of space. Books, I decided, must not over-run the house, must not be found in stacks or be crowded into rooms where they would be out of place, but when the shelves which lined my study chest-high had been filled there would always be the warehouse, which could be turned into a library. Thus a most profitable and ancient pursuit could continue unchecked till my death should come—at a suitably remote date, I hoped—to disperse the collection. The envelopes which I would welcome most, I foresaw, would be those which contained booksellers' catalogues, and the local auction sales I would attend would have books among the items of furniture offered.

Although it has not, of course, worked out like that, there has been sufficient truth in the picture for me to feel that I have had more pleasure from book-collecting in my two years here than at any time previously. The long, leisurely hours needed to clean and look after books, to notice the collector's points about them, even, if pushed to it, to read them, have not been mine and perhaps never will be. (I distrust all hobbies which can only be enjoyed 'when I have the time'.) But I have been able to consider them as the fruits of many years' search and selection, to examine them and add to them and read them because I want to do so, and not because I need to turn up some reference. I have, at last, enjoyed them.

2

I do not know why book-collectors seek to justify their passion for first editions with curious arguments, saying that they wish to possess a book as it appeared on the morning of its publication two centuries ago, to read the very type which the contemporary critics may have read, to turn the sheets which Dr. Johnson perhaps turned, to note the defects which the 'Scotch reviewers' found. This seems to me a mite sentimental and specious. Nor am I much impressed by the contention that the original editions of books should be collected as the originals of pictures are, or early impressions of prints. I do not think that first-edition collecting needs any justification, for it is an end in itself, but it may well be remembered that it gives deep and lasting satisfaction, it performs some service to literature, it is an interest which never grows stale, and it stays the selling-up to people of less impoverished or better-managed countries of a part of our national heritage.

For me it has had a special advantage—it has enabled me to continue collecting books since boyhood, in bad times and good, to form a library which would have been wholly beyond my means if I had not, while still in my teens, begun to gain the strange esoteric knowledge which is the stock-in-trade of the antiquarian bookseller and collector. When I 'lisped in numbers' it was of the misprint on page 116, the twelve advertisement sheets at the end of the first issue, the date of the rare second edition. I prattled of 8vo and 12mo, of boards uncut and incunabula, and with this miscellaneous knowledge added to a student's acquaintance with literature, I was able to trust my wits against the booksellers, I was able to pay for the books I wanted to keep by selling at a profit the books of value I had bought with them. Except during the years when I had a bookshop I have never made any monetary profit from buying and selling books, but on the other hand I calculate that my collection has cost me nothing in money, and the time I have given to it has been some of the most happily spent in my life.

It is still possible for anyone who is interested in books to do this; it may even be easier today than in the years when I went to country auction sales and conscientiously examined every bundle or looked round the shelves of small bookshops. But where, I wonder, are the young collectors of today? Or the old ones, for that matter? The great antiquarian booksellers of twenty and thirty years ago have become mere exporters, buying up our private libraries and shipping the books to the United States as fast as they can be packed. There are English collectors left, of course, but few of them can afford to compete with the Americans, who can buy for five dollars a book which is priced at two pounds. In a calculable number of years there will scarcely be a book of any distinction or value left in private hands in England; the rows of calf-bound volumes which, shut away in a rather gloomy room called the library, were a feature of every country house, will have vanished from English shelves, and instead of our first folios and beautifully bound sets we shall have the coloured comics and Westerns which we import from America for the dollars earned by the sale of fine editions.

This is no forced Jeremiad, as any honest bookseller will admit, or any post-office clerk dealing with the vast and never-ceasing outward flow of book-parcels. But it is not entirely a question of economics. For some reason hard to perceive, our interest in books, in the actual and physical things, has ebbed.

'Do you collect books, then?' I asked a woman who was explaining to me the difficulty of packing them and moving them to her new home.

'Well, I have belonged to a book society and a book club for eight years, and have all their monthly choices,' she replied brightly, speaking, it seemed to me, a farewell to the age of bibliophiles.

What an age it was! I am glad to be old enough to remember it, at least in its later glories, when all the world, it seemed, was interested in Stevenson's falling market or the sudden rise in Herman Melville's prices, or the steady increase in the best eighteenth-century stuff or the unprecedented figure paid for a first of Adam Smith's *Wealth of Nations*. When on the Stock Exchange they could quote the current price of a *New Arabian Nights* almost as readily as that of New Pioneer mining shares. When the T. J. Wise forgeries were as widely discussed as a contemporary murder, and booksellers' catalogues were studied by passengers on the Underground as fervently as are strip cartoons today. Nowadays book-collecting is a more lonely hobby.

3

I can explain the limits and aims of my collection in a very few words. I collect books on two special subjects—gypsies and cookery. I collect first editions of those modern authors whose books I expect to want to read more than once. For the rest and of the past I try to form a library of standard works. This means self-discipline, a refusal to be attracted to the superficially desirable book which may be eagerly read but need not be possessed. It means also stern discrimination and economy of shelf-space, but no foreseeable time at which the collection will be considered complete—a lamentable cul-de-sac which, in the end, the bibliophile never has to face.

Most collectors have one or two highly personal specialities—books on brewing or butterflies, Africa or aeronautics; books with fore-edge paintings or in signed bindings; missals or manuscripts; books with coloured plates or early children's books. The advantage of this, apart from its absorbing interest, is that the collector soon becomes a specialist with a greater knowledge of values in his particular field than the general bookseller. Moreover, as his accumulation grows, new discoveries are more and more exciting as they become rarer. It is essential, I think, not to choose a subject so wide that it is discouraging and demands a library too large for a private house, but on the other hand a subject can be so specialized and limited that a year's search will exhaust most of its potentialities.

My own—the subject of English gypsies—was started because I became intersted in them at a time when it was almost as cheap to buy books as to belong to one of the lending libraries which supply reference books on obscure subjects. I bought in the conventional way from a bookseller who had advertised my wants in the trade paper and quoted to me at a small profit the books offered to him, for a collection of books on a specialized subject can scarely be made by any other means. Now and again something may be unearthed in a shop or offered in auction, but for the most part it must be found for the collector by the bookseller. This is not to say that it is a poor investment; rather the contrary, for whereas a number of items in one category may be worth, individually, very little, an important collection of books on one subject may be most valuable.

I have written elsewhere * of the literature of the gypsy and tried to pay a late tribute to some of the men who followed Borrow, like Charles Godfrey Leland, a quaintly erudite American; like Francis Hindes Groome, an Archdeacon's son who twice ran away with gypsy girls and who wrote three books about gypsies which seem to me classics; like John Sampson, that scholarly librarian who made a rich anthology of gypsy literature, *The Wind on the Heath*, and wrote the best book on the Romani language, *The Dialect of the Gypsies of Wales*. It has been delightful to get together their books and all the others on the people they loved. A subject of this kind has an appeal so limited that the *Journal of the Gypsy Lore Society*, a brave biennial which has fought its way through seven decades, has a world-wide circulation of only a few hundred copies. But from the book-collector's point of view there is a curious advantage in this —none of my books has been quoted to me as an 'association' copy; indeed, no bookseller would think such associations worth mentioning in a catalogue, yet most of them have belonged to some other of the small devoted company of gypsy-lovers whose names are familiar to me. My copy of Charles Godfrey Leland's *Gypsy Sorcery and Fortune-Telling* (1891), a folio decorated and illustrated by the author, belonged to John Sampson, and has his signature on the title-page. That strange unsuccessful novel by Francis Hindes Groome which he so mistakenly insisted on calling *Kriegspiel* (1896) bears, in my copy, a presentation signed by Groome. A little vellum-bound monograph by William Chambers called *Exploits and Anecdotes of the Scottish Gypsies* (1886) belonged in 1896 to Herbert Wilson Greene, a contributor to the *Journal of the Gypsy Lore Society*, while Paul Bataillard's monograph *Nouvelles Recherches sur l'Apparition et la Dispersion des Bohêmes en Europe* (1849), as well as Raper's translation of Grellmann's *Dissertation on the Gipsies* (1787), belonged to Bath Charles Smart, one of the joint authors of *The Dialect of the*

* *The Moon in My Pocket* (Sampson Low).

English Gypsies (1875). An exhaustive account of Scottish Romanies and their associates called *The Tinkler Gypsies* (1907) has a signed presentation from its author, Andrew McCormick, and R. A. Scott Macfie's *With Gypsies in Bulgaria* (1916) contains an inscription in the beautiful handwriting of that fine scholar and writer, the inscription being to Fred Shaw, whose photographs of gypsies illustrate many a *rai's* book. Charles Godfrey Leland's *The Gypsies* belonged to Charles Strachey, who wrote an essay on 'Shakespeare and the Romany' in 1892, while Archdeacon F. G. Ackerley, one of the true *rais*, used for his review and annotated my copy of that excellent, forgotten novel of gypsy life by E. S. Stevens, *Allward* (1915). A long-ago crank named James Simson, who wrote pamphlets to prove that Bunyan and Mrs. Carlyle were gypsies, has inscribed my copy of one of these, and it has since belonged to Lady Eleanor Smith, while a pamphlet by T. W. Thompson, *The Ceremonial Customs of the British Gipsies* (1912), bears his own signature. Of gypsy-lovers, at least, the cliché may be repeated—it *is* a small world.

This collection of English gypsy books is not, thank heavens, complete; but it cannot easily be added to. The shelf of books on cookery, food and wine, on the other hand, contains only a small nucleus of the innumerable books which may one day swell its numbers. It is good to be starting an accumulation at the time when another has reached the stage of long waiting and rare acquisitions.

4

A 'library of a standard English works' sounds a formidable and dusty thing, but can be less awe-inspiring than it sounds. The poets, at least down to the middle of the last century, are accessible in a supremely well-printed and annotated collection: the famous Aldine Edition, which one of the great publishers of the last century, William Pickering, produced in the 'thirties and 'forties. It was later taken over by Bell and Daldy, who changed Pickering's sign—a reproduction of the anchor and dolphin of the original Aldus Manutius, the fifteenth-century Venetian publisher—to the swinging bell which may be seen on books

published by George Bell and Sons to this day, but continued
to have them printed by Whittingham at the Chiswick Press.
Pickering's collection had fifty-three volumes, but Bell added to
them more recent poets.

What magnificent printing and book production this was!
The notes separate from the text, the type clear, the ornamental
capitals and end-pieces neither too affected nor too formal, the
size of the book, small 8vo, making it most convenient to hold,
the paper of the right thickness and purity, the margins adequate
but not ostentatiously wide.   There have been more lavish, more
original, perhaps more beautiful books before and since the
Aldine Edition, but none in which the text is more clearly visible,
more seductively easy to read.

My own Aldines, the original fifty-three of them, are bound in
half crimson morocco, and cost just eight pounds. I have
found some of Bell's later additions—Shelley and Coleridge, for
example—which are differently bound, thus serving to break the
long lines of crimson on the shelves, while a few other poetic
works, like those of Browning, issued in volumes of identical
size, continue the line.   Thus in forty inches of shelf-space it is
possible to have most of the English poetry of six centuries
aligned, a shining phalanx of coloured morocco and calf.

Fashion had its influence, even here. The Aldine Edition
contained no Blake and no Donne, no Skelton, none of the Meta-
physical or Restoration poets, no Gay, Herrick, Moore or
Christopher Smart.   On the other hand, Charles Churchill, a
rhyming satirist of the eighteenth century, has two volumes, and
Henry Kirke White, James Beattie, Thomas Parnell and Mark
Akenside have one apiece.   This is the penalty for collecting so
much in a uniform edition, but it is a penalty I gladly pay by
buying the Nonesuch editions of Blake and Donne and filling in
the other gaps as cheerfully.

There is a 'best edition'—in the bookseller's phrase—of most of
the classics, a very popular *Works* of Sterne, for instance, is the
1803 edition in four volumes, which is often found in a fine
ding. If I had been given my choice I would probably
ess this, but it happened that many years ago in Stirling I

looked in the windows of a furniture shop to see a set of ten volumes bound in plain old calf standing on a bureau, to give it an air of authenticity, perhaps. I bought them for a pound—the 1780 edition of Sterne. Such are our natural tricks of rationalization that I am convinced now that I prefer it to any other.

I cannot say that of my four-volume Poe, which is printed in poor type on discoloured paper and was issued in New York in 1881 by a publisher with the curious name of Widdleton. It belonged, it seems, to someone called Belle Gore, who has written " Poor fellow!" beside Poe's portrait. Even its handsome calf binding scarcely compensates for its dim type.

It is not always realized that eighteenth- and early nineteenth-century books were issued in paper or boards and that the ornate leather bindings in which they are usually found were added by their owners. What craftsmanship our binders had then, and what a superb display of it there must have been in any great library! My set of Chesterfield's Letters, for instance, though none too well printed by John, the brother of Robert Dodsley, is bound in calf with red and green labels and backstrips exquisitely tooled in gilt. A similar though even more elaborate and brilliant binding adorns my Collected Works of Peter Pindar (John Wolcot), that lovable, voluble, irrepressible character who started life as a physician, became a parson in Jamaica, returned to be a doctor in Truro and a satirist in London. Joseph Addison's work is in six volumes of navy-blue calf, and Goldsmith in four of very simple design.

I would like to form a Collection of Unpopular Classics, for I seem almost alone in wanting a number of them. I am told that I am either a freak, a bore or a liar when I venture to say that I have read—nearly always with interest and pleasure—the novels of Scott which line a whole shelf in twenty-five calf-bound volumes of the Centenary Edition of 1871. 'Furniture, of course,' said a bookseller friend when he saw their gleaming gilt labels, but I resent the term most bitterly as applied to any book which I own, and particularly to these. Also among the unpopular or unfashionable would be the four volumes of Works of Douglas Jerrold, or the three of Oliver Wendell Holmes, the collected writings of James Hogg, the Ettrick Shepherd, and some novels by Maria Edgeworth, including her four-volume *Patronage*, a wordy story with the overpowering Lord Oldborough stealing the show.

Would the novels of George Eliot be consigned to the same library nowadays? It is hard to name a more unfashionable author or one who commits more literary sins, if her work is judged by today's standards. She will even 'hear her reader exclaim' or generalize philosophically for whole paragraphs, or write as if she were chiefly concerned with making her prose a suitable hunting-ground for the calendar-maker who wants a quotation for every day in the year. But I would not be without a tall blue-cloth Library Edition published by Blackwood in 1901.

A collector would have to be lucky today to find the Thornton Edition of the novels of the sisters Brontë at anything but an exorbitant price. It is in twelve very handsome volumes, bound in buckram with a heavy design in gilt; its type is bold, its paper rich and deckled. Moreover, the Brontës are 'in', while poor George Eliot is 'out'. But when I discovered that set stacked in a corner of a Cheltenham auction-room it was knocked down to me for the price of so many cheap editions. The excellent Knutsford Edition of the works of Mrs. Gaskell was bought at the same time, and gave me my first introduction to those good novels *Mary Barton*, *Sylvia's Lovers*, and the rest of them, which have been so overshadowed by *Cranford*. Richard Bentley issued my neat green-cloth library set of Jane Austen's novels. And so on through other classics.

I believe, then, in the standard set, I am not afraid of the uniform edition, I do not think that a row of books in identical binding strikes a chill of anticipated boredom in the mind. I would rather not own a book, would rather depend on loan or purchase when the need arises, than crowd my shelves with cheap editions. Everyman, World's Classics and the like, excellent for their purpose though they may be, clearly printed and neatly bound, seem to me books with little spaciousness or dignity about them. , weight, large type, a worthy binding seem to me essentials ll reprinted classics.

5

Which brings me to a few shelves of books which by no means
conform to all these puritan standards of utility I have set myself.
I would not presume to call this a 'collection' of fine bindings,
indeed the few I own have come fortuitously for the most part.
But now and again I have not been able to resist the temptation to
keep one of these rococo adornments of the library, these exquisite gewgaws of 'leather or prunella'. Sometimes their
contents are worth the craftsmanship devoted to them, occasionally, I must confess, they are not. I am content to look at the
binding itself.

There are a few early bindings and some rich eighteenth-
century ones, but it is in a period slightly later than these that I
take most pleasure, and in books which could be collected before
the war at a few shillings each and even now are often marked at
a not wholly exorbitant price, little books in the quite matchless
binding of Regency times with plates, usually, by one of the great
illustrators who flourished then. For instance, a 12mo *Junius*
bound for the Marquis of Lothian of that time and so, not
surprisingly, incorporating a thistle in its minutely detailed
tooling. Or a tiny apple-green book which contains the poetical
works of a certain John Cunningham who wrote a successful
farce called *Love in a Mist* and anticipated heroes of motor-
racing with the verse—

> 'Tis strange, the many-marshal'd stars,
> That ride yon sacred round,
> Should keep among their rapid cars,
> A silence so profound!

This is from the Chiswick Press of that great printer Charles
Whittingham, so is a minute Bacon's Essays with a Stothard
title-page engraved by (John) Romney. This is bound in
beige morocco, and uniform with it, except in details of binding,
is that best-seller of the time, *Elizabeth, or the Exiles of Siberia.*
They were issued, I find now, in 'Whittingham's Cabinet
Library', of which a score of titles are listed at the end of *Elizabeth*,
'in a neat pocket size with embellishments by Corbould, Westall,

Stothard etc.' Any part of the library, the publisher generously says, 'may be had separate'; today it could only be 'had separate', but what a pleasant, comparatively inexpensive and rewarding piece of collecting it would be to get together the whole of 'Whittingham's Cabinet Library' once more.

Whittingham also printed for the publisher John Sharpe a number of slightly larger books with Westall plates which are nearly always found in fine bindings. I see prices like one shilling still written in these by the booksellers who sold them to me before the war: Falconer's *Shipwreck*, Young's *Night Thoughts* and so on—best-sellers in their day. Alike in size and binding, though inevitably with shamrock leaves and harps in evidence, is Moore's *Irish Melodies*, and in plum-coloured morocco another forgotten but once hugely popular book, Campbell's *Pleasures of Hope*.

These and other odds and ends of binding are no more than enough to whet the appetite. However expensive and difficult it may be to possess fine bindings, more collectors at home, one hopes, will be attracted to them, for only collectors can provide the means of saving them from being turned into blotters and cigarette boxes, or being shipped to the United States—a traffic which seems to me little less criminal than the slave-running of a century ago.

There is another kind of book which, in a good library edition, should, I think, form part of a general collection like mine, that is the 'one' book of certain authors whose other work is less important or readable or could only be kept at hand if space were almost unlimited. Charles Reade, for instance, wrote a number of novels, of which *The Cloister and the Hearth* was his third. I suppose that a conscientious student might wish to read *Peg Woffington* or *Hard Cash*, but almost anyone interested in the fiction of the last century needs to refer to *The Cloister and the Hearth*, that strangely persuasive narrative, so full of sick prejudice yet so triumphantly a good story. Then who but a biographer of Charles Kingsley would find opportunity, in a hurried lifetime, to read more of his work than *Westward Ho!* and the *Water Babies*, unless perhaps, recovering from an illness in a lonely cottage in which it was the only printed thing, *Hereward the Wake*? It is surprising to find how many writers there are whose sole valuable output can be contained in a single volume, or, to be less dictatorial, from whom I wish to possess no more than one book, or at the most two. Like Bunyan, whose *Pilgrim's Progress* I have in a modern illustrated quarto, while *The Holy War* is in an old calfbound volume. Like *The Decameron*, which is charmingly illustrated by Thomas Derrick. Like *The Deeds and Sayings of the Giant Gargantua and his Son Pantagruel*. Like *The Surprising Adventures of Baron Munchausen*, which is in a pleasant edition published by the Medici Society. Or *The Compleat Angler*. Or *The Life of Lazarillo de Tormes*. Or De Coster's *The Legend of the Glorious Adventures of Tyl Ulenspiegel in the Land of Flanders and Elsewhere*, which is as frequently taken down as any book I have. It is a white cloth quarto beautifully produced by Chatto and Windus, translated by Geoffrey Whitworth, illustrated by Albert Delstanche.

But this goes on, I find. Who would really read much more of De Quincey than *Confessions of an Opium-Eater*, even if the whole of his works in their sixteen volumes stood at hand? I once possessed a first edition of the *Opium-Eater*, an insignificant-looking little book, the sale of which realized enough to buy a dozen of the edition I have, a handsome small folio with a long introduction by George Saintsbury, who loved literature almost as much as wine. I do not know whether Joel Chandler Harris ever wrote anything more than *Uncle Remus*; the one beloved volume, as Grant Richards issued it in 1902 with J. A. Shepherd's illustrations, is enough for me. Nor do I want to study the prejudiced and pompous literary criticism of Edmund Gosse, but his *Father and Son* in the Booklover's or first illustrated edition of 1912 I greatly prize. Perhaps in having, alone of James Morier's novels, *The Adventures of Hajji Baba of Ispahan* I am discriminating foolishly; I am more confident that although *John Halifax, Gentleman* is a favourite novel of mine (its gentleness, sincerity and rich Victorian atmosphere are a tonic after a diet of febrile moderns), I do not lose much by possessing no more of the novels which Mrs. Craik (Dinah Maria Mulock) wrote after marrying a partner in the publishing firm of Macmillans. Does this book still sell, I wonder? My edition was issued in 1897, a sumptuous thing with illustrations by Hugh Riviere. *Uncle Tom's Cabin*, with Cruikshank plates, seems as fresh and lively as it was a century ago, when Mrs. Beeton's husband brought it to England, but somehow I cannot work up much interest in Harriet Beecher Stowe's *Agnes of Sorrento* unless it is to wonder what that magic word in a title inspired so long before Hugh Hastings used it for a naval play of notable authenticity.

There must be an end to this enumeration of 'one' books; indeed, I am amazed to find so many, and I reflect regretfully that hard-working novelists like G. P. R. James and James Payn, who wrote upwards of a hundred and sixty novels between them, are in oblivion now because among all their titles no book can be singled out in this way. But I cannot forget *The Ingoldsby Legends*—or does anyone read Barham's novel *My Cousin Nicholas*? Nor Mary Russell Mitford's *Our Village*, one of the books which Hugh Thomson distinguished with his immortal drawings. Or are there readers for *Belford Regis* and the rest? Nor Gilbert White's *Natural History of Selborne*.

I have kept my most treasured 'one' book till last—Joseph Henry Shorthouse's *John Inglesant*. This seems to me one of the greatest curiosities of our literature, a novel of quiet underground power which would seem to be written for a small circle of sympathetic readers, but which became a best-seller, a novel suffused with a highly esoteric kind of religiosity, full of curious and occult matters and remote erudition, yet a novel read as an exciting narrative. It is almost formless, it ignores the unities, it has steady but never high tension, yet it was acclaimed by most critics and a huge public. I remember the first time I read this singular book at the age of fourteen, reading far into the night with a shaded torch, with impatient wonder and almost feverish excitement. My copy is of the limited large paper edition in two volumes bound in olive buckram with a new preface which was issued in the year after its first publication. Both volumes are inscribed identically 'Florence P. Anderson, with every good wish from the Author and Mrs. Shorthouse. J. Henry Shorthouse. Sarah Shorthouse. Lansdowne, Edgbaston, June 5th 1900.'

'The oddments and decorative pieces in my study'

7

Though many people deplore the decline in English book-collecting, the dwindling of private libraries of fine old books, there are less who regret the almost vanished cult of the modern first edition. It was an artificial thing, they say, promoted for quick profits and speculation. It applied a spurious valuation to contemporary literature, boosted certain writers out of all proportion to their worth and allowed slumps in the value of others which had no relation to the quality of their writings. It encouraged certain unscrupulous dealers to play the market at the expense of sound investment; it was a gamble, a stunt, a calamity.

But if early first editions are to be collected, surely it is legitimate to try to pick from among contemporaries those whose values will be augmented by time. As new books appear it is as easy and inexpensive to buy a first as a second edition, and this may at least keep its value, instead of being worth no more than pence. There is satisfaction in finding one's taste, rare and unpopular at the time, endorsed later. I remember Michael Sadleir once telling me that he collected W. B. Maxwell's first editions. He was probably alone in this, and until now nothing has happened to corroborate his judgment, but it was a challenge surely well worth making. Admittedly there has been a good deal of dodgy behaviour by dealers; I remember hearing of a firm which had 'laid down a bin of H. G. Wells', for instance. There have been sudden spurts promoted by the trade which have sent the first edition prices of not very significant writers soaring to absurdity, like the boom in Mary Webb, but they need not discourage one from this expression of interest in the best work of our time, this way of paying a small tribute to the writers one admires, this mark of trust in the permanence of their appeal. Its satisfactions are personal. No one but their owner is likely to take much pleasure in a row of cloth-bound volumes which look like all others, or to rejoice in the inverted numeral on page 108 which shows that some book is a first issue, but that should not lessen the collector's pride and happiness in having found them, or his joy in the chase.

P

When the bottom dropped out of the market in modern firsts the book trade as a whole rejoiced, feeling that its artificial fluctuations had encouraged speculators rather than collectors. Never again, they said, will there be such crazy lack of proportion, and quoted some of the freak prices of the late nineteen-twenties—very large sums for Galsworthy or Arnold Bennett firsts, premiums for A. A. Milne or D. H. Lawrence. A scarce book will keep its price, they maintained, but collectors will not be asked for a guinea for a book which only a week or two before was in the bookshops at seven and six. In that I concur, though the value of my own collection has fallen with the rest. I do not want to see the return of false values and gambling in books, and I admit that few enough books published of recent years seem to promise much to the future. But I believe that the reaction has gone too far and that at the moment modern first editions offer the small investor with critical judgment a very promising field. At least he will enjoy himself.

8

I have been collecting modern first editions since I was a schoolboy. Many of the authors whose books are about me now are out of fashion both in the small world of bibliophiles and in the larger one of readers, so that it may seem mere pig-headedness which makes me regret none of them. A few are almost unknown or quite forgotten, others have become booming best-sellers. They must stand, nevertheless, as an index of my taste. It will be difficult to enumerate them without allowing a collector's comments to become at times a critic's, but I want to think of them chiefly as books in the concrete, physical sense.

By 'modern' first editions I mean, roughly, books published in or since the 1890's. It is an inadequate definition, but it will serve. It includes, for instance, Thomas Hardy, whose work I collect in the grand, tall Wessex Novels edition published by Osgood M'Ilvaine but augmented with uniformity by Harpers and Macmillans. Several volumes in this, like *Jude the Obscure*, are first editions, and the whole is a good thing to collect, since it may be found cheaply in odd volumes and once completed becomes valuable. Two books supplementary to this are a first American edition of *Life's Little Ironies*, which I keep because it belonged to Ellen Terry and has her signature and the date 1894 on the title-page, and a limited American edition of a tale called *Old Mrs. Chundle* which is inscribed by Hardy's widow.

There are two novelists of the end of the last century whose work I would dearly like to collect, but I have to be content with such of their books as chance sends me, so rare have they become. They are Henry James and George Gissing. The three-deckers of the former in their original binding have all been sent, I think, to the native land of that gentlemanly old *émigré*, while poor unsuccessful Gissing, who wanted so desperately much the fame and rewards which were his right, was published in small editions. W. H. Mallock, who wrote *The New Republic* and some rather dated novels, is easier to find.

William de Morgan, a verbose, sentimental yet lively story-teller who published his first novel at the age of sixty-seven, is not difficult to collect, though his *Joseph Vance* (1906) is a fairly rare book. Much harder to come by, and even now highly priced, are the five books which make up the whole literary output of Kenneth Grahame. A director of the Bank of England in his spare time, he applied himself to writing his dreamily beautiful children's books and one book of essays, *Pagan Papers*. It has taken me twenty years to find all of these, and even now some of my copies would not be considered by a bookseller to be 'in fine state', but here they are, their dates showing the minutely small output of the man, for his work came all within fourteen years. *Pagan Papers* (1894), *The Golden Age* (1895), *The Headswoman* (1898) (this was no more than a long short story), *Dream Days* (1899), and *The Wind in the Willows* (1908). I have also the limited large-paper edition of *The Wind in the Willows* signed by Kenneth Grahame in 1931, and a biography by his friend Patrick Chalmers, whom I remember as another banker who wrote some happy rhymes.

Then (George) Louis Becke—does anyone else collect his first editions now, I wonder? My copy of *By Reef and Palm* is signed, and seven other books of his have not been easy to accumulate.

But what a good, virile writer he was, and though his stories are set in a vanished world—the South Seas of eighty years ago—how green and living they seem today. No less so are the stories and sketches by his contemporary Hubert Crackanthorpe, but here we come in from far places to London and the stuffy and would-be sinful atmosphere of the 'nineties. The very titles seem to indicate the poised pen and tinted prose of the Yellow Age—*Wreckage : Seven Studies* (1893), *Sentimental Studies* (1895), *Vignettes* (1896) and, after his untimely death *Last Studies* (1897), with a valedictory preface by Henry James.

Less obscure now is the name of Stephen Crane, that meteoric American who stirred even Conrad to enthusiasm in the 'nineties and died with the century. My copy of his first little book of poems *The Black Riders* (1895) is inscribed by him to a friend—'Not at all reluctantly but with enthusiasm—From Stephen Crane, May 26, 1895'. *The Red Badge of Courage* (1895) and *George's Mother* (1896) were first published in America, and I am lucky to have them as issued there, but *The Third Violet* (1897) was brought out by Heinemann while Crane was over here. No two of his books came first from the same publisher, however, and *The Open Boat* (1898) was published in New York.

Another American, a baroque eccentric who could write so badly that the reader bites his lip in embarrassment, but also with a sort of high-powered, breathless inspiration which makes some of his work, it seems to me, unforgettable, was Edgar Saltus. He is the subject of surely the oddest biography ever written, a study of him by his second wife, who calls him ' Mr. Saltus' throughout the book and includes a portrait of herself with the caption, 'Marie Saltus, Sitting at the Table on which her Husband wrote his Books, burning Incense before a Siamese Buddha and Meditating on a Stanza from the Bhagavad-Gita.' But nothing could have been too bizarre as a memorial to Saltus; the man was an exotic, while his books were full of grandiose unreality, and had titles like *The Pomps of Satan*, *Mary of Magdala*, *Imperial Purple*—an almost hysterical piece of writing about the Caesars during which the author does not seem to pause once to take breath—*Love Throughout the Ages*.

Yet another American of the time whose books I collect with an assiduity that has already caused two shelves to be filled is Jack London, that madly generous success-boy whose Socialism was the real thing—a bare-knuckle crusade for the under-dog. He, too, could write excruciatingly badly—but Lord, how good he is at his best.

That is more than can be said of his two neighbours in my shelves—M. P. Shiel and Leonard Merrick. Every attempt to popularize their work has mysteriously failed. A collected edition of Merrick, each volume with a preface by a famous writer, was as unsuccessful as their original publication had been, and still memorable is Victor Gollancz's gallant but unsuccessful attempt to reissue the novels of Shiel. Yet Merrick's fault would not harm his reputation today, for it was only pessimism, after all—a yellow miasma of personal gloom which pervaded everything he wrote. Shiel was too lavish, perhaps, in design, in imagination, and most certainly in words. 'A world with ruby mountains and coloured moons, where all the lads are forever blowing the oboe and ring-doves roll their soft rondeaus,' is a quotation from, if not a specimen of, his dialogue. But the books of each of these two men in the picture-cloth bindings of the time are rare, quaint and readable.

Still in the first two decades of the century there is an embarrassment of wealth. I think there is no time in our literary history when so many and such varied fine novels were published in so short a period. Now the names crowd in as one looks back. Joseph Conrad, for instance, I collected before his prices rose to their phenomenal levels in the 'twenties, continued to collect during his boom and have collected during his present, surely very temporary, eclipse. 'You can still get a high price for a good *Nigger*,' a bookseller told me rather ambiguously the other day. He was thinking of that rare item, a first edition of *The Nigger of the Narcissus*, but the implication was that the days when any early Conrad was wanted by collectors are no more.

For three novelists of that time I have had to content myself with choosing the books which have meant most to me, since a complete collection of any of them would cover a wall. Of

Maurice Hewlett I have thrown out twenty or thirty good books and kept only the five little masterpieces—*Earthwork out of Tuscany* (1895), *The Forest Lovers* (1898), *Richard Yea-and-Nay* (1900), *Little Novels of Italy* (1902), *The Queen's Quair* (1904). I regret the necessity for this bitter discrimination, but inside one of them is a manuscript letter from Hewlett dated 1910 in which he says 'I don't think there are any more novels to come out of me', so perhaps I am less unreasonable than might appear. Of Wells I have kept only *Tono-Bungay* (1909), *The History of Mr. Polly* (1910), *The New Machiavelli* (1910) and *Kipps*, while with Arnold Bennett I have pared down even harder and have only *Riceyman Steps* (1923) and *The Old Wives' Tale* (1908).

There was a son of the then Archbishop of Canterbury who became a Catholic and wrote some interesting short stories and novels, Robert Hugh Benson. He befriended Frederick Rolfe 'Baron Corvo' (whose only book not achingly dull seems to me *Hadrian VII*). Benson wrote some excellently creepy stories of the occult. Another Edwardian was 'Saki', H. H. Munro, but he is far from forgotten, his gay, malicious humour sounding across the last thirty years unembittered and undated by the world's changes.

When I was about to leave for South America as a boy of nineteen, J. C. Squire summoned me to the office of the *London Mercury* and gave me some very good advice. But the words of it which I remember best and which have meant most to me were 'Read Cunninghame-Graham'. I think if I had—God forbid— a literary nephew or niece, bound for Argentina or not, it is the advice I would most like to give him or her, for that crystal style, the cool, limpid river of words which is Don Roberto's prose, could be a most valuable literary influence in this age of violence and interjection. Yet his first editions have not been difficult to collect, and of all my books I am most sure of their appreciating value. Three other widely different writers share only this with the old Socialist Hidalgo, that they are primarily stylists, excelling in the sweet economy of their prose to whatever end each may devote it. Virginia Woolf (though I suppose she has supporters who feel such categorization almost a slur on her airy genius),

Lytton Strachey (though perhaps there are critics who have
mistaken him for a historian), and Katherine Mansfield (or is stylist
too cold a word for her warm-hearted humanism?). First
editions of the second two, just now, may be bought at no great
premium, though some of Virginia Woolf's rare books remain
highly priced.

9

Let me turn next to two long rows of books, each collected
with a disciple's devotion, since their authors were in some sense
heroes of mine and gave me encouragement in the lonely and
dubious years of first efforts. My collection of Rudyard Kipling
first editions has none of the freak rarities, the Lahore *Echoes*, the
Allahabad *City of Dreadful Night*, the items printed in small numbers for copyright protection, but for all working purposes it is
complete and it has, folded into some of its volumes, letters from
Kipling, one of them inviting me to come and see him at Bate-
man's, the house which is not five miles away from mine now.
The other writer who was kind to me when I started writing was
John Galsworthy. My tea with him and his wife at Grove
Lodge was an annual event, and his letters to me were a vast
encouragement through several difficult years.

I never knew Arthur Machen, and bitterly regret having been
uanble to accompany a friend who was visiting him not long
before his death. *The Hill of Dreams* still seems to me a small
classic, while the scholarly ghost stories are as harrowing as when
I read them on a tram going from Lewisham to London as a boy
of seventeen. I have heard a first-hand account of that queer
volatile fellow Richard Middleton from Henry Savage, who was
his friend and biographer.

Rather half-heartedly I collect D. H. Lawrence, that shrill
Messiah of masturbation whose tautology and drilling emphasis
can yet sometimes be calmed to serene and memorable passage.
And, with more confidence, Henry Handel Richardson, a sad,
uncompromising writer who never 'lets up' in her mirthless but
deeply impressive revelations of the flesh's weakness.

Other writers who are for the most part of the century's earlier decades, and whose work I collect, can be no more than listed, to provide suggestions, perhaps, to other, I hope younger, collectors. They are C. E. Montague, Forrest Reid—a voice so quiet and well-modulated that it never made itself widely heard—James Stephens, whose book *The Crock of Gold* used to be a rare prize for collectors, Willa Cather, the Kai-Lung books of Ernest Bramah, F. W. Bain, whose beautiful quartos were once greatly collected, and may now be found on shilling trays, J. D. Beresford, though not, I fear, with any great conviction, so infuriatingly unable to let himself go does he seem, and Sinclair Lewis—my American first edition of *Babbitt* being greatly treasured.

Again I have kept back two names because they mean so much to me. May Sinclair, whose books are probably being pulped for paper on which to print some new discovery, seems to me to have been the best woman novelist since the Brontë sisters—and I am forgetting nothing. Such infinite subtlety, such calm, unfrightened appraisal of the worst and most degrading and most terrifying in man, and such soaring knowledge of the best, such cunning in her craft that she keeps her readers panting for each new revelation and incident—this woman had everything. Pick up any book of hers, from *Audrey Craven* (1897) to *The Life and Death of Harriett Frean* (1922), and you at once find yourself with truly distinguished creativeness. I have only a score of her books, and as many letters in her firm, round writing, but I put all my faith in them. Work of this quality will not die while English is read and human beings remain human.

The other is a lesser figure, but still one too soon forgotten— Stacy Aumonier, who died in his early forties soon after the First World War. There may be more profound and exacting short-story-tellers—there are no more entertaining ones. In the eight volumes which contain all that remains of his are at least a dozen stories like *Miss Bracegirdle Does Her Duty* and *Where Was Wych Street ?* which once read are unforgettable.

10

There are 'one' books of this period, too. Richard Whiteing's *No 5 John Street* (1899) and *The House With Green Shutters*, that sombre masterpiece by George Douglas.   Less rare, perhaps, and as a first edition very well worth buying, is that unique and fascinating novel *The Wooings of Jezebel Pettyfer* by Haldane MacFall.   It was recommended to me twenty years ago by Charles Lahr, a bookseller whose grubby little shop in Red Lion Street was a meeting-place for many of us who were trying to get a living by writing in the 1920's, and I have read it more than once since then.   A more usually 'collected' book is Frank T. Bullen's *Cruise of the Cachalot*, of which Kipling said, 'It is immense—there is no other word.'

There are still one or two writers of the last seventy-five years whose first editions I collect in a desultory way but about whom other collectors are, or were, more enthusiastic.   I would like to mention them before talking of living writers in case—as I greatly hope—I may have readers who will accept this chapter as one of suggestions.   There is the mysterious Ambrose Bierce, for instance, with his *Cobwebs from an Empty Skull* and *In the Midst of Life*.   There is an almost forgotten writer of Tynedale sketches called Austin Clare, and an inspired chronicler of Cockney life, Arthur Morrison, whose *Tales of Mean Streets* and *A Child of the Jago* are still read quite widely, I believe, as they well deserve to be.   I am less sure about William Clark Russell and his sea stories, which seem to me almost mechanically proficient.

There are two critical writers who must by no means be forgotten—Dixon Scott, who was killed in the First World War after writing a score of essays on his contemporaries which were collected after his death in a volume called *Men of Letters* (1916) with a preface by Max Beerbohm.   Some of the most creative and percipient criticism of the century is in that book.   Then, I think, I have managed to collect everything by or about one of the most spectacular of writers—Lafcadio Hearn.   His father was an Irish soldier-doctor, his mother a Levantine, and he saw neither of them after he was ten.   Sent to the States at nineteen, he worked his way to a professorship at Tokio University, married a Japanese girl, and left a Hiberno-Japanese son who must now be a man of nearly sixty if he is living.   As an interpreter of the East to the West in his *Glimpses of Unfamiliar*

Japan (1898), *In Ghostly Japan* (1899), *Japan : An Interpretation* (1905) he is unmatched, but his work is far more than mere observation of an unknown land and people—for one feels in reading it that he would still have been a creative writer if he had never left Ireland.

II

Of living writers it is less easy to write as a collector of first editions without seeming invidious, prejudiced or childishly partisan. I am fortunate enough to have as friends or to know sufficiently well several of those whose work I collect, and so have copies inscribed to me of some of the books which I should, in any case, most deeply value.

Somerset Maugham, throughout an eventful life, has shown in his writings that he is unable either to suffer fools gladly or to let pretentiousness go unscathed; he takes delight, I believe, in making himself appear forbidding and aloof—but all this is no more than a protective armour to save him from the irritating consequences of having an exceptionally kind heart. Evidence of it is on the fly-leaves of his books in my shelves—he has not been content merely to inscribe and sign them, but in almost every case has added notes, some of them of great bibliographical interest. In *Cakes and Ale* (1930) he has written, 'Its author's favourite novel for a fellow novelist.' In *Ah King* (1933), 'The last volume of Far Eastern stories.' In *Then and Now* (1946), 'A propaganda book!' while in *The Razor's Edge* (1944) he has flatteringly written, 'Who knows his India' after my name. Such inscriptions would give a deep pleasure to the most cursory of book-lovers, and to me, who read *The Bishop's Apron* under the lid of my desk at school, they make reasonable and rewarding all these years of book collection.

My row of Compton Mackenzie's first editions is no shorter, and these, too, are inscribed. There can scarcely be a writer of my generation who has not been deeply influenced by *Sinister Street*; I have read it every five years or so since I was a boy. There was a to-do about it then, I remember, because some of the lending libraries banned it as too daring, and it might have been forbidden in my home if my father had not been at St. Paul's School himself. Greater rarities in their first issues, however, are *The Passionate Elopement* (1911) and *Carnival* (1912), books which gave me years of pursuit.

A third novelist, of less popular appeal but in my eyes of no smaller eminence, is that master of sound and image, Oliver Onions. I have twenty of his books, and these, too, are inscribed. They have been more difficult to accumulate, not because they are keenly collected but precisely because they are not, so that one has to depend on chance discoveries. Here is a fine opportunity for the collector; such books as *Widdershins* (1911) or *Poor Man's Tapestry* (1946) must appreciate in value as their great and lasting qualities are recognized.

Miss Rose Macaulay, though having no patience herself with such fal-lals as book-collecting, is kind enough to tolerate it perplexedly in another, and drove across London one afternoon in order (as she put it) to 'sign those books' for me. Sign them she did, talking about Spain most of the while, since both of us know the country well. She horrified me by saying that when she was abroad she never wanted to go shopping, and I shocked her scarcely less by admitting that I detest bathing in the sea unless it is at least as tepid as the Indian Ocean. Her novels fill a shelf.

Claude Houghton, a writer with a special talent for surrounding a story with an air of breathless suspense so that as you read you continually expect a thunderstorm to break, inscribes his *This Was Ivor Trent* (1935) while another inscribed set is that of the novels of H. E. Bates, including the bound proofs of his delightful *My Uncle Silas* (1939), in which he has written to me, 'Who, if I say orchards, Czechs, pears, wooden trains, rabbits, darts, rain and children, will understand what I mean.' H. E. Bates's books have always been listed by those dealers who sell modern first editions and have rightly kept their value even since he has become a best-seller. But I do not know what the collectors do about Gerald Kersh. If he is not among the younger writers 'wanted', an opportunity is being missed, for such a novel as *The Thousand Deaths of Mr. Small* (1951) will surely enough live. His inscriptions are brief and modest, while Sheila Kaye-Smith, who has no more patience than Rose Macaulay with this nonsense of book-collecting, has simply signed my copies across the half-title. They include her rare first book *The Tramping Methodist* (1908).

One other collector's treasure with an inscription in it, is a sumptuous large-paper *Helena* (1950) bound in white buckram which Evelyn Waugh gave me, and which stands beside the best of his books from *Decline and Fall* onwards.

For the rest, I collect as they come John Collier (now, alas, bewitched by filmland, but once one of our most exciting younger writers), Graham Greene, Rhys Davies, Walter de la Mare, Frederic Prokosch, Clemence Dane, Max Beerbohm, James Branch Cabell, Ernest Hemingway, Carl van Vechten, William Plomer, Richard Llewellyn, Rebecca West, Denton Welch and William Sansom—enough to keep one's shelves swelling and one's collecting instincts on the alert.

12

I am left staring with something like dismay at four long rows of modern poetry and drama, realizing that even in this superficial book-lover's catalogue I cannot do justice to them, or show what they have meant to me as I have collected them, or what they mean to me now in a country house in which I am cut off for weeks from the kind of conversation in which they might occur. One volume recalls Sean O'Casey as he was, riding with me on the top of a bus through Sloane Square and blinking down at the memorial there to say, 'You see that? The sword on the cross. That'll be the title of my next play, *The Sword on the Cross*.' Another makes me remember shy, awkward Harold Monro breaking into a conversation in a Soho restaurant because we were talking about poetry. Yet another reminds me of Dylan Thomas bubbling with beautiful rhetoric among blank, mistrustful faces in a bar.

There is something enchanting about these thin books, so few of which have been produced at anything but a loss. Imagination has gone to their design, their wide margins and fine type, but though reputations have been founded on them, scarcely one of them has sold more than a score or two of copies. Here, too, are the anthologies, from the variegated volumes of *Georgian Poetry* to *The Faber Book of Modern Verse* (1936).

One collection among these is of particular bibliographical interest—a complete set of the first editions of Lord Alfred Douglas, who was a kind and generous friend to me for thirty years and, as I knew him, a man of saintly life and sweet and humorous disposition. His books are annotated in his hand, and there are a number of his manuscripts and countless letters. Since his death in the early years of the war, mean little detractors who dared not open their mouths in his lifetime have been spitting at his memory, but nothing can defame the beauty of his poetry, which is as likely to be for all time as any other written in this century. There can, alas, be nothing more of his to collect, but they are all here, from the Mercure de France *Poèmes* (1896), *Perkin Warbeck* (1897), the rare and anonymous *City of the Soul* (1899) down to the *Nine Poems* of which A. J. A. Symons had fifty copies privately printed in 1926, and the last collected edition. These, I think, would be the last books I would part with if my collection were sold in some nightmare auction, book by book, over my head.

Life in the House

THERE is a room of the house which has not yet been mentioned, though not because of any delicacy or Victorian primness; it is that compartment known in England by a variety of terms—'the lavatory' (though it is not a lavatory), 'the W.C', 'the loo', the 'if-you-want-to-wash-your-hands', or, in schools and the services, by less refined names. D. H. Lawrence said that the only time the English mentioned any kind of excretion was when they shed tears, and Aldous Huxley slightly shocked the 'twenties by introducing a character into one of his novels whose hobby was the study of sanitary plumbing. I respect the reserve of which Lawrence apparently complained, but accept the Huxley character because he is entertaining. The topic is a dull rather than a disgusting one, and most efforts to enlarge on it by decorating water-closets with originality have not been very successful. The lavatory may be provided with reading matter carefully chosen— I know a house in which *The New Statesman* is kept there in a special rack—or it can be regarded as having the one wall-surface suitable for photographs. But attempts to enliven it further are apt to seem self-conscious, an expression of schoolboy, or perhaps undergraduate, humour.

When I first saw the lavatory in my house, with its mayoral mahogany throne, I noticed that its walls were lined with boards running horizontally round it. They had been painted in some drab colour by the previous occupants, and it seemed to me that they should be replaced by a plain plaster surface. But this would be expensive, and I was already reaching the end of the sum which I was licensed to spend. So I decided to substitute a flippancy. I searched paintshops for lacquers in a sufficient number of colours, then had each board painted in a new one,

so that the walls from ceiling to ground resembled a gigantic
Neapolitan ice. This, I decided, should be my visitors' book.
Guests whose visits I wanted to remember should be given a
brush and a pot of paint of their own choosing and invited to
sign their names on the wall, adding a design if they wished.
There is no one, I argued, man or woman, old or young, who has
not at some time felt the queer perverted urge to scribble on
lavatory walls. Here would be the opportunity.

The notion was, of course, facetious, mock-arty, adolescent,
in bad taste, what you will; but Lord, let us sometimes forget
our dignity, our fear of making ourselves look ridiculous, our
canons of polite behaviour, even our natural discrimination and
cynicism. Let me have one thing in the house which, however
silly and affected, gives me the giggling pleasure with which very
small boys hear dirty stories. So the paint went up, to the horror
of the painters, and now visitors spend five or ten minutes, paint-
brush in hand, assiduously commemorating their visit in a colour
which contrasts with its background.

2

Scarcely less childish is the pleasure I derive from the cupboards
in my dressing-room. Any wall-cupboard, it seems to me,
needs the very simple and cheap addition of a lighting point so
that a bulb over the door shines inwards on its contents, but I
begin to wonder whether this is an idiosyncrasy of mine, or the
outcome of something rude and Freudian, because I rarely see it
done in other houses. For the outlay of a pound or so, a little
bright shrine is created, a room within a room which has its own
mysterious existence in darkness when its door is closed, but which
springs to life as it is re-illuminated. I like to have a cupboard
papered in a pattern contrasting with that on the walls of the
room, further to emphasize its separate entity. This seems to
enlarge the house.

When I first appropriated my pair of little rooms leading one
from the other I saw that the bedroom had a built-in cupboard
beside the fireplace and the dressing-room a set of wooden
cupboards which completely covered one wall. I could not wait

—as we fatuously say—to get lights put in them all, then to make the one in the bedroom, somewhat anomalously, into a small armoury. I have never set out to collect knives and muzzle-loading pistols, but somehow have achieved a sizeable accumulation bit by bit. There is, for instance, an old ivory-handled knife which I bought in Mombasa and which, I like to think, was once stuck in the belt of a Zanzibar pirate or slave-dealer. There is a Commando knife given to me by my friend Sergeant Tommy Ludlow of the Fifth Commando, with whom I was in Madagascar. There are Indian knives, jewelled, crystal-handled, jade-handled, which were the gifts of the young Rajah of Akalkot, in whose palace in the Deccan I spent a very happy month's leave. There is a horrifying little weapon called 'the tiger's claws', a sleeve-knife with razor-sharp claw blades to protrude between the fingers. It is supposed to have belonged to Shivaji, the great Mahrata hero, who made a kingdom while Charles I of England was fighting to keep one. There are old swords from India, some four foot in length, and an ancient flintlock pistol. A round embossed shield and a lacquered Persian helmet, two policemen's truncheons—one French, one English—a miscellany of odds and ends, offensive and defensive, which I do not wish to keep loose in the house, have been arranged behind the cupboard's wooden doors.

In the dressing-room, however, the contents of the cupboards are more conventional. A thick brass rod runs the length of the longest for clothes-hangers, while the other cupboards are shelved.

Country life has revived in me a young man's pleasure in loose and rebellious clothes. In London all loud and unconventional male garments look shabby, affected, would-be bohemian. One thinks at once of the charlatanry and ostentatiousness of bearded men wearing corduroys with filthy feet in sandals and a manner alternating between obsequiousness and insolence. One thinks of dull pubs round the Tottenham Court Road and tedious arguments on mighty issues of Life and Death or the necessity of an immediate small loan. In London or any big city the only possible clothes for a man are the clothes of the day, the dull suit which has scarcely changed its shape in this century. Only by

'A painted specimen-case in an angle of the stairs'

obeying convention can one enjoy freedom from a vulgar conspiciousness, a freedom well worth attaining. But in the country, even in country towns, one need not revere common usage so obtusely. One does not feel theatrical or silly if one is not dressed like every other man.

This has always been a hobby-horse of mine. Before the war I used to contribute a monthly article to a periodical called *Man and His Clothes,* and looking through old numbers now I see that I advocated the wearing of such *outré* oddments as a waistcoat of rawhide tanned with the red and white hair still on it, which I had seen on a farmer in Kilkenny; white 'Gandhi' caps for the seaside; old flowered waistcoats cut to a modern shape; a suit seen in the West India Dock Road—'purple was a mild word for it and it had a pin-stripe of the richest daffodil yellow'; a fur coat; check trousers strapped under the shoes; German peaked student-caps; opera cloaks, stocks and leather shorts.

Sobered by six years in uniform, perhaps, and with the remains of a pre-war wardrobe moth-eaten and tight in the waist, I still find it pleasant to pull on a pair of corduroy trousers which, in country places, can be topped with a number of easy things—a roll-top pullover, a lumber jacket, a check shirt, an American airman's wind-jacket which I once bought from a Polish burglar, and which still shows the ghost of the airman's flashes, a shirt and tie, a sports jacket (but without the idiotic twin vents of a 'hacking' jacket, unless the jacket is for hacking), a pull-over of towelling with a loose collar. I still like to dress in summer, for the house and garden, in the vastly wide trousers of softest cotton which are worn by Indian Muslims, and with them a *shivani,* the long, tight, many-buttoned coat with a straight collar like the collar of a German uniform. Or an *atchkan,* the shorter version of that coat, which can be worn with ordinary European trousers. Or Tyrolean shorts with horn buttons and white stockings. Or, indeed, any carefree or highly coloured clothes which would be eccentric in more severe surroundings.

It seemed to me at one time that our emancipation in this matter might come from America, but since the war that hope has receded in a flashy sunset of ties which look like Edwardian

Q

wallpapers and pansified silk blouses in colours and designs once considered suitable only for cretonne curtains. Men's clothes will never grow more gay or imaginative by imitating women's, and if we are ever to escape from the twin drainpipes of our trousers, the strait-jacket coat, the halter and gyves of collar and cuffs, it will be by inventing something less funereal but not less virile. Nor will it come while innovators study only men in their twenties. Men's appearances were most cheerful when in the seventeenth and eighteenth century they wore wigs and clothes which blurred their age-distinction. Nothing will gain much support from conservative males which only emphasizes the youth of the young.

3

There is an omission in this book which will not have been unnoticed by any reader who has worked his way through to this chapter. It must seem strange to him that I can have gone on so long talking of water-closets and water-colours, of drink and the devil, without saying what animal inmates the house has, what cats, dogs, birds, fish or monkeys. I have not thrust them on the reader because there is no greater bore than the man or woman with a series of anecdotes about his pets, examples of uncanniness on the part of alarmingly intelligent dogs, descriptions of long-dead cats and their curious wiles, discourses on the mating habits of birds. Second in tedium only to reconstructions of dreams, these are almost inescapable if they are once started, and I promise you that you shall be subjected to no whimsy stories about my dog's gifts of reasoning or my cat's nocturnal promiscuity. Still, if I am to say what makes the life for me, I cannot very well leave out altogether this most essential part of it.

When I was making plans for this house I had the somewhat stagey fancy that any pets I might keep should be white. Almost immediately my sister, far more interested in animals than in houses, gave me a white kitten bred in her Hertfordshire riding-stables, so that before I had more than played with this over-ornamental notion of a white collection, it had begun. The kitten was, of course, a charmer, though, even at that early age and in his first weeks away from his family, more than naturally independent. I soon discovered that he was stone deaf, and was harshly told by an authority on cats that I ought to have known this. All white cats are deaf, he said, a rule with no exception. He could not tell me why. Other cat-lovers held less categorical opinions—that white cats with green eyes are deaf, or that sometimes white cats are only a little hard of hearing. But mine, there can be no doubt, is deaf as a trunkmaker. This leads to rather uncanny situations, as when in the morning someone enters the kitchen in which he is asleep to find that pots and pans can be rattled for several mintues before he suddenly wakes up. Accustomed to cats for ever on the alert, one feels that his complete detachment is a little other-worldly.

He is called 'Poona' because it is a right-sounding name for a cat and because I spent some months in that pleasant Deccan city. (I never gave its name as my address when writing to England, I remember, for its blimpish associations are so strong that my leg would have been endlessly pulled.) 'Poona' has a dark interior life of his own in the silent world he knows, and is probably no less happy than cats able to hear themselves addressed in the fatuous squeaks which human beings use when addressing them. He is by no means dumb, having one of the most imperious of miaows with which to demand entry, exit, food or milk. He was our sole guest from the animal world for the first six months here.

I wanted a dog, of course. The bright all-yellow Alsatian which I had owned for six years before the war, about whose intelligence and love I could tell a hundred stories, was to have gone to a dogs' home when I joined the army, but the wife of a Canadian general, a Mrs. Pearks, in England only for the duration of the war, kindly volunteered to look after him for me. When I was in hospital abroad I received a letter from this lady saying that she had given up her furnished house and moved into a hotel in which dogs were forbidden, so that, rather than give Dingo to strangers, she had had him painlessly destroyed. I have kept this letter among war souvenirs. A white Alsatian, then, I wondered? But although I do not believe that a breed exists more beautiful, more fiercely faithful, or more trainable, than this, there had been,

I remembered, certain episodes in Dingo's life, certain discreditable incidents connected with sheep, which made me hesitate to commit myself to another of his breed. There had been a time when a farmer, though fully compensated for his loss, had taken the matter of some sheep to Court, and only the skilful pleading of a friendly solicitor had saved Dingo from a destruction order. I did not want to face these anxieties again.

There was only one breed to compare with the lithe Alsatian, I considered, and its graces and traditions were so different that one wonders how a single species can contain such diverse animals. If, indeed, the Pekinese is a dog at all, a matter on which I have the gravest doubt, though I would not attempt to decide what reincarnated primeval spirit may be his. The aristocrat of all canines, his imperial lineage running back unmixed and uninterrupted to an age when China's civilization was the only one capable of supporting dogs as pets, the Pekinese has a history which makes the very hounds of Orion parvenus. Exclusively bred by the Chinese imperial family, he has been known to the outside world for a comparatively short time, but there are stories of ceremonial dog-fights in the lacquer pavilions, among the gilded pagodas, in the flowery gardens, and if there is truth in them, their scenes must have been some of the most elegant in the ancient world. I knew that there was no dog more captivating and spirited, more exquisite and yet more courageous, than this small, silky piece of ancient *chinoiserie*.

A white Pekinese, then, it had to be, and when I heard of a male puppy eleven weeks old, I bought him. Without any doggy sentimentality, I feel vaguely uncomfortable when I think of this transaction, as though I had been guilty of dealing in human life. Let no one ever own a Pekinese who wants a fawning pet, an obedient ornament, a pretty plaything, or who thinks that dogs should know their places. For he will bring home in that tiny body, small enough to stand in a pint pot, the soul of a Chinese prince, a creature so proud and so resolute, so full of character, so consciously winning and yet so manly, that no household remains unchanged by his presence. It is not a matter of 'spoiling' a Pekinese; I doubt if that would be possible. It is a matter of respecting him, as an individual, as a highly civilized co-inhabitant of one's home, as a being with certain rights.   He will learn his duties and manners as a well-behaved foreigner in a strange country learns his.   He will give his love to you because you are to be his life-long companion.   He likes a joke.   He is energetic and waggish.   But he must not be mistaken for a dog or treated like one.

In his first weeks with me the puppy who is called Tito (again because the name has the right sound, though it represents rather the Spanish diminutive than the Yugoslav surname) was a source of embarrassment, causing shrill cries of 'Oh, isn't he *sweet?*' whenever I took him out, and being twice snatched out of my arms by strangers who *had* to stroke him, they said.   But he grew quickly, his white plumes waving like a lancer's, his hair becoming long and silky.   I often wonder who he may be.

It seemed that white fantail pigeons would make a fairly obvious additon to these, and I found that it is as easy and almost as cheap to buy a live pigeon from a pet-shop as a dead one from a poulterer's slab.   But a good pigeon-cote must be made by a skilled carpenter, for it is a prominent thing in the garden which can follow a traditional pattern or look like a chicken-house. Mine is of the ancient kind on a high pole with separate compartments inside;   it was constructed from weather-boarding, which, I was astonished to find, may actually be purchased without a by-your-leave from any timber merchant.

There are great white possibilities.   Only one pair of white peacocks remains in England, at Buscot Park, and I wait somewhat anxiously to see if they survive and produce healthy progeny. A friendly circus proprietor has promised me a pelican if I can ever afford to feed it.   I enquired from an animal-dealer the price of a stork, and was told that one could be imported for £80, or a pair for £150.   Even though I can think of no other means by which the human population of my house is likely to be increased, I find this a forbidding price.   A white canary, a little ghost of the yellow one, is easily bought, but a rather melancholy sight, I think.

There are larger possibilities, but they are best not visualized too clearly if life is to retain its realism.

4

Gertrude Jekyll wrote a book, I seem to remember, on flower decoration. Hitherto the subject had interested me only bibliographically, because this book had long been out of print and was a 'wanted' item. But now it has a more direct importance, for this is a house which demands abundant flowers, not in the window-blocking, stuffy, hot-house way in which they used to be crowded in the cottages of my childhood, but to emphasize the very airiness of the rooms. Constance Spry, someone said, was an authority on this among many subjects and gave courses of instruction in the art. It had become an important one in the last few years, I was told, for while the sales of most so-called luxuries had decreased as the pound lost value, those of flowers were booming. So I gathered that there were fashions in this, as in so many things, and I began to notice in London flats curious white-plaster receptacles with lozenze-shaped rims and conch-like bases which appeared to be in the mode, also painted baskets with vast hoop-like handles in which mixed flowers were arranged with rather conscious originality.

'A girl from the florist's comes once a week to do them,' explained a hostess standing beside a cone of colour such as Victorians perpetuated in wax.

It was not, I realized sourly, an art in which I was likely to be at all proficient, and I was becoming somewhat anxious. Then suddenly I remembered that in India this cult, which has recently come to inspire books of instruction here, is as old as the very race, that garlands were made to adorn stone carvings in the happy days before history, and that every Indian is brought up to accept the most exquisite arrangement of flowers as part of the daily religious and social life of his communtiy. Flowers—why, they were everywhere in India, garlands round every picture or statue, Hindu or Christian, garlands for bride and bridegroom, garlands for the parting guest, the person to be honoured, garlands for the dead. No Indian woman so poor but could afford a flower or two most beautifully arranged in her hair, no shrine without its flowers.

'Who makes the garlands in India?' I asked Joseph slyly.

'The men, of course. It is an expert thing, a special calling. The flower-sellers can make any garland, from a little chaplet of jasmine to a garland for a state occasion which might cost a large sum of money.'

'You never tried it?'

'I daresay I could make a fairly ordinary one. I used to do the flowers for my sister's hair sometimes.'

'What about vases?'

'Oh yes. It's not difficult.'

It is not, for him. With a few thousand years of training behind him, he has managed to dispense with the necessity of taking lessons from Mrs. Constance Spry.* The effects are brilliant. He is not consciously unconventional, because he does not even know our conventions, and when he uses the tall, creamy-coloured flowers of the rhubarb plant or the rich purple and grey leaves of pickling cabbage among flowers it is because he finds it logical to do so.

But success in this seems to me to depend in great part on having a large variety of vases and jars from which to choose as each purpose presents itself, and the discovery in a Tunbridge Wells antique shop of four fan-shaped glass vases on short, twisted stems—fragile and lovely things of Georgian times—has made arrangement easier. Urns, great urn-shaped china buckets which once fulfilled some unmentionable purpose in a 'toilet set', earthenware straight-sided jars, coloured jars once supplied by a famous firm of marmalade-makers with seven pounds of their product for three-and-sixpence, now sold by the cheaper antique dealers at half-a-guinea, copper jugs, glass bowls—each of them has its purpose.

A painted Hepplewhite specimen-case which had been lined with lead for flowers seemed difficult to place until, in the corner half-way up the staircase, a supporting angle of the stair was made for it. This is given an abundant display which climbs the wall sometimes or droops almost to the stair itself. I write this in

* But Joseph admits his debt to her two fine books *Winter and Spring Flowers* and *Summer and Autumn Flowers*.

October, and Michaelmas daisies are in it with great heavy tassels of love-lies-bleeding among them and falling from between them.

I remember so many of the flower arrangements of summer—hollyhocks trimmed and tall with cardoons on equally long stems just breaking into flower; great swords of gladiolus among the three-foot Cape hyacinths and, more conventionally, marigolds with cornflowers, a dazzling contrast of blue and gold.

Moreover, Joseph has discovered, by what mysterious dowsing I do not know, where to find things growing wild in our neighbourhood which keep the house alive in the most difficult months. In November spindleberries, which he trims of all foliage and unnecessary twigs; in December the holly and evergreens of Christmas decoration which surround the little illuminated stable of his crib; then, with spring, branches of pussy-willow, horse-chestnut branches whose virgin leaves break out of their sticky buds, primroses and Ponticum rhododendrons which grow wild by our roadside. Honeysuckle, short-lived foxgloves and wild ferns bring us round to our own time of garden plenty.

5

'Don't forget to have your house blessed when you have moved in,' wrote a friend, 'and make sure that the priest blesses every room.' The second part of his caution was unnecessary, for our local priest, who spent the war in Dover and has seen more houses destroyed than most of us, is not the man to skimp a job. Arriving on his noisy little Corgi motor-cycle, he said a general prayer in the hall which closed with the words: 'And may the Angels of Thy Light dwell within the walls of this house and may they protect it and those who dwell herein.' Then he entered each room with a brief benediction.

'Well, *really*,' said a sternly rationalistic friend who was staying in the house, 'Talk about superstition and Popery! I've always supposed you to be a moderately intelligent man. Now consider the logic of this. . . .'

But what a bore is logic. And in any case the priest who had just rattled away could have out-reasoned him, I daresay, even by scientific standards.

Life in the Country

I

LOOKING through the chapters I have written, I am alarmed to find the word 'plan' used so often, and I wonder now whether I have given the impression that life here conforms to schedules and blue-prints, to some business-like curriculum, or is regulated by charts or time-tables. The impression would be wholly false. Planning or, to use a better word with all its implications, *scheming* has been necessary to reconstruct the house, make it habitable and create in it the means to follow a certain kind of existence, but there is very little detailed planning about the life itself. Day follows day in a rotation which is neither retarded nor accelerated by design, and the comfortable round is regulated by no psychologist's Bradshaw. The idea has been to live as well as it is possible to do in an over-taxed and over-organized country, to follow personal inclinations unintimidated by persuasions and threats made by the propagandists of human uniformity, to put civilization before civics. It has not been to produce my own ant-hill on which to tread out in isolated discipline my track.

It is ironic, when one remembers the derivation of the word civilization, that such a life should be easier in the country than in a city, and it may be that there is but an illusion of greater freedom here, that the impudent minions of bureaucracy are only better concealed, that our village policeman dutifully standing by his bicycle at 'turning-out time' only seems a less menacing figure than the sometimes overbearing and highly regimental police force of a city which, one remembers, has so often been adapted in other countries to more sinister purposes than traffic-control. But whether illusion or not, there is this sense of greater freedom and mutations of season are more insistently noticeable here than alterations of front, or of Government, or of policy, in London.

Time runs by, changing his shoes for the weather, but keeping his even pace, and I realize only now and again that a month, a year, two years have passed, with nothing but a few feet of the wistaria's growth, a book or two completed and a puppy grown to a dog, as signs of their passing.

A book or two completed—that is the real issue.   Sitting here with a thousand books by others standing reproachfully around me, I write without fear that the telephone will break out or that friends will drop in; I write for four or five hours a day; I write contentedly because, when all is said, it is what I like doing most between sunrise and darkness in any day or in any place.   This lunacy of sitting over a table making hieroglyphics while there is sunlight outside and while the years are being stolen can be cured by no shock treatment, like the less unreasonable obsessions of those actually certified, nor would I wish it cured, for without its irresistible impulse the other pursuits which I have described would lose their significance and savour.

So I write while Tito watches me perplexedly and Poona yawns outright.   Then, getting up from the table, I walk out into the garden, which, in its second year, begins to repay the arduous work of early days.   Each rhododendron tree is a pillar of fire, and across the lawn the roses burn with a confident inner glow.

'I think we must have some aconites next winter,' I say to Stanbridge, who is hoeing in the vegetable garden.   But before he has answered I can see his face and know what he feels about it.

'That's a thing you can *never* get rid of,' he says inevitably, and, turning to pleasanter subjects, tells me of Mrs. Benatar's irises, or the reward which Mr. Akers-Douglas is reaping from having manured his ground last winter, or of the swift growth of Lord Goschen's hedge or of Mrs. Walford's lilies.

I take some thyme and a bay-leaf into the house for a *mirepoix* which is being made, and find that the postman has left a large flat packet which looks like the little water-colour I ordered on approval, then, when I have examined it for a few minutes, I return to my desk. House, garden, kitchen, books, pictures recede for a time, as I tackle this last chapter of the longest book I have written.

2

Yet my isolation in this house is not to be compared with that which its occupants in previous centuries must have known, for while they could go no farther than the village on foot or perhaps to Tunbridge Wells in a pony-trap, I have a car. Again I am warned by my own leaden experience in hearing men talking of their cars that anecdotes about dogs and dreams are only just ahead of this topic in the scale of tedium. A nausea, like sea-sickness and the fatigue which follows a route march mixed in a yellow gloom, comes over me. 'Must have been doing about seventy', or 'My old bus never lets me down', or, 'It may not *look* much . . .' In spite of the grim hours of paralysed ennui which I have spent listening to such talk, I must pay some swift tribute to the battered grey machine which has carried me so long and so far. I bought it in 1938, an Opel Cadet which was a German product of General Motors, its export subsidized by Hitler. Its low saloon body had a shape ahead of its time, so that even today it still looks modern, and in spite of its lightness it has a 12-h.p. engine. I began to realize that I had an unusually fast and reliable car when I went in that last pre-war autumn down to Marseilles, then up the east side of France to Alsace, where I stayed to work for a month, journeying to Kassel in Hesse and to Switzerland. Through the summer of 1939 the car pulled a caravan trailer as I followed Rosaire's Circus, and when war broke out I left it in an open barn on a Kentish farm, meaning to come back for it in a month or two, and so not even bothering to jack it up or take out the battery. Six years later I returned from the East to find a rusty skeleton from which everything removable had been stolen, but within a month or two it was on the road again, and has since done four years' hard and daily service in London and two in the country, with one journey to the north of Norway and two to the south of France. I can still leave here for Brighton at eight o'clock on a winter's night with reasonable confidence that it will bring me home over the thirty-five miles of lonely road after midnight.

From the days of my bookshop I remember a series of books

published in the early years of this century called *The Badminton Library of Sports and Pastimes*. Of all its volumes those on 'Motoring' and 'Archery' were the ones most keenly sought. Motoring was a sport, you notice, as much as yachting or shooting. So in my mind it is still, and so it will remain. The internal combustion engine is for me an alchemical mystery, and in spite of countless drowsy lectures in the army and well-meaning efforts by friends, I have never yet learnt why pouring petrol in the thing makes it go. But I am happy driving it, finding in that both an anodyne and a pastime.

3

Besides, it takes me to the cinema, and for us in the country that is no trivial matter. For us the cinema is neither the convenient place of darkness where curious, and one would say practised, inter-lockings accompany intermittent whispers, nor is it the home of the Great Art of Tomorrow, the hope of those who think both the novel and the theatre have had their day. It is our escape from nature, our opium den, our weekly or bi-weekly ascent into a braver world.

I ask only of a film that I may be able to believe in it, that I may live for a time with its sublime adventurers, that it may never for a moment degenerate into a number of men and women acting on a set, but may carry me with it into the bedroom of an American boarding-house, an oasis in the Western desert, the forest home of the seven dwarfs or a thieves' kitchen in Soho. I am not hard to convince—I will go as far with the director as a sane man can; I am willing to believe that the male population of the United States is about equally divided between depraved gangsters and heroic G men, or the female between women of spectacular hideousness and great age and girls of alluring beauty and almost embarrassingly youthful appearance. I will accept the existence of large English country houses with a dozen servants apiece, of gentlemen in fancy waistcoats called sheriffs and of high-wire performances in the forests of Africa—all provided that the film has that secret amalgam of sincerity, con-viction, authenticity, drive, which is able to bewitch me into forgetting my doubts and criticisms, into living the story.

The up-to-the-minute topicality of a film does not matter, for I shall not be called upon at any cocktail party to criticize yesterday's first performance, and if films are discussed at all it will be 'the one showing at Tunbridge Wells this week', or at Hastings, or Battle, or Cranbook, our nearest cinemas. I shall not have to stand in a queue or pay eleven shillings to see a recent importation, but shall be told that 'there's plenty of room in the three-and-a-pennies'. I shall not need to study the acidulated pasquinades of Miss Lejeune, because by the time that the film has reached this area I should have forgotten in any case whether or no she found some praiseworthy moment in it. I can, in fact, finish dinner at home, drive to the cinema and for a couple of hours gape and laugh and weep in comfort, untroubled by any doubts about Art, or Production, Dramatic Licence, Composition or Treatment. Which may be just as well.

4

My car also carries me, when rightly guided, to any one of a dozen pubs dotted conveniently round my home, and in them I shall find no fellow-writers waiting to discuss literary movements or a promising new firm of publishers 'who will pay the earth to get any sort of name on their list, old boy', but decent drinkers, intent on swallowing beer, with conversation sensibly limited to commonplace topics discussed in crudely emphatic terms. This pub has a pleasant landlord but a shrill landlord's wife, that one reverses the two; another will be warmed with a great log fire, while in yet another the darts are of a high standard. One will be crowded with hop-pickers in season; one has a boastful moron as a landlord but a jolly landlord's daughter; one gleams with polished brass, another is dark and dirty. Idiosyncrasies must be studied and discussed as the merits of current plays are studied by townsmen, but the pub which fits the occasion may usually be found.

It must have a dart-board, though. I once wrote a book on the alluring game of darts, and was shocked to find that because it was the first book to be written on the subject, it was given more prominent reviews than any novel of mine had then achieved. I still find the game enjoyable, but lack of practice has made my play erratic, and I am dismayed by the intense team-work of this area, in which there are league matches and competitions and char-à-bancs which have brought representatives from other villages standing outside each pub once or twice a week. This means that the contemporary touch of regimentation has been added to what was at one time the most free-and-easy of pastimes.

5

Then, once or twice a year, comes the circus. Its little posters have appeared in incongruous places, blotting out orders to 'stick no bills', ornamenting telegraph or signposts or being shown in the windows of our local shops in return for a free ticket. The circus lorries rumble past in the early morning, and by lunch-time the flag on the big tent is visible above the house-tops. It will be one of the smaller, the family circuses which will stop here, but for me it will bring much more than the entertainment in the ring, for I 'on honey-dew have fed and drunk the milk of Paradise'. The elusive circus, gone at dawn to another county, the romantic, the indomitable circus fighting its way across an indifferent or hostile countryside, combating its eternal enemies—wind, fire and the tax-inspector—indefatigable, irrepressible: it has had my allegiance since I first came to know it and its gallant men and women two decades ago. I am an initiate now, even forgiven by circus folk for having written books about them, at home in any living-waggon, able to exchange the parry and thrust of crude repartee which is circus talk, able to hear and give scraps of news and gossip, understanding the strange necessities of the life. And the show itself, when I see it, I enjoy as heartily as the children crowded along the benches, finding the primitive humour of the clowns more to my taste than the diamond wit of a modern comedy, and the acts of strength and daring of the acrobats, the wire-walkers, the trapeze artists, more breath-taking than the fabricated suspense of a drama in the theatre.

6

Often, too, I receive visits from another breed of nomadic people; for gypsies, passing this way, will come to the door and ask for me, and we spend an hour exchanging the gossip of the *tans*. There is no connection between them and circus folk, let me emphasize, and neither have any direct relationship with the fair-ground, nor any of the three with the fourth kind of nomad on the road, the professional tramp or mumper who spends his life on foot.

News travels fast among the living-waggons of the Romanis and the half-bred *didakais* who are their surviving relatives now that the pure-blooded have almost disappeared from the Home Counties. It was not long after I had moved here that the first shy callers came. Or driving home at night along one of the quieter lanes about here I see the horses grazing the roadside grass and pull up to be greeted instantly, before one would have thought that I was visible, with 'That you, *rai*?' to find myself with Boz'l and Cinny, whom I may not have seen for years, or with some of the Bartons, the Scamps, the Hildings, the Smiths or the Brazils.

'I heard you'd come to live round here,' one of them will say, and I am flattered to think that my movements have been a part of the talk exchanged by wayfarers. I must know several thousand of them in different parts of the country, and never find their visits a nuisance, though I may be expected to write a letter, produce tobacco or some old clothes, or listen to lamentable histories of illness and death, or livelier stories of a brush or two with the police, or 'trouble' in an unfriendly pub. With these people I am at ease; I know them and their language, and they know me. I have travelled with them and worked with them, written about them* and studied their long history. Though they have had opportunities enough, they have never stolen from me or betrayed a trust. Life in the country without the gypsies would be less picturesque for everyone; for me it would be less eventful, too.

7

I came here in fretful exasperation with London, but now I find one of the chief joys of country life is an occasional visit to the capital. Seen from this distance it seems to regain some of the

---

* *Glorious* (Jarrolds). *The Moon in My Pocket* (Sampson Low).

brilliance and geniality which once belonged to it. An evening at the theatre has a suggestion of the magic of a childhood's 'outing', as it must have for most country dwellers, while little drinking-clubs seem less spiv-ridden and more sophisticated. In the streets the clothes of men and women look less cobbled and ugly, the shop-windows more promising, and even the food in restaurants not quite so nasty. It is faintly exciting to drive away from here towards the crowded, lighted streets, and though I will never again be one of the population of London, yet for one night, now and again, I can at least find something to do in it. I manage to feel like a stranger, I greet my friends as one from a great distance who has not seen them for many years; as a guest I am pitifully easy to please, content to see a new face or two. I want to do simple things for which I never had time while I lived in London, like walking through Bond Street when the shops are open, or even having a meal at the Caprice or the Ivy, where the most noisily publicized inhabitants of the florid world of entertainment are on show. I learn the new names from hoardings, see the new rhyming play, hear the latest droll story, rush to a crowded party, where I drink an iced concoction in which, I fervently hope, there is enough alcohol to glaze the faces about me, while I hear discussed the latest autobiography of an escaped prisoner of war or a new American novel. I go to an art Exhibition almost willingly, since I shall not have to do so again for six months. I am amused to find that there is a change in the attitude of my friends towards me, especially when they are discussing their social projects. 'But of course you won't be here,' they say, perhaps with relief, while they smile at me in the manner that used to be called quizzical, as if doubtful whether to envy or pity me. I hear the scandal—that A is living with B, that C has a new book coming out, that D has been disgracefully rude to E, that F never *stops* borrowing money, while G has fallen in love with a sailor. I am asked with friendly patronage how the garden is getting along, but before I can answer I am told about H being turned out of the I club. I listen gravely, remembering contentedly that I shall soon be back in my house sitting by the fire with a book while outside the world is asleep.

Oh yes, I say, I like coming up to London, and that is true enough, so far as it goes. I believe that London is getting a little less mournful at last. You can even spend an evening in it without being coshed, arrested, pushed off the pavement, blackmailed, robbed or thrown into despair. In time it may be possible to eat there again, to go to the theatre after dusk instead of in the afternoon, even to smile civilly without being mistaken for a ruined lecher who is trying to get off with the nearest shop-girl.

Or is it just the same? Is it that for me it provides what is called 'a nice change' now and again?

8

That cuts the other way, too. The hurried and ginny sort of entertainment which is all that can be offered to friends in London leaves everyone unsatisfied, but here, five miles from a railway station, I must invite them to spend time, to eat, to stay, or not invite them at all. A visit is something more than a rush to the door, a swallowing of liquor, an exchange of carefully chosen conversation and a quick departure : it becomes leisurely and reminiscent of more spacious times. We in the country look forward to the arrival of visitors and prepare for it, while those who come, for however long or short a time, move for a time at our more tranquil tempo.

Even our parties, if they are given for friends who have come from town or from distant homes, as is usually the case, cannot be limited to the two hours stipulated on an invitation card, but must continue into the night. This means that instead of stuffed olives or snippets of anchovy on pink paste, an honest meal must be provided which in itself suggests something of kindlier times and manners than today's.

In common with most country-dwellers, I like the spare room to be occupied for short periods, but frequently. When I read in a novel by Jane Austen or one of her contemporaries of visits which lasted several months I perceive, I must confess, that there are consolations in the accelerated way of living which we have now evolved. I can think of no one whom I would like to entertain for more than a week or two, and find that 'the week-end' is an admirable period if it is properly interpreted. But friends whom I saw several times a week in London bloom with surprising new qualities when they stay here and escape the over-bearing domination of the wrist-watch. They cease to fidget, they need not ask if they will be able to find a taxi, they do not remember the trials of tomorrow, and so become generous talkers, amiable and expansive people, good friends. Then I feel smug, thinking that my ambition to create a household with a warming effect on its inmates, temporary and permanent, has been successful.

10

But neighbours—that's another matter. Here in Sussex we keep ourselves *to* ourselves, an arrangement which suits me admirably. A writer who must earn his living in his own home is somewhat at the mercy of people who do not realize this and think that he will be delighted to 'have a little chat' at any moment. I must quickly salute the ladies and gentlemen of Ticehurst, who have known so much better that they have left me in peace quite uninterrupted for two years. The 'people from the manor' came, and a writer who lives here, an inventor of excellent thrillers named Seldon Truss. Otherwise my isolation has been splendid. I am told that for his first twenty years in the village a newcomer is ignored, a system which I welcome, especially if I do not remain here for twenty years, since—let it be faced—most exchanges of calls and counter-calls in an area of this kind are deathly dull, and most ladies and gentlemen who live with determined gentility in the country are pretentious and unattractive. Whatever else I hoped for when I came to Sussex, it was not to enlarge a somewhat mixed acquaintance, which already has to embrace most nationalities and callings, and includes gypsies, clergymen and criminals. So we are content. And when I am told that Mrs. This or That would so much like to call on me 'but of course she cannot because there is not a lady of the house and her husband is not home during calling hours', I say, 'There! What a pity!' not without a secret smirk. There does not, after all, seem to be much reason for any-one to spend time with those people who by a mere geographical chance live near him. Nor am I greatly flattered by local curiosity, which has been known to inspire rides on the buses passing my house because only from their upper deck can the garden I have made and the new appearance of the house be viewed.

II

Other country pleasures are more specialized. An auction sale in the garden of an old house on a summer day is not everyone's idea of a deliriously happy occasion, nor, perhaps, is mowing the lawn with a hand-mower, though both of these please me. So, in their various kinds, do market-days in a nearby town, walking through the woods in winter, driving away in the car to spend a couple of unplanned days in the southern counties, playing canasta for stakes slightly larger than I can afford, looking round antique shops, lying in the sun, picking my own beans, peas or fruit, digging my own potatoes, and polishing up old metal articles. For others less squeamish than I there are shooting and fishing, but although I can if necessary bear to see creatures killed and am not distressed to think of ferreting, for instance, I can kill no living thing myself— not even an insect. This is not a matter of high principle, as with the Jain sect in India, or as with certain vegetarians, but rather it is a kind of fastidiousness which I am unable to shake off.

Certain indoor occupations, now almost universally followed, gain significance in the country, and of these 'listening to the wireless' must be the foremost. In this house, however, the only programmes heard more than rarely are the six o'clock news and an occasional concert. Television seems to me a painful bore; on the few occasions when I have looked into the witch's crystal of a friend's set my eyes have smarted and I have developed a headache only for the sake of seeing some race-horses canter by in a thick fog, or of watching the open mouth of a woman singing, or staring while sparks and splinters of light play like demons on the screen and someone says 'It's that damned car going by!' I was recently persuaded to see a televised play in which a number of people sat huddled close together for what seemed like hours of dialogue, and it was explained to me that this was for the sake of the camera-man, who had to keep them all in focus. When I venture to hint that television appears to provide somewhat limited entertainment, seems in fact designed to amuse the feeble-minded, I am beset by assurances that it is the thing of the future. Then I'll wait for the future, I say disagreeably, and hear myself called anti-progressive.

'Wasn't the cinema jerky and painful to watch at first? Did we not all have to have ear-phones when wireless began? Well, then. . . .'

It was and we did, but we should have saved ourselves a good deal of pain and boredom if we had waited for them to become proficient. I am not difficult to entertain, but I do not relish watching a very old film through the wrong end of a dirty telescope. My heart fails to leap up when I behold eggs broken in a cookery lesson proceeding behind a rain-splashed windscreen, and I cannot frankly (after a glance at several) understand why anyone should want to *see*—however dimly—the members of any band or orchestra. This way of spending 'the long winter evenings', in fact, is not for me, and when I am asked if I do not need something 'to pass the time' in the country I cease to understand what my interlocutor is talking about.

It is not because the invention is slightly older that I prefer the gramophone, but because with this I can at least exercise some control over the entertainment provided and because I can listen to a symphony without seeing and hearing it announced by a well-meaning woman intent on modulating her voice attractively or seeing the musicians' faces while it is played. If—as happens with shameful frequency—I find myself one of several million people enraptured by a new 'number' (as I have learnt to call a tune), I can play it as many times in a day as I wish, until it sickens me as much as it has already done Mrs. Rummery and Joseph. The gramophone is adaptable to one's moods, in other words, while radio and television remain perforce indifferent to them. So here you will find a record spinning more often than an announcer spieling.

12

Where is this catalogue of country delights to stop? Newspapers are not merely the mean and scrappy sheets which bring us details about our latest humiliations abroad, another ship sunk by Albanians or Chinese, more British property commandeered in the Middle East, rebuffs in Argentina, American admirals appointed to command our ships, and whatnot. For we have time, here, to read the paper—even the third leader in *The Times* —and to do the Crossword. A novelist once told me that the hardest moment of his day was when he *had* to put aside the *Times* Crossword and start working; he spoke for me, too.

But we have a special joy in the country—our local papers. So rewarding do I find them that I take three and read them more avidly than any daily. Apart from telling me what films are showing and what auctions are being held, they describe the proceedings at various Council Meetings and I learn which Councillor disagreed with the Mayor on what grounds. They give details of the local Courts and I learn with alarm that a neighbour has been fined five shillings for riding without a light or a youth has been imprisoned for poaching. I read in the advertisement columns that an eight-bell grandfather clock and a quantity of creosote are for sale; I observe the births, deaths and marriages of the district. Then, with open impatience, I turn to that column, rich in poetry and sentiment and headed *In Memoriam*, and for the hundredth time resolve to make an anthology drawn from it.

> Sweet are the memories, silently kept,
> We smile with the world but never forget

I read. Then, because I am sufficiently expert to dismiss the perennially popular lyrics, I look for novelty.

> Asleep in God's beautiful garden,
> Sheltered from all sorrow and pain,
> Some day when life's journey is over,
> We'll meet you, dear Mum, again.

These are *vieux jeux*, but next week there will be original verses, there will be newly-phrased sentiments. I should hate to miss my local papers.

13

A last confession to end these complacent details of what makes 'the life for me'. It is a confession because the habit I wish to acclaim has been so much frowned on by our legislators that it has a brimstone aura about it and bids fair to be categorized with 'wine' and 'women' as the gravest of human vices. I mean, of course, tobacco-smoking. Successive Chancellors of the Exchequer have seen in the Englishman's love of smoking a profitable weakness to exploit. 'They can't stop it!' these gentlemen must have said with glee. 'However much they are taxed they can't stop smoking! Whoopee!' And they piled it on until the few wisps of tobacco bound round with paper which are sold as cigarettes cost more than twopence each. 'If you don't like paying the tax', say the Chancellors of the Exchequer with hollow laughter, 'give up smoking!' Then wink to their wives or colleagues as much as to say, 'That's settled 'em!'

The trouble about this kind of infantile reasoning is that it ricochets uncomfortably, and a man who is being forced to spend a pound at least every week on cigarettes is not going to be satisfied long with his wages of five pounds. But such considerations belong to the department of life so curiously named 'politics'.

I have smoked since I was eleven years old and have tried most instruments and materials from a meerschaum pipe to a straw-bound cigarette, from Toscanos to Woodbines, from an Indian hubble-bubble to a Turkish hookah, from the gold-tipped Balkan cigarettes of pre-war Germany to the black Maryland cigarettes of France, from shag to honeydew, from Corona to Naval Issue. For thirty years I smoked cigarettes, and during the last twenty years of this time my average consumption was not less than fifty a day. It occurred to me one morning, as such things annoyingly do, that it had become a nervous itch, a drastic and domineering necessity, that it gave me no positive pleasure, but only assuaged a neurotic longing. All this had been pointed out to me before, and I had smiled with superior knowledge, mildly surprised that anyone should bother to explain such things to an habitual smoker. That morning, however, they were attended by a thought which made them more persistent. Suppose that I did not give up smoking, but changed its manner and method? Suppose that instead of these little tubes of paper-bound tobacco which are of comparatively recent popularity and have come to dominate instead of satisfy mankind, suppose that instead of these I smoked something long, soothing, perceptibly pleasurable—in a word, a cigar?

I enjoyed a cigar. I very much enjoyed a very good cigar, enjoyed a passable one and quite enjoyed the most ordinary. If, then, I could change over . . . but conscience at once reminded me that in a few days I should be smoking as much in sheer weight of tobacco as I was then. So I resolved to give up smoking altogether for three months, then, when the break was made, to allow myself a couple of cheroots a day.

I will not harrow you with stories of those three months, of how I became stupefied and silent, an obsessed idiot who for several weeks could not concentrate long enough on the spoken word to answer a commonplace question; how I passed from stupefaction to irritability, to misanthropy, to sullenness and depression; how I did no work for five weeks, and how, at the end of two months, I wanted to smoke almost as much as before I gave it up. In the end I had to prolong the period of no smoking at all to six or seven months—only then did I dare have a cigar. But it has been worth the agony and strain, for the thing has worked. Now, two years after smoking my last cigarette, I have three cheroots a day, and actively and consciously enjoy every one of them. The economics of the change are interesting, too. Whereas on cigarettes I had to spend from £3 to £3-10 a week, my everyday cheroots, long, well-rolled things sold by Wills called Castella Panatellas, cost exactly one shilling each, or a guinea a week. I keep a few good cigars for more splendid occasions, but even so I spend on smoking a hundred pounds a year less than previously and am fitter and happier for the change. To the pleasure of a book and a brandy by a log-fire after dinner on a winter evening has been added this, while the house, instead of retaining the staleness which comes from yesterday's cigarettes or the unpleasant railway-carriage odour that even the best pipe-tobacco leaves behind, has an opulent perfume which blends with that of the pot-pourri.

14

There can never, fortunately, come a time when the whole thing is complete, when the house and garden need no more changes or additions, when there are no new features of country life to explore. Now, after nearly two years, I am conscious of a great deal yet to do.

There is, for instance, that high, timbered, eighteenth-century warehouse which stands behind my house and from which I first saw 'the view'. In all this time no change has been made in it; its pine-lined walls have not been cleaned down and oiled, as they might so easily have been, its windows are still dusty and the collection of ancient cigarette-cards stuck on a door is undisturbed. For, as they say, I have 'not got round' to this.

What is it to be, I ask myself now, as I did on that first spring day when I came here alone and imagined it put to this or that purpose. Shall it be what the Americans call a rumpus room in which raucous parties can be held out of the hearing of our sedate village? Or a more English playroom, with table-tennis and darts? It would make a fine studio, with its north light, its airiness and remoteness—if I were a painter. Or a music-room with a grand piano hauled up by the gantry to dominate it—if I were a musician. I suppose that as a writer I ought to think of making it into a library with the carpenter's bench, twenty feet long, as the largest writing-table in existence, perhaps, but that would mean that I should have to go up there in isolation to work, and years of writing amid disturbances have made it positively irksome for me to be in complete silence and solitude.

It would make a good clubroom, and I have been tempted to adapt it to this. It could be decorated in a pleasantly Scandinavian way with a wooden balcony overlooking the view, and, with a licence, might attract the more spirited inhabitants of the area. But do I want this? It is well suited to be a show-room for antiques, if I had time to buy them, or books, if I wanted to deal in them again. It has, in fact, so many possibilities that I can decide on none, so that it stands there reproachfully waiting. But I like it so. I feel that while it is empty I have not begun to exhaust the potentialities of this place.

Whatever its purpose, the old warehouse would have to be connected with the house, and a covered passage could run along the wall behind the courtyard. Then there would be an entrance room at one end of its ground floor and a passage running along to the other divisions of it. There is stabling here for two horses, but that, too, is empty. So I can promise myself that one day, when sufficient library subscribers have demanded copies of my books in sufficiently peremptory tones, I shall be able to keep a horse on which to do a little staid hacking round about. This, I have always known, is the pleasantest kind of exercise possible here, and ever since I owned a horse called Firpo, which I bought for 50/- from an itinerant sweet-seller in Argentina more than twenty years ago, I have wanted to possess one again. His presence, over there in the stable, would bring that tall building into the household, as it were. There is nothing, I am told, much more unpatriotic and selfish than keeping a horse to ride. The only horses not actively disapproved by authority are cart-horses. Race-horses are inevitable, since more than half the electorate 'do a bit' on the races. Hunters are anachronistic, but any talk of the abolition of hunting seems to rouse such purple ire in country places that the animals must be endured. A horse kept for a man to ride, though; what justification can there be for that? It earns no dollars and grows no food and is no part of any plan. It gives exercise or relaxation only to the one man who owns it. Let it be almost an impossibility, then. Taxation and the price of fodder can nearly eliminate it and propaganda can do the rest. Still, I never look at those two stalls without a resolution that they shall one day be filled.

15

This, then, is the life for me. Or should I qualify the phrase and say the 'exterior life'?—since I have not been concerned with essentials which in a book of this kind would be out-of-place and embarrassing. I have not written of love or religion, literature, morality, friendship or death. I have been occupied only with the circumstances and surroundings of a certain kind of life, its embellishments and everyday delights. If it all seems no more than escapism, if the making and enjoyment of a home appears foolish in view of the threatening grimaces of the nations, I can point to a good many more permanent monuments left by mankind which must have seemed even more supposititious when they were planned.

It might be thought sometimes, from present-day comments, that we believe ours to be the first civilization in history that has been threatened with obliteration by barbarians. Every civilization of the past has grown to its meridian under just such a threat, which, often enough, has materialized. But that never prevented men of braver days from making their lives ornamental, from developing their tastes and faculties, and it is cowardice which sees now in a restless and menacing world a reason for accepting the stereotyped, the second-rate, the popular.

'You muddled with books and pictures, an' china an' etchin's and fans,' said Kipling's dying ship-owner to his son, with the heartiest contempt; but how would he have felt now, I wonder, if he saw the struggle that men must make for the right to 'books and pictures', the precariousness of all ownership, the hostility with which all imaginative living is watched? We have fought two wars for 'books and pictures', and a few other things, and must still make sacrifices and efforts for the privilege even of discussing them where and when and in what terms we please.

So, in this home which I have made with such disproportionate devotion, when I take an apprehensive glance at the headlines before turning to the ecstasy of a virgin crossword puzzle, I wonder sometimes whether perhaps I am fiddling while Rome burns. If so, there still seems no reason why I should not fiddle as well as I can. Careless playing of poor music on a cheap little violin will do nothing to check the flames. No, I feel no sense of guilt or even of being malapropos in doing what I have done and in describing it. So far as it is anti-social it has served society. So far as it is out-of-date it is ahead of time. So far as it is self-indulgent it is disinterested. Or even if it has no significance at all it has been entertaining, and for me, in this grim middle-century, that is enough.

FINIS

PRINTED IN GREAT BRITAIN BY
RICHARD CLAY AND COMPANY, LTD.,
BUNGAY, SUFFOLK.